T5-DGK-207

JOURNAL FOR THE STUDY OF THE OLD TESTAMENT
SUPPLEMENT SERIES
135

JSOT Press
Sheffield

JSOT Press
Sheffield

Israel in Egypt

Reading Exodus 1–2

Gordon F. Davies

Journal for the Study of the Old Testament
Supplement Series 135

Published by JSOT Press
JSOT Press is an imprint of
Sheffield Academic Press Ltd
The University of Sheffield
343 Fulwood Road
Sheffield S10 3BP
England

Typeset by Sheffield Academic Press
and
Printed on acid-free paper in Great Britain
by Billing & Sons Ltd
Worcester

British Library Cataloguing in Publication Data

Davies, Gordon Fay
Israel in Egypt: Reading Exodus 1–2.—
(JSOT Supplement Series, ISSN 0309-0787;
No. 135)
I. Title II. Series
222

ISBN 1-85075-337-7

CONTENTS

ACKNOWLEDGMENTS AND DEDICATION

I thank my Archbishop, the Most Reverend A.M. Ambrozic, DD, his predecessor, the Most Reverend G.E. Cardinal Carter, DD, and the former Chancellor of the Archdiocese of Toronto, now the Archbishop of Winnipeg, the Most Reverend L.J. Wall, DD, for their fatherly encouragement. Nor will I forget my gratitude to the people of the Archdiocese of Toronto, who made my long term of study possible.

The Dominicans and students of the Ecole biblique et archéologique française provided me with friendship and advice. Mr Ezra Ozery knows my debt to him for his patience in our study together of the Hebrew-language articles. I owe thanks to Caren Greenberg for help in typing and, much more, for her faith.

Written entirely in Jerusalem, this book is dedicated to the Palestinian and Jewish peoples.

ABBREVIATIONS

AJSL	*American Journal of Semitic Languages and Literatures*
AnBib	Analecta biblica
ANET	J.B. Pritchard (ed.), *Ancient Near Eastern Texts*
AOAT	Alter Orient und Altes Testament
AusBR	*Australian Biblical Review*
BASOR	Bulletin of the American Schools of Oriental Research
BDB	F. Brown, S.R. Driver and C.A. Briggs, *Hebrew and English Lexicon of the Old Testament*
BETL	Bibliotheca ephemeridum theologicarum lovaniensium
Bib	*Biblica*
BJRL	*Bulletin of the John Rylands University Library of Manchester*
BJS	Brown Judaic Studies
BR	*Biblical Research*
BTB	*Biblical Theology Bulletin*
BZ	*Biblische Zeitschrift*
BZAW	Beihefte zur *ZAW*
CAT	Commentaire de l'Ancien Testament
CBQ	*Catholic Biblical Quarterly*
ExpTim	*Expository Times*
GKC	*Gesenius' Hebrew Grammer*, ed. E. Kautzsch, trans. A.E. Cowley
HALAT	W. Baumgartner et al., *Hebräisches und aramäisches Lexikon zum Alten Testament*
HUCA	*Hebrew Union College Annual*
IDB	G.A. Buttrick (ed.), *Interpreter's Dictionary of the Bible*
IDBSup	*IDB*, Supplementary Volume
Int	*Interpretation*
JBL	*Journal of Biblical Literature*
JNES	*Journal of Near Eastern Studies*
JNSL	*Journal of Northwest Semitic Languages*
JQR	*Jewish Quarterly Review*
JSOT	*Journal for the Study of the Old Testament*
JSOTSup	*Journal for the Study of the Old Testament*, Supplement Series
JTS	*Journal of Theological Studies*
Leš	*Lešonénu*
MUSJ	*Mélanges de l'université Saint-Joseph*

NedTTs	*Nederlands theologisch tijdschrift*
OBO	Orbis biblicus et orientalis
Or	*Orientalia*
OTS	*Oudtestamentische Studiën*
RB	*Revue biblique*
REJ	*Revue des études juives*
RHPR	*Revue d'histoire et de philosophie religieuses*
RivB	*Rivista biblica*
SB	Sources bibliques
SBL	Society of Biblical Literature
SBLDS	SBL Dissertation Series
SBLSP	SBL Seminar Papers
SBT	Studies in Biblical Theology
Sem	*Semitica*
SJOT	*Scandinavian Journal of the Old Testament*
ST	*Studia theologica*
TBü	Theologische Bücherei
THAT	*Theologisches Handwörterbuch zum Alten Testament*
ThWAT	G.J. Botterweck and H. Ringgren (eds.), *Theologisches Wörterbuch zum Alten Testament*
TQ	*Theologische Quartalschrift*
VT	*Vetus Testamentun*
VTSup	*Vetus Testamentum*, Supplements
WMANT	Wissenschaftliche Monographien zum Alten und Neuen Testament
WBC	Word Biblical Commentary
ZAW	*Zeitschrift für die alttestamentliche Wissenschaft*
ZTK	*Zeitschrift für Theologie und Kirche*

INTRODUCTION

1. *The Importance of Exodus 1–2*

Practical needs directed the choice of the first two chapters of Exodus as the material for this study. They were not chosen for any special beauty or depth of thought. But once the work of reading is underway, one notices their spread in the tissue of the Bible.

The two chapters join Joseph's death to the birth of the Israelites as a people and, beyond, the Patriarch to the Exodus. They set out the oppression of the Israelites, that from which they are liberated in the Exodus. That event is 'the definitive deliverance and the type of all the rest [that] mythically...is the only thing that really happens' in the Hebrew Bible.[1] Exodus 1–2 describes the chaos from which integration is achieved in the 'source, [the] original version' for modern Western revolution.[2]

> The burning-bush contract introduces a revolutionary quality into the Biblical tradition, and its characteristics persist through Christianity, through Islam, and survive with little essential change in Marxism. Of these characteristics, the most important are...a belief in a specific historical revelation as a starting point. Israel's story begins here and in this way; Christianity begins with Christ and not, say, with the Essenes; Islam begins with the Hegira of Mohammed, Communism with Marx and not, say, with Owen or Fourier...[Another] is the dialectical habit of mind that divides the world into those with us and those against us.[3]

1. N. Frye, *The Great Code* (New York: Harcourt, Brace & Jovanovich, 1981), p. 171: 'As the various declines of Israel through apostasy and the like are not acts so much as failures to act, it is only the rises and restorations that are real events' and, of these, 'the primary and model form is the deliverance from Egypt and the creation of the nation of Israel that formed part of this deliverance'.
2. M. Walzer, *Exodus and Revolution* (New York: Basic Books, 1985), p. 133.
3. Frye, *The Great Code*, p. 114.

2. *Methodology*

Source-Oriented and Discourse-Oriented Methods

What follows is a synchronic analysis of Exodus 1–2. As an interdisciplinary exercise, it should be defined in relation to the rest of biblical scholarship and literary criticism.

This 'text-immanent'[1] approach seeks dialectic rather than conflict with historical studies of the Bible. It recognizes that 'source-oriented' and 'discourse-oriented' methods ask different questions of the text.[2]

> [The first] addresses itself to the biblical world as it really was... [I]nterest focuses on some object behind the text—on a state of affairs or development which operated at the time as a source (material, antecedent, enabling condition) of biblical writing and which biblical writing now reflects in turn... [The second method] sets out to understand not the realities behind the text but the text itself as a pattern of meaning and effect... What image of a world does the narrative project? Why does it unfold the action in this particular order and from this particular viewpoint?... And, in general in what relationship does part stand to whole and form to function?[3]

The paths of the two methods diverge where 'the story lines cross the boundaries commonly set down by source analysis'.[4]

Often discussions about the value and provinces of the two kinds of analyses are hampered by the terms used for the biblical genre and the connotations that these elicit. To call the Bible 'literature' or 'fiction'

1. J. Cook, 'Text and Tradition: A Methodological Problem', *JNSL* 9 (1981), p. 6.

2. Cook, 'Text and Tradition', p. 11. The terms in quotation marks are from M. Sternberg, *The Poetics of Biblical Narrative* (Indiana Literary Biblical Series, 1; Bloomington: Indiana University Press, 1985), p. 15. Excellent summaries of historical-critical research on Exodus are available in H. Schmid, *Die Gestalt des Mose: Probleme alttestamentlicher Forschung unter Berücksichtigung der Pentateuchkrise* (Erträge der Forschung, 237; Darmstadt: Wissenchaftliche Buchgesellschaft, 1986), pp. 1-56, for the period from 1960 to 1984, and W.H. Schmidt, *Exodus, Sinai und Mose* (Erträge der Forschung, 191; Darmstadt: Wissenchaftliche Buchgesellschaft, 1983), pp. 1-15, to 1982.

3. Sternberg, *Poetics*, p. 15.

4. C. Isbell, 'Exodus 1–2 in the Context of Exodus 1–14: Story Lines and Key Words', in *Art and Meaning* (ed. D.J.A. Clines *et al.*; JSOTSup, 19; Sheffield: JSOT Press, 1982), p. 56.

strikes many as frivolous, irreverent and 'a fundamental perversion'.[1] Others answer that it is just as 'problematic to define the Bible as a religious text [...since it is] a set of texts which in its abundant narrative and poetic portions uses manifestly literary means to serve chiefly religious—it might be more accurate to call them covenantal—ends'.[2] 'Rhetorical' is an apt name,[3] if it is taken in its proper sense of 'calculated to persuade' (*OED*) and removed from the unfortunate depreciatory notion of 'mere rhetoric'. It is 'ideological',[4] but this word alarms English-speakers.

Perhaps the best route is around the taxonomic obstacle and into the heart of the issue. For Frye, the Bible is 'deeply rooted in all the resources of language'. It is a unique idiom, 'oratory on the highest level of oracle'.[5] Like all rhetoric, it is a 'mixture of the metaphorical and the "existential" or concerned, but unlike practically all other forms of rhetoric, it is not an argument disguised by figuration'. It rather demands assent by dividing the world of life from the world of death. Its only self-definition is its terminus of faith, and the most fitting way to read it is to enter this trajectory and lay bare its mechanisms.

It is true that the Bible does not classify itself as literature. But neither does it call itself history or theology, because it makes no distinction among the three. Everywhere, including in those narrative portions where its 'organizing principles are literary',[6] it promotes a theocentric understanding of history as present reality projected back to the time of causes'[7]—of which the first and ultimate is God himself.

Critics of a 'purely literary' approach are correct that 'biblical

1. J. Kugel, 'On the Bible and Literary Criticism', *Prooftexts* 1 (1981), p. 233. His debate with A. Berlin is one of the best discussions of the issue: A. Berlin, 'On the Bible as Literature', *Prooftexts* 2 (1982), pp. 323-32, and J. Kugel, 'James Kugel Responds', *Prooftexts* 2 (1981), pp. 328-32. See also R. Alter's defence of the designation 'fiction' in *The Art of Biblical Narrative* (New York: Basic Books, 1981), p. 24.

2. R. Alter, 'How Convention Helps us Read: The Case of the Bible's Annunciation Type-Scene', *Prooftexts* 3 (1983), p. 116.

3. It is used by E. Fox (*Now These are the Names* [New York: Schocken Books, 1986], p. xvii) and by I.M. Kikawada ('Some Proposals for the Definition of Rhetorical Criticism', *Semitics* 5 [1977], p. 67).

4. Sternberg, *Poetics*, pp. 84-128.

5. *The Great Code*, p. 29.

6. Alter, 'Convention', p. 116.

7. Kugel, 'On the Bible and Literary Criticism', p. 230.

stories...emerge from society and serve the purposes of society' in ways essential to their interpretation.[1] But often these purposes are precisely the exaltation of God through the plot and narrative techniques as best observed by a synchronic reading.

I am here claiming the middle ground that will be mine throughout the study. It stands on one side of the line between diachronic and synchronic analyses, but also at a distance from those who attempt a merely aesthetic evaluation of the Bible and discount references to extra-textual sources.

Reader-Response Criticism

This study will operate along another axis of critical coordinates. The literary world is engaged in a debate over the origin of meaning, an abstruse topic but of necessity mentioned here because the study applies the working techniques of some of the participants.

A roughly grouped circle called 'reader-reponse' critics maintains that a text cannot 'be understood apart from its results'.[2] 'The basis of the method is a consideration of the *temporal* flow of the reading experience, and it is assumed that the reader responds in terms of that flow and not to the whole utterance.'[3] For example, 'Nor did they not perceive the evil plight' in *Paradise Lost*, 1.335 is logically equivalent to 'They perceived the evil plight', but the prominence of the 'nor' and the unexpected second negative have an effect on the reader's interpretative progress through the line. Surprise and hesitation momentarily subvert the logic of consecutive reading here. Fully considered, a literary work lies between two poles, the text created by the author and the realization accomplished by the reader.[4] Much about this position is common sense and will be defended practically in the chapters to follow.

Here too I choose moderation. The step that I do not make leads

1. J. Neusner, 'Beyond Historicism, after Structuralism: Story as History in Ancient Judaism', *Henoch* 3 (1981), p. 192.

2. J.P. Tompkins, 'An Introduction to Reader-Reponse Criticism', in *Reader-Response Criticism* (ed. J.P. Tompkins; Baltimore: Johns Hopkins University Press, 1980), p. ix.

3. S.E. Fish, 'Literature in the Reader: Affective Stylistics', in Tompkins (ed.), *Reader-Response Criticism*, p. 74, whose example from pp. 72-73 follows.

4. W. Iser, 'The Reading Process: A Phenomenological Approach', in Tompkins (ed.), *Reader-Response Criticism*, p. 50.

beyond the reader's activity as instrumental to the understanding of the text, a fulfilment of what is already implicit in the structure of the work. Some, agreeing with S. Fish, declare that the act of reading is itself the source of all literary value.

> Meaning. . . is not something one extracts from a [work. . .] but an experience one has in the course of reading. Literature, as a consequence, is not regarded as a fixed object of attention but as a sequence of events that unfold within the reader's mind. . . [T]he question to answer is not 'what do poems mean?' or even 'what do poems do?' but 'how do readers make meaning?'[1]

This last question cuts language from reality and collapses hermeneutics into introspection. Interpretation vanishes, murdered by mere 'response'. The sense of a text would become that which gives satisfaction for 'the present location of the reader. . . [M]eaning is dynamic and *final meaning* continues to recede'.[2] In effect, '*anything can be said about anything*'.[3] For example, with this method a play by Pinter has been entirely analysed in terms of one commentator's sexuality. And '[t]here is no need to claim that the [biblical] Joseph story is "about" ambivalent feelings of sons toward fathers, since it is obvious that this describes [another scholar's] experience of the story'.[4]

Such radical reader-response criticism and its vanishing extreme, deconstructionism, is 'in the final analysis *the death of God put into writing*'.[5] It cannot be argued against because its 'playful abolition of the stable subject contains a logical circularity'.[6]

Instead I prefer to neutralize such radically subjective approaches with the force of common sense, the 'moral intuition' that there can be no 'striving towards intelligibility. . .[without] a postulate of *meaningfulness*. . .We must read as if the text before us had meaning', and so

1. Tompkins, 'Introduction', pp. xvi-xvii.
2. E.V. McKnight, *Post-Modern Use of the Bible* (Nashville: Abingdon Press, 1988), p. 60.
3. G. Steiner, 'Real Presences', in *idem*, *Le Sens du Sens* (Paris: J. Vrin, 1988), p. 75.
4. S. Elliott and T. Jordan, cited approvingly by D. Bleich, 'Epistemological Assumptions in the Study of Response', in Tompkins (ed.), *Reader-Response Criticism*, p. 153, pp. 156-57.
5. C.A. Raschke, quoted by E.L. Greenstein, 'Deconstruction and Biblical Narrative', *Prooftexts* 9 (1989), p. 52.
6. Steiner, 'Real Presences', p. 80.

we find it. We may make a 'Cartesian–Kantian wager' that sense is not random. We cannot master meaning or exhaust its complexity. But we can take responsibility for our action as readers and face the text pragmatically as a real singularity, a source of significance because its elements encode valuable experience.[1]

Interpretative Interest

Once we trust in our own literacy, we can look again at the musings of the deconstructionists and co-opt them for rational use as 'speculative instruments'[2] in the exegetic enterprise. Perhaps the most valuable nugget to be sieved from so much broken rock is that, for all its validity, 'meaning' is a controvertible word. While upholding our right to use it in principle, we may be prudent to leave it aside when describing our purpose in analysing Scripture. We need a precept that does not exalt the ego or tolerate error, but recognizes that 'no one interpretive strategy can lay claim to meaning at the expense of other strategies'.[3] S. Fowl suggests a practical solution: we should define our work by our 'interpretive interests'.[4]

Some scholars may want to expose an author's conscious intentions, for example, Luke's 'communicative aims in presenting Jesus in the way he does'. Others may study a text's 'contextual connections to the material or gender-based means of its production'. The result is more profitable debate because '"What we once thought to be one topic is really several topics"'.[5] Disagreements will remain but be more manageable.

The interpretative interest of this study is to examine the confluence of narrativity and theology in Exodus 1–2, the inseparability of story and argument. It will look for the chapters' conception and judgment of the events and characters as formed by the pericopes' structure, language, focalization and management of information. These are not used decoratively but ideologically, where 'ideology' is defined as 'a

1. Steiner, 'Real Presences', pp. 83, 85, 86.

2. I.A. Richards, quoted by E. Freund, *The Return of the Reader* (London: Methuen, 1987), p. 156.

3. S. Fowl, 'The Ethics of Interpretation, or What's Left Over after the Elimination of Meaning' (SBLSP, 27; Atlanta: Scholars Press, 1988), pp. 69-81 (75).

4. Fowl ('The Ethics of Interpretation', p. 70) credits J. Stout with the idea.

5. Fowl, 'The Ethics of Interpretation', p. 72, quoting Stout.

system of ideas concerning phenomena' (*OED*).

No pretense is made that the entire Bible or even the whole Pentateuch has the same ideological goals.[1] Even within the first five chapters of Exodus, a similar method could be and has been specified for each hypothetical source, J, E, P and dtr.[2] But I maintain that a coherence of concerns is detectable in Exodus 1–2 with ordered streams of allusion to Genesis and the later chapters of Exodus. These ideas are at once the product and burden of the literary techniques.

The involvement of the audience is an operative principle of the study without any claim to epistemological or biblical revolution-making. For every pericope, a 'right' way of reading has been sought '—"right" in the only sense that criticism can recognize, as the way that conforms to the intentionality of the book itself and to the conventions it assumes and requires'.[3] Hence methodologies are in service for some parts that are not called for elsewhere, like rhetorical analysis for Pharaoh's speech in 1.8-14, and a study of the symbol of water in 2.1-10.

Of course, much of the effect on the original audience has been lost to us. Conclusions must be cautious, and the 'self-conscious sense of historical perspective which is part of our modern intellectual equipment [can help] against the danger of modernization of the Bible'.[4] Every methodology runs risks: synchronic analysis in turn can remind redaction-historical critics that the meaning of a passage should not be equated with the intention of its author, nor the expressed intention with its fulness.[5] For this reason, I speak of the 'text's' message, not the author's or redactors'.

1. Note F. Langlamet's criticism of Sternberg, *Poetics*, on this subject in his recension, 'Poétique du récit biblique', *RB* 99 (1987), pp. 466-77, and take as an example *Poetics*, pp. 88-89.

2. P. Weimar, *Die Berufung des Mose* (OBO, 32; Freiburg: Universitätsverlag; Göttingen: Vandenhoeck & Ruprecht, 1980).

3. Frye, *The Great Code*, pp. 79-80.

4. Alter, 'Convention', p. 117.

5. See the discussion of various intentions, the overt authorial intention, the 'components of the author's intended meaning of which he or she is not fully conscious', 'unattended meaning which the author would surely have acknowledged, had it been brought to his attention', and 'a still deeper level, viz. subconscious meaning' in N. Watson, 'Reception Theory and Biblical Exegesis', *AusBR* 36 (1988), pp. 46-49.

As an expositional strategy, I will apply the fiction that the actual reader is the same as the implied reader. That is, for the sake of simplicity of approach, I will always treat the text as though the readers of this book join me in the choice to go along with the implied author's appeal to the implied reader. One recognizes, of course, that 'suspicious' as opposed to accepting approaches can also be adopted.

3. *Delimitation and Unity of the Chapters*

Time has shown the importance for biblical rhetorical criticism of a speech by J. Muilenburg in 1969. In calling for new directions of study, he stressed that a preliminary and essential task is the delimitation of the passage, 'if we are to learn how its major motif, usually stated at the beginning, is resolved'.[1]

The first two chapters of the Book are the prelude to the story of the Exodus and are unified in form and nature.[2] They divide into seven segments, whose brevity and diversity contrast with the long scene at the Burning Bush (3.1–4.17), with its unity of time, place and characters. The narrative in chs. 1–2 is usually reserved in its information and always clear in its transition from one episode to the next. Aaron is the only main character to be introduced after Exodus 2.

Muilenburg drew special attention to inclusions as markers of units.[3] Exodus 1–2 begins with the genealogical list of ancestors' names and ends with Moses' naming his descendant. At the outset, the sons of Israel grow according to God's promise. This covenant is then explicitly mentioned at the end. Joseph died, and now Pharaoh dies. Pharaoh had been afraid that the Israelites would go up from the land; instead their cry goes up. Pharaoh did not know Joseph; God does know. Chapter 7 (on 2.23-25) will expose other threads of thematic and stylistic unity.[4]

1. J. Muilenburg, 'Form Criticism and Beyond', *JBL* 88 (1969), p. 9.

2. What follows owes much to M. Greenberg, *Understanding Exodus* (Heritage of Biblical Israel, 2.5; New York: Behrman House, 1969), pp. 57-60.

3. 'Form Criticism and Beyond', p. 9.

4. Some commentators place Exod. 2.23-25 with Exod. 3 and following. Weimar (*Berufung*, p. 333) calls it the thematic exposition of Moses' call and the first scenic unit of a section that runs from 2.23 to 3.6. Cassuto (*A Commentary on the Book of Exodus* [trans. I. Abrahams; Jerusalem: Magnes Press, 1967], p. 28) entitles it the 'Exordium' of what comes next in Exod. 3. B.S. Childs (*The Book of*

4. *Technical Notes*

The general format has been to translate the pericope in a very literal way as a first approach to the text, then to comment on any translation difficulties, to delimit the pericope, and to analyse the narrative structure, the point of view, the lexical, semantic and thematic symmetry, and finally the vocabulary.[1] In addition, each unit except the last has at least one special narrative feature: in 1.1-7, repetition and a deep structure overlapping with Genesis 50; in 1.8-14, public rhetoric; in 1.15-22, narrative speeds and order; in 2.1-10, narrative stages, perspective and symbolism; in 2.11-15, a deceptive deep structure; and in 2.16-22, the question of 'type-scene'.

The literal translation is divided into sense lines or units according to the criteria of H. Schweizer.[2] The relevant rules are these. A unit has only one finite verb or it can be nominal. A new unit begins after the introduction to speech. And a subordinate clause with a conjunction is also separated. Elements put in recognizable parallel are separated. Infinitive constructions, such as 'in order to', are not. Every member of the predicate can be separated in its function as an adjunct of some kind: coordinating, descriptive or explicative.

Some exegetes limit the term 'chiasm' to the strict inverted repetition of identical words. When the figure involves an inverted parallelism of synonyms, or pronouns standing for nouns, this study will use the broader adjective 'chiastic' and justify itself by reference to the vocabulary and definitions in works by J.W. Welch, R.A. Lanham,

Exodus [Philadelphia: Westminster Press, 1974], p. 32), however, rejects the NEB and the NAB, who also attach these verses to the new section. He says that they relate primarily to what has already been recounted and conclude it by returning to the earlier theme of Israel's misery. J.I. Durham (*Exodus* [WBC, 3; Waco, TX: Word Books, 1987], p. 24) calls it a 'Postscript on the Oppression'. I too believe that the points made in the text above and later in Chapter 7 are sufficient to maintain the unity of Exod. 1–2.

1. 'Theme' is taken here as a synonym for 'motif', a significant phrase or set description frequently repeated in a work. See M.H. Abrams, *A Glossary of Literary Terms* (New York: Holt, Rhinehart & Winston, 3rd edn, 1971 [1941]), p. 102.

2. H. Schweizer, 'Wovon reden die Exegeten? Zum Verständnis der Exegese als verstehender und deskriptiver Wissenschaft', *TQ* 164 (1984), pp. 161-85.

M.H. Abrams and A.R. Ceresko.[1] All these authors allow for a parallelism beyond the literal in chiastic structures.

The working document has been the Masoretic Text, although reference has been made to other versions where appropriate. For easier comprehension of the Hebrew, I have at times added the transcription in brackets after words whose Masoretic spelling might be ambiguous without vowel points. Thus רע (*rēa'*). Since I am not doing genre research or creating canons of literary criticism, I have also been free in my terminology—'unit', 'story', 'pericope' and 'episode' are interchangeable, as are 'focalization' and 'point of view'.

1. J.W. Welch (ed.), *Chiasmus in Antiquity* (Hildesheim: Gerstenberg, 1981), esp. p. 9; R.A. Lanham, *A Handlist of Rhetorical Terms* (Berkeley: University of California Press, 1968), pp. 22-23; A.R. Ceresko, 'The Chiastic Word Pattern in Hebrew', *CBQ* 38 (1976), pp. 303-11; Abrams, *Glossary*, p. 150.

Chapter 1

EXODUS 1.1-7

1. *Literal Translation*

1a	Now these are the names of the sons of Israel who came to Egypt,
1b	with Jacob each with his household they came:
2	Reuben, Simeon, Levi and Judah,
3	Issachar, Zebulun and Benjamin,
4	Dan and Naphtali, Gad and Asher.
5a	All the persons issuing from Jacob's loins were seventy persons,
5b	whereas Joseph was [already] in Egypt.
6	Then Joseph died and all his brothers and all that generation.
7a	Yet the Sons of Israel bore fruit,
7b	they teemed,
7c	they multiplied,
7d	they grew powerful—exceedingly, yes, exceedingly
7e	so that the land was filled with them.

Notes on the Literal Translation

Verse 5a. נפש: 'person'. The word is used in an enumeration to mean a collective for persons.[1] However, as A. Johnson points out, even in this technical use, it maintains its close connection to the verb חיה and to a 'person' in the sense of a 'unit of vital power'.[2] It thus contributes to the passage's vocabulary of fruitful and potent life.

1. *HALAT*, III, p. 673; BDB, p. 660.

2. A.R. Johnson, *The Vitality of the Individual in the Thought of Ancient Israel* (Cardiff: University of Wales Press, 2nd edn, 1964 [1949]), pp. 18-20; also C. Westermann, 'נפש *næfæš* Seele', *THAT*, II, pp. 88-89; W. Gottlieb, 'The Term "Nepes" in the Bible: A Re-appraisal': *Transactions of the Glasgow University Oriental Society* 25 (1973–74), pp. 75-76. Writing of Gen. 46.26, a verse parallel to this, A. Murtonen (*The Living Soul: A Study of the Meaning of the Word næfæs in the Old Testament Hebrew Language* [Studia Orientalia 23.1; Helsinki: Societas Orientalis Fennica, 1958], pp. 15-16) notes the importance of the collective sense but adds that 'above all, action is characteristic of the soul'. A. Lacocque (*Le Devenir de Dieu* [Paris: Editions Universitaires, 1967], p. 28) translates the word here as 'vies'.

Verse 5b. ויוסף היה במצרים: 'whereas Joseph was [already] in Egypt'. As the first element in a w^e... *qatal* construction, the ו implies here that the second verb is anterior and contradistinct.[1]

Verse 7d. במאד מאד: 'exceedingly, yes, exceedingly'. This translation, suggested by Fox,[2] is used here to show the important feature of repetition about which more will be said in Section 5.

2. *Delimitation*

The section forms a transition between the end of Genesis and the return to fuller narrative style in Exod. 1.8. Genesis has made a round conclusion with the death of Joseph. This section begins with a summary of previous action and a genealogy. These establish unity between the books, but also mark the passage between them.[3] The genealogy in Exod. 1.1-4 could be profitably understood as a link in a chain of genealogies in Genesis 12–50, where, according to N. Steinberg, the return to a state of equilibrium is provided through a genealogy that marks the movement from one generation to the next. But this resolution immediately brings on a new start in the cycle.[4]

Ancient authors sometimes used surface patterns as a system of 'indicators' that are effective in either oral or written presentations to

1. R. Meyer, *Hebräische Grammatik* (Sammlung Göschen, 763, 764, 5764, 4765; Berlin: de Gruyter, 3rd edn, 1972 [1915]) §112; P. Joüon, *Grammaire de l'Hébreu biblique* (Rome: Pontificium Institutum Biblicum, 1982 [1923]), §118d; A. Niccacci, *The Syntax of the Verb in Classical Hebrew Prose* (trans. W.G.E. Watson; JSOTSup, 86; Sheffield: JSOT Press, 1990 [originally published in Italian as *Sintassi del verbo ebraico nella prosa biblica classica* (Studium Biblicum Franciscanum Analecta, 23; Jerusalem: Fransiscan Printing Press, 1986)]), §40.

2. *Names*, p. 10.

3. D.T. Olson argues that genealogies, *toledot* formulae and census lists are the 'overarching editorial structure' of the Tetrateuch. P. Weimar sees this genealogy as the true conclusion of the Jacob cycle. This list is the end of the final sub-unit of the third section that began with the 'Toledothformular' of Jacob in Gen. 37.2. See D.T. Olson, *The Death of the Old and the Birth of the New: The Framework of the Book of Numbers and the Pentateuch* (BJS, 71; Chico, CA: Scholars Press, 1984), p. 188; P. Weimar, 'Aufbau und Struktur der priesterschriftlichen Jacobsgeschichte', *ZAW* 86 (1974), p. 200.

4. N. Steinberg, 'The Genealogical Framework of the Family Stories in Genesis', *Semeia* 46 (1989), p. 43.

do the work of emphasis and division that we assign to italics, headings and the like.[1] The present study will point to many examples. One here is that יוסף and וימת form 'linking-words' between Genesis 50 and Exodus 1.[2] In a chiastic inclusion within Exod. 1.1-7, 'the sons of Israel' come to 'Egypt' in v. 1, and then 'the land is filled with them' in v. 7.

The next unit is set off from this one by the introduction of a character, the king, who breaks with the past because he 'does not know Joseph' (1.8). The second episode is signalled by a פ indicating a פתוחא or open paragraph.[3]

3. *Narrative Structure and Gaps*

Deep

Amid a welter of competing terms stand two fundamental parts in the construction of a narrative. Every plot can be shorn of its distinctive dress in features like setting and characterization to reveal basic compositional 'units',[4] 'structural building blocks'[5] or 'functions'.[6] One can consider the actions of the characters independently of the diversity of the characters themselves.[7] This compositional girdering does not have a self-sustained existence.[8] But it is useful to abstract it from

1. H.V.D. Parunak, 'Oral Typesetting: Some Uses of Biblical Structure', *Bib* 62 (1981), p. 154.

2. Specifically Gen. 50.26 and Exod. 1.5b. On 'linking-words' or 'mots-crochet', see H.V.D. Parunak, 'Transitional Techniques in the Bible', *JBL* 102 (1983), p. 531.

3. However, C. Perrot ('*Petuhot* et *Setumot*: Etude sur les alinéas du Pentateuque', *RB* 76 [1969], p. 81) warns against a simplistic notion that these signs always introduce a new theme or idea. For our purposes here, his most appropriate 'critère d'ordre formel' is that the פתוחא can introduce pericopes that are important for the liturgy, theology and history of the people (p. 84).

4. V. Propp, 'Structure and History in the Study of the Fairy Tale' (trans. from Italian by H.T. McElwain) *Semeia* 10 (1978), p. 72.

5. C. Conroy, *Absalom Absalom!: Narrative and Language in 2 Sam. 13–20* (AnBib, 81; Rome: Pontificium Institutum Biblicum, 1978), p. 10.

6. On 'fonctions': V. Propp, *Morphologie du conte* (trans. M. Derrida *et al.* from the 2nd Russian edn [1969]; Collection Points, 12; Paris: Editions du Seuil, 1970), p. 31.

7. Propp, 'Structure', p. 62.

8. Propp, 'Structure', p. 71.

the story to clarify the dynamics of the plot, especially where it turns around repetition, as in the plot summary and genealogy here.[1] In these verses, we can better understand their relation to Genesis and the subsequent growth of the Israelites if we first reduce the plot to a skeletal structure.

An extended example of the difference between plot and basic composition is offered by Vladimir Propp, who did work on the patterns underpinning the Russian heroic fairy tale.

> Suppose that a dragon steals the king's daughter. The king seeks help, and the son of a peasant decides to find her. He set outs on his journey, and along the way he encounters an old woman who proposes that he tame a herd of savage horses. He is successful, and the old woman gives him one of the animals as a gift; the horse takes him to an island where he finds the kidnapped princess. The hero slays the dragon, returns home, and the king rewards him by offering him his daughter's hand. This is the 'plot' of the tale. The 'composition' on the other hand may be delineated as follows: some misfortune takes place; the hero is asked to help; he goes off on his quest; along the way he encounters someone who puts him to the test and then rewards him with some magical agent; thanks to this magical medium he finds the lost object; the hero returns and is rewarded.[2]

'Propp chose the name "function" for those elements of a tale that are constant.'[3] He discovered that, in his chosen genre, a multiplicity of characters meets a paucity of functions, function being understood as the action of a character, defined from the point of view of its significance in the unfolding of the plot.[4] It is a unit of action that is meaningful for the progress of the whole tale.[5] The sequence of these constitutes the compositional scheme of the tale.

Legitimately one asks if this Proppian structural-formalism can be applied to Scripture. In a review of the various attempts to do so, P.J. Milne concludes that most fail because they overlook Propp's insistence that the details of his conclusions were valid only for heroic

1. Propp, 'Structure', p. 83; S. Chatman, *Story and Discourse* (Ithaca, NY: Cornell University Press, 1978), p. 92.

2. 'Structure', pp. 71-72.

3. P.J. Milne, *Vladimir Propp and the Study of Structure in Hebrew Biblical Narrative* (Bible and Literature Series, 13; Sheffield: Almond Press, 1988), p. 72.

4. Propp, *Morphologie*, p. 31.

5. H. Jason, cited in Milne, *Vladimir Propp*, p. 73.

folktales.[1] They look throughout biblical narratives for the same composition that he found in his corpus of fairy tales. Furthermore, narrative macro-structure is usually examined on a broad scale 'to study the universal, or at least general, properties of literature',[2] for example to classify stories[3] or whole typologies of plot.[4] However, the Bible resists easy sorting into genres.[5]

Some even take structuralism as a hermeneutic tool for the interpretation of all reality.[6] But, alone, it might do a disservice to the theological purpose of biblical narratives. Among the censures of structuralism by G. Strickland is the judgment that—beyond the level of the single word—it ignores an utterance's setting, context and therefore its intention.[7]

The purpose in this study is more modest and less derivative. Two biblical chapters are under scrutiny, not entire genres. No master theory

1. Propp, p. 141 and n. 9.

2. D.W. Fokkema and E. Kunne-Ibsch, *Theories of Literature in the Twentieth Century: Structuralism, Marxism, Aesthetics of Reception, Semiotics* (London: C. Hurst, 2nd edn, 1979 [1978]), p. 12.

3. R.C. Culley (*Studies in the Structure of Hebrew Narrative* [Semeia Supplements, 3; Missoula, MT: Scholars Press, 1976], p. 71) grouped 14 stories together as 'miracle stories'. But he also said that the aim of this kind of analysis remains a question (p. 114).

4. Chatman, *Story*, pp. 84-95.

5. On this subject, and about Exod. 1–2, consider the position of G.W. Coats, that Moses' story is an heroic saga, and note his consequent debate with M. Noth, B. Anderson and others in 'The Moses Narrative as Heroic Saga', in *Saga, Legend, Tale, Novella, Fable* (ed. G.W. Coats; JSOTSup, 35; Sheffield: JSOT Press, 1985), esp. pp. 34-36. See also his *Moses: Heroic Man, Man of God* (JSOTSup, 57; Sheffield: JSOT Press, 1988), pp. 47-48.

6. For example, C. Bremond, 'La logique des possibles narratifs', *Communications* 8 (1966), p. 76: 'Cet engendrement des types narratifs est en même temps une structuration des conduites humaines agies ou subies. Elles fournissent au narrateur le modèle et la matière d'un devenir organisé qui lui est indispensable et qu'il serait incapable de trouver ailleurs.'

7. G. Strickland, *Structuralism or Criticism*? (Cambridge: Cambridge University Press, 1981), p. 17, citing E. Benveniste; Strickland, *Structuralism*, p. 158, citing S.H. Olsen. L. Doležel (quoted in Fokkema and Kunne-Ibsch, *Theories*, p. 30) cautions against inflexible structuralist systems: 'There is no fixed and universal "grammar" of narrative; at the same time there is no unlimited freedom for the author's idiosyncracy. Every narrative act is simultaneously norm-obeying, norm-creating and norm-destroying.'

of narrative is sought, just a first step in understanding the plot of these units. Following Propp's principles, we will strip the characters' actions into their component parts, but without trying to impose Propp's own function categories or induce any critical generalities from the results. Such an application of Propp is not unfair to him; as the structuralist R. Scholes says, the greatest contribution of Propp's method is simply its exhortation to 'look at plot-functions and character-roles with an eye for their rigorous and narrowly defined interconnections'.[1]

Viewed from the high ground of this theoretical landscape, Exod. 1.1-7 is clearly not structured as an independent dramatic narrative. The segment has a plot, if plot is defined as 'the dynamic sequential element in narrative literature'.[2] But the internal element of causality is missing. From this text alone we do not know why the sons of Israel went down to Egypt or why their descendants should reproduce so extraordinarily. And without that information we can neither understand the plot nor reduce it to its deep structural functions.

The narrative requires us to supply data from the previous pericope. We must remember the story of Israel and his sons and the promise that God made to propagate Abraham's descendants.[3] Only with these data can we satisfy our natural curiosity about the reason for the events here. And then we can detect that Exod. 1.1-7 represents the second parts of twin functions: 'danger–escape from danger'; and 'promise–fulfilment'. 'Escape from danger' is a repetition of what we already know, that in Egypt Israel and his sons found safety from the famine. 'Fulfilment' is a realization of what we expect, that God will multiply the patriarchal family. They are properly called a set of twin functions because they are matching and interdependent actions.[4]

As other narrative elements in Exod. 1–2 often will, this deep structure tells the story with a kind of Wagnerian melody by deriving its new developments from variations on motifs from Genesis.

1. R. Scholes, *Structuralism in Literature* (New Haven: Yale University Press, 1974), p. 67.

2. R. Scholes and R. Kellogg, *The Nature of Narrative* (London: Oxford University Press, 1966), p. 207.

3. Gen. 12.2; 13.15; 15.4-6; 16.10; 17.2, 4-7, 16, 19-20; 21.13, 18; 22.16-17; 26.3-4; 26.24; 28.3-4; 28.13-14; 35.11-12; 46.3; 48.3-4.

4. The idea of twin functions is not Propp's. It seems called for in biblical texts, perhaps because of their propensity to scenes with only two actors. On this characteristic, see Alter, *Narrative*, p. 72.

Surface
Scholars have long recognized the important idea of tension in the study of the biblical story. Licht calls the building and resolution of tension one of the two foundations of biblical narrative.[1] C. Westermann spoke of an arc stretching through the narrative and giving it dramatic resilience.[2] As it rises and tightens, it entangles the principal characters or the events of their lives. It presents a crisis in relations, a menacing turn of events, or a confrontation that demands and holds the anxious curiosity of the audience.[3] Exod. 1.1-7 is not a full narrative because it lacks a crisis that elicits this suspense.[4]

4. *Point of View*

Exod. 1.1-7 uses a different angle of perspective from what precedes and follows. At the end of Genesis 50 we were with Joseph in Egypt when he predicted that God would 'bring [his brothers] up out of this land' (Gen. 50.24). We were given a glimpse of the inner life of the characters: 'He comforted them and spoke to their heart' (Gen. 50.21). But now we do not see through the eyes of any character; we stand beside the narrator above the action and its natural flow of time. In v. 1, the narrator begins his report with an external, unpersonified focalization. ואלה שמות, 'these are the names', is presented to the reader panchronically.[5] By v. 6, by changing the relative adjective, the narrator has taken the position in time; we look back on 'that generation' (הדור ההוא), seen now as past. But the narrator is not yet

1. Licht, *Storytelling in the Bible* (Jerusalem: Magnes Press, 1978), p. 26. The other principle is the exposition of dialogue and action with a minimum of description.

2. C. Westermann, 'Arten der Erzählung in der Genesis', in *idem*, *Forschung am Alten Testament* (TBü, 24; Munich: Kaiser Verlag, 1964), pp. 33-34.

3. G.W. Coats, 'Tale', in Coats (ed.), *Saga, Legend, Tale, Novella, Fable*, p. 65.

4. Westermann ('Arten der Erzählung', p. 34) says the same about Gen. 13.14-17. Looking across the whole story of the Exodus, however, G.W. Coats ('A Structural Transition in Exodus', *VT* 22 [1972], pp. 138, 142) finds an arc of tension beginning here and coming to an end in Exod. 12.

5. S. Rimmon-Kenan, *Narrative Fiction* (London: Methuen, 1983), p. 78: 'External focalization is panchronic in the case of an unpersonified focalizer'. The next chapter will devote more attention to this and other matters of focalization.

fixed in space. The journey of the sons of Israel is a movement neither to nor from the narrator; for בוא (v. 1) can mean either 'to go in' or 'to come in'.[1]

5. *Repetition and Narrative Gaps*

As 'escape from danger' and 'fulfilment', the incomplete deep structure of Exod. 1.1-7 both unites and separates Genesis and Exodus. It unites the books by repeating material. It separates them by presenting that information from a different point of view and by altering it subtly in ways we will see. The deep structure and the external focalization set in motion a process of filling in gaps. M. Sternberg has worked on this important narrative reality:

> From the viewpoint of what is directly given in the language, the literary work consists of bits and fragments to be linked and pieced together in the process of reading: it establishes a system of gaps that must be filled in. This gap-filling ranges from simple linkages of elements, which the reader performs automatically, to intricate networks that are figured out consciously, laboriously, hesitantly, and with constant modifications in the light of additional information disclosed in later stages of reading.[2]

The narrative can control this ambiguity by closing some gaps. 'Incongruity is brought out by reference to one...feature, then resolved by appeal to another of the same scope.'[3] These sources of affirmation are variously 'directions', that is, infallible indications from the narrator; 'half-directions', like comments from the characters who are often unreliable; or 'indirections', such as metonymy, analogy, verbal echo or generic frame.[4] Our case is of the third kind. We determine analogously why the events in 1.1-7 happen by recalling their origins in Genesis.

The insufficiency of the information in this prelude encourages us to make further correlations. Now that God has honoured his assurances of fertility, we can hope as well for the other two blessings. He promised land, often in the same theophany. And he undertook not to

1. *HALAT*, I, p. 109; BDB, p. 97.
2. *Poetics*, p. 186.
3. Sternberg, *Poetics*, p. 254.
4. Sternberg, *Poetics*, p. 259.

abandon them.[1] Since the promises made to the patriarchs are often together and are the most common motif in Genesis 12–50,[2] it is allowable to anticipate all the benedictions in the fulfilment of one. In the pericopes to come, numerous verbal clues will furnish 'indirections' along these lines of association. On his deathbed Joseph has just predicted the eventual departure of his family from Egypt (Gen. 50.24-25). Less happily, we also recall that God said to Abram they would be oppressed for four hundred years before coming out (Gen. 15.13). By deriving hope and anxiety from gaps and repetition, the story can see forward by looking back, as in a mirror.[3]

This expectant repetition hints as well at the thematic presuppositions on which the story of the oppression and the Exodus will rest. The closing scenes of the Joseph cycle in Genesis bring his brothers before him after the death of their father. The brothers are afraid that Joseph will avenge himself and they bow to him, calling themselves his 'slaves' (Gen. 50.18). Joseph assures them, 'Do not fear. Am I in the place of God?... God meant it for good to keep alive a numerous people' (Gen. 50.19-20). The struggle for the Hebrews' liberation will show that Pharaoh cannot win because he is guilty of precisely the

1. Mention of God's promise of land is in Gen. 12.7; 15.7-21; 24.7; 50.24; promises of land and posterity are mentioned together in 13.14-17; 17.4-8; 22.17; 26.3-4, 28.3-4, 13-14; 35.11-12; 48.4. His presence is assured in Gen. 31.3, together with one or both of the other promises in Gen. 12.1-3; 17.1-11, 17-20; 26.3, 24; 28.15; 46.3; 48.21.

2. C. Westermann, 'Promises to the Patriarchs', *IDBSup*, p. 691. D.J.A. Clines (*The Theme of the Pentateuch* [JSOTSup, 10; Sheffield: JSOT Press, 1978], esp. p. 29) believes that the principal theme of the Pentateuch is 'the partial fulfilment—which implies also the partial non-fulfilment—of the promise to or the blessing of the patriarchs'. He speaks of a single threefold promise. Olson (*Death of the Old*, p. 113) also finds that the promise is a major theme, but accuses Clines of unstructured and unverifiable methodology (p. 190). W. Brueggemann ('The Kerygma of the Priestly Writers', *ZAW* 84 [1972], p. 412) has studied the genealogies in P texts and concludes that they generally make the connection between the times of a promise and its fulfilment.

3. These sentiments born of implication are the closest that this unit comes to suspense. But they do not crystallize around an issue until 1.8-14, and thus do not form the kind of dramatic tension that allows one to chart its structural development. See 'Narrative Structure—Surface' above. In his diachronic analysis, T.C. Vriezen ('Exodusstudien Exodus I', *VT* 17 [1967], p. 343) also writes that this unit looks both forward and backward, but for smoothness to bridge a gap in the tradition.

hubris that Joseph rejects.[1] Pharaoh will say, 'Who is YHWH that I should heed his voice in sending away Israel?' (Exod.5.2). Reverence toward God will be set against foolish pride, and subjugation will be compared to freedom (Exod. 15.1-18).[2]

Note too Joseph's reflection that his brothers 'meant evil on [him] but God meant it for good...'[3] Providence will continue to figure in the story to follow. We will see how every act of oppression by Pharaoh leads to increased growth among the Israelites. As the narrator will say, 'And the more they oppressed them, the more they increased' (1.12).[4]

Two more elements in the prelude mark and specify the repetition it entails. These are the opening words and the genealogy.

The syndetic construction of the opening verse, ואלה שמות, records syntactically the close connection between this passage and what comes before.[5] The ו is all the more important to confirm the link that repetition will amplify because stylistically the end of Genesis is quite different from the beginning of Exodus. Genesis closes with narrative that uses direct speech, character interplay and a shift in focalization, all of which are absent from these first seven verses of Exodus.[6]

The role of the genealogy in the delimitation of the unit has already been discussed. As a repetition, it digests and supplements what the narrative has already told us. Israel's sons have already been listed in

1. Greenberg, *Understanding Exodus*, p. 22.

2. D. Daube, *The Exodus Pattern in the Bible* (All Souls Studies, 2; London: Faber & Faber, 1963), p. 12; Cazeaux, 'Naître en Egypte: Exode 1–7, 7—Etude littéraire', *RHPR* 60 (1980), p. 406.

3. O.S. Wintermute ('Joseph, son of Jacob', *IDB*, II, p. 984) considers this verse the most complete expression of the theology of the Joseph story. See also the note on Gen. 50.19-20 in *The New Oxford Annotated Bible with the Apocrypha* (rev. edn; ed. A.G. May and B.M. Metzger; New York: Oxford University Press, 1977 [1962]).

4. Refer to the logically subsequent observation in Chapter 3, 'Narrative Structure', that every mention of the proliferation of the Hebrews is followed by a new rise in tension.

5. Joüon, *Grammaire*, §§159-60; E. Kautsch (ed.), *Gesenius' Hebrew Grammar* (trans. A.E. Cowley; Oxford: Clarendon Press, 1910), §49b n. 1. This work will henceforth be referred to by the standard abbreviation GKC.

6. We have already noted the shift from external focalization focused out to that focused inward in Gen. 50.21: 'Thus he comforted them and spoke to their heart'. More will be explained about these technicalities of focalization in Chapter 2.

Genesis 35 and 46. In fact, Gen. 46.8 uses the exact phrase ואלה שמות בני ישראל. In Genesis 35, the sons' names were explicitly ordered according to Israel's wives Leah and Rachel, then their maids Bilhah and Zilpah. In Genesis 46 the order is the sons and grandsons of Leah and her maid Zilpah followed by the sons and grandsons of Rachel and her maid Bilhah. Neither is the same as the order of birth given in Genesis 29–30 or of the blessings in Genesis 49.

The list in Exod. 1.1-7 is original. It follows the broad 'genealogical framework of Genesis 46,[1] but drops the details of the sons of the sons. It copies Genesis 35 in citing the sons of the wives before those of the concubines, the eldest to the youngest by each mother. But it drops the explicit mention of the women. The result is the creation out of the Genesis tradition of a simplified and implicit hierarchical order, detailed chronologically.[2]

This ordered genealogy repeats the record of the past interpretatively.[3] And in doing so it introduces the growth of the sons of Israel from a family into a people.[4] That is, the sons of Israel are becoming a nation by a process in which principles and events are coconstitutive. Like the genealogy itself, the Exodus story will be construed history.

1. Childs, *Exodus*, p. 2.

2. S. Talmon ('The Presentation of Synchroneity and Simultaneity in Biblical Narrative', in *Studies in Hebrew Narrative Art Throughout the Ages* [ed. J. Heinemann and S. Werses; Scripta Hierosolymitana, 27; Jerusalem: Magnes Press, 1978], pp. 14-17) takes Exod. 1.1-5 as an example of 'resumptive repetition' safeguarding the 'linear continuity of the narration' while also promoting 'the synchroneity of the events related' (p. 17). However, his interest is not in the subtle changes in the Genesis and Exodus genealogies. According to Greenberg (*Understanding Exodus*, p. 18), their variations mean that 'whatever significance may have inhered originally in the ranking of the twelve had become blurred by the time the traditions were fixed'. He does not attempt to find a principle in this redaction of the list.

3. This is not an unusual function for a genealogy according to K.F. Plum, 'Genealogy as Theology', *SJOT* 1 (1989), p. 85. She maintains that genealogies in Scripture show that history has a meaning and purpose.

4. M. Noth, *Exodus* (trans. J.S. Bowden; Philadelphia: Westminster Press, 1962), p. 20; Coats, 'Transition', p. 135; Lacocque, *Devenir*, p. 32. W.H. Schmidt (*Exodus*. I. *Exodus 1–6* [Neukirchen–Vluyn: Neukirchener Verlag, 1985], p. 7) neatly terms it the 'Volkwerdung Israels'. Hence the format in the literal translation of בני ישראל changes from 'sons of Israel' to 'Sons of Israel'.

It will be the past understood in function of God's mercy.[1]

The narrator's repeating of what we already know, but in summary form and from a strictly impersonal point of view, enhances his authority as a trustworthy storyteller.[2] This is an indispensable condition of biblical poetics that promotes a 'rhetoric of glorification'. 'The very choice to devise an omniscient narrator serves the purpose of staging and glorifying an omniscient God.' 'The narrator stands to the world of his tale as God to the world represented in that tale, each reigning supreme in his own sphere of activity.'[3] Sternberg may state the correlation between God and the omniscient narrator too strongly and generally. But the coherence and reliability we see here in the narrator's repetition does in fact match God's faithfulness, he who has begun to make good his word to his people.

6. *Narrative Symmetry*

The narrative uses the fertility of the Israelites as the setting for the continuation of the story and the reason for Pharaoh's oppression. Under the section entitled 'Delimitation', I mentioned a chiastic construction between v. 1 and v. 7. Framed by that pattern, the Israelites' growth is described in a series of reversals. With the people transformed from the countable (70) to the innumerable, and with the list of proper names being matched by a list of verbs of increase, the passage shifts from the static to the dynamic. Joseph had been alone in Egypt; now his people fill the land. The original generation dies off; their successors are powerfully fertile.

The verb forms break into two groups, a division that amplifies these reversals. From v. 1 to v. 5b the verbs are in forms other than *wayyiqtol* (except for ויהי). From v. 5b on, the verbs are all in *wayyiqtol* (except for פרו). The meaning of the verbs also changes at

1. M. Fishbane (*Text and Texture* [New York: Schocken Books, 1979], p. 64) calls Exod. 1–19 'a literary construct fusing saga and history. . . focusing selectively on specific events and people, endowing the encounters with a paradigmatic cast and infusing historical process with the wonder of supernatural events'.

2. M. Sternberg, 'The Repetition Structure in Biblical Narrative: Strategies in Informational Redundancy', *HaSifrut* 25 (1977), pp. 116-17 (Hebrew).

3. Cf. Sternberg, *Poetics*, pp. 91, 89, 83, for the last three quotations respectively; also his 'Repetition', p. 136, where he cites Gen. 1.3-31 as the clearest example: 'God said, "Let there be light". And there was light.'

v. 5b. Before then, they all speak of coming, going and being. After v. 5b, they are about fruitfulness and filling. The one verb outside this pattern of semantic fields signals the transition, וימת.

Verses 5b and v. 7a both begin with a ו copulative: ...ובני ישראל ויוסף. These two constructions bracket and stress the crucial news of the death of Joseph, his brothers and all that generation in v. 6. Their passing is the first step in the plot beyond the events of the Joseph cycle in Genesis. The story is now free to advance.[1] We noted too that the focalization took a position in time here, looking back on 'that generation' now past.[2]

This balance between the name 'Joseph' and בני ישראל perhaps also encourages our conclusion that, by this stage in the unit, through the device of synecdoche, the latter is more a proper name than a description. It is better translated freely 'Israelites' than 'sons of Israel'.[3]

A number of lexical repetitions and a minor chiastic pattern provide a bit of added cohesion to the loose but serviceable symmetry of the unit: בני ישראל, מצרים, בוא, נפש, יוסף, יעקב, כל and מאד.[4] The patriarch is called, in order, Israel–Jacob–Jacob–Israel.

1. Lacocque (*Devenir*, p. 30) writes that in the Pentateuch, an entire generation must pass to clear the way for the birth of a history that is new but in continuity with what has gone before. Coats ('Transition', p. 131) says a death notice announcing the end of a generation commonly stands at the end of a major redactional unit.

2. Without a detailed stylistic analysis, Childs (*Exodus*, pp. 2-3) writes that v. 7, not v. 6, functions as a hinge verse by pointing in both directions. It serves as the fulfilment of the Genesis promise and the background for the events initiating the Exodus. But Greenberg (*Understanding Exodus*, p. 19) sees that the true sequel to the end of Genesis sets in only at v. 6. My analysis is an alternative to Schmidt's conclusion (*Exodus*, p. 10) that v. 6 does not fit in stylistically. For him it anticipates the threatening future and adds nothing to the purpose of 1.1-7 (to report the growth of the people). Vriezen ('Exodusstudien', p. 335) also excludes v. 6 from vv. 1-7. He attaches it to v. 8 as a part of a unit which is a 'Bindeglied' between the patriarchal and Exodus stories.

3. E.W. Bullinger (*Figures of Speech Used in the Bible* [Ann Arbor, MI: Baker, 1968 (London, 1898)], p. 624), on synecdoche, citing בן in this verse: 'Words of a limited and special sense are used with a wider and more universal meaning'.

4. The last is in fact an instance of epizeuxis, 'the repetition of a word with no other word in between'. The definition is from Lanham, *Handlist*, p. 125. See also Bullinger, *Figures of Speech*, p. 189.

7. *Vocabulary*

All the semantic fields here will reappear in later pericopes:

> Nationality: בני ישראל, מצרים (2×), ארץ
> Fertile Life and Family: בני ישראל, בית, אח, דור, ירך, פרה, שרץ, רבה, נפש
> עצם, מלא (*niph.*)
> Affliction: מות
> Motion: בוא (2×), יצא

בני ישראל figures under both 'Fertile Life and Family' and 'Nationality', because, as we will see, its signification changes in the course of these verses. ירך has been classified under 'Fertile Life and Family', because 'thigh' here means 'loins, as seat of procreative power'.[1] Joseph's death in old age is not a tragedy in itself, and on first glance it seems strange to classify it as 'Affliction', except that that semantic field that will be important throughout Exodus 1–2, and the passing of his generation is the first step towards Israel's disaster.

שרץ normally describes the movement of small animals.[2] A. Ahuviah suggests that it implies the Hebrews were barely surviving.[3] This seems unlikely here, since they are not yet oppressed. In fact they are 'powerful'. It may have been used here because of its previous occurrences in Genesis, as the paragraphs below will explain.

In the plot, the proliferation of the sons of Israel is according to God's earlier pledge, as we have seen. But in the broader terms of its style, the passage is the convergence of seven key-words used already in Genesis in various combinations and places.[4] Some but not all of these recurrences have been the promises of fertility. Until now they have never been all together.[5]

1. BDB, p. 438; *HALAT*, II, p. 419.
2. Schmidt, *Exodus*, p. 3.
3. A. Ahuviah, '"I Will Bring you up from Egyptian Affliction"', *Beth Mikra* 74 (1978), p. 302 (Hebrew).
4. I.M. Kikawada, 'Literary Convention of the Primaeval History', *Annual of the Japanese Biblical Institute* 1 (1975), p. 14.
5. C. Houtman, *Exodus* (Commentaar op het Oude Testament; Kampen: J.H. Kok, 1986), I (on 1.1–7.13), p. 222.

The key-words are פרה, שרץ, רבה, עצם, מלא, ארץ, and the adverbial expression במאד מאד.[1]

We find the key-words in Genesis in two contexts: created life and the ancestors of the sons of Israel.

About created life, the words apply to the waters (1.20); to 'the great sea monsters and every living creature that swarms (שרץ), with which the waters swarm' (1.21; with the birds, 1.22); and to 'all flesh...all the swarmers that swarm upon the earth...and every living person' (7.21; also 8.17, 19).

As for the ancestors, they are Adam (1.28), Noah (9.1, 7), Abraham (17.2, 6, 8; 18.18; 22.17; 26.4, 24), Ishmael (17.20), Jacob-Israel (28.3; 35.11; 48.4; with his family, 47.27), Hagar (16.10), Isaac (26.16, 22), Joseph (41.52; 49.22).[2]

The diction of Exod. 1.1-7 joins the passage to all that comes before it—the Creation and all the patriarchal stories. The narrative technique of repetition, and the genealogy especially, showed that Israel grows into a nation by divine promise as part of an historical process. The vocabulary, for its part, stresses that this process is a continuous act. The entire past is constitutive of the present in Exod. 1.1-7, and both are witnesses to God's free cooperation with humankind. The nation that is born here will soon come into its own identity. But that identity, like the fertility that prepares for it, are not arbitrary products of the divine. God's will is proved omnipotent, but it will be realized in the Exodus story through human history because the promises of growth are fulfilled ineluctably, but in language made familiar to us from descriptions of the past in Genesis. God is not dependent on the Israelites. But he chooses to involve them in his plans. He who in Genesis existed before Creation bends here to the human measure of time, where the present flows out of the entire past.

A final item of vocabulary calls for notice. ותמלא (v. 7e) is a *niphal wayyiqtol*: 'so the land was filled with them'. The *niphal* means that the Israelites are not the direct agent of action. It is perhaps a theological passive where God himself is the implied actor. The same gram-

1. See the Appendix, 'Combinations in Genesis of Key-Words in Exodus 1.1-7', at the end of the volume.

2. The number 70 is merely an approximate figure. See M.H. Pope, 'Seven, Seventh, Seventy', *IDB*, IV, p. 295. It is worth noting that Gen. 46 and the LXX of this verse both give the total as 75.

matical construction with מלא and ארץ is to be found in Gen. 6.11: ותמלא ארץ חמס.[1] There the earth was filled with violence due to humankind's sinfulness, prompting God's punishment. Now, through no merit of the Israelites, the land is filled with them as a sign of God's faithfulness.

8. *Conclusions*

By its repetition and vocabulary, Exod. 1.1-7 joins the opening chapters of Exodus to what has preceded in Genesis, laying down the conditions for the furtherance of the story. The reader knows the authority of the narrator and the truth of the divine promises to the Israelites. How will the propagation of the Hebrews now affect their condition and induce the redemption of the other pledges?

1. ותמלא is a *niphal* 'à sens statif' (Joüon, *Grammaire*, §118a). The accusative is used after 'verba copiæ' (Meyer, *Hebräische Grammatik*, §105.3a; GKC §117z, 121d; Joüon, *Grammaire*, §125d). The second object of a doubly transitive verb stays in the accusative when the verb is used passively (Meyer, *Hebräische Grammatik*, §109.2; Joüon, *Grammaire*, §128c).

Chapter 2

EXODUS 1.8-14

1. *Literal Translation*

8a Now a new king arose over Egypt
8b who did not know of Joseph.
9a He said to his people,
9b 'Behold, the people of the Sons of Israel are too many and too mighty for us.
10a Come,
10b let us deal shrewdly with them
10c lest they multiply
10d and,
10e if war should happen to us,
10f they as well join our foes,
10g fight against us
10h and go up from the land.'
11a And they set taskmasters over them to oppress them with their burdens.
11b They built store-cities for Pharaoh,
11c Pitom and Raamses.
12a And the more they continued to oppress them,
12b the more they increased and
12c the more they spread
12d so that they came to shudder in horror at the Sons of Israel.
13 The Egyptians made the Sons of Israel work with rigour.
14a They made their life bitter
14b with hard work,
14c with mortar
14d and with bricks
14e and with every work in the field,
14f all their work
14g which they had done by them with rigour.

Notes on the Literal Translation

Verse 9b. ממנו: 'too...for us'. The sense could also be comparative: 'more numerous and mightier than we'.[1] Considerations of the rhetorical situation, to be studied later, have guided the preference shown in this translation.

Verse 10e. תקראנה: 'should happen'. This verb is most directly explained as a feminine third-person plural used with מלחמה considered as a collective.[2] The Samaritan Pentateuch, Targum Onkelos and the Syriac Peshitta have the feminine third-person singular with suffix: תקראנו: 'should happen to us' (GKC, §47k).

Dahood turned to קרא[3] and suggested the *qal* passive of the energic mood: *tuqrā'annâ*, 'when war is declared'.[4] Lacocque accepts this possibility.[5] Schmidt[6] does not.

Verse 10h. ועלה מן־הארץ: 'and go up from the land'. One translation overinterprets this phrase as 'rise from the ground', explaining in a note that the meaning is perhaps 'rise from their wretched position'.[7]

1. Meyer, *Hebräische Grammatik*, §98.3a; BDB, p. 582; C. Brockelmann, *Hebräische Syntax* (Neukirchen: Moers, 1956), §111g; cf. M. Dahood ('Ugaritic-Hebrew Syntax and Style', in *Ugarit-Forschungen* [ed. K. Bergerhof *et al.*; Neukirchen–Vluyn: Neukirchener Verlag, 1969], I, pp. 21-22), who makes v. 10b comparative by juxtaposition as well: 'Let us show ourselves shrewder than him'.

2. Schmidt, *Exodus*, p. 3; F. Michaeli, *Le Livre de l'Exode* (CAT, 2; Neuchâtel: Delachaux & Niestlé, 1974), p. 29 n. 2. For the common phenomenon of plural verbs with singular collective nouns, see, e.g., Meyer, *Hebräische Grammatik*, §94.3c, 4b, 5d; §97.2f.

3. *HALAT*, III, pp. 1053–55: קרא I = 'rufen, schreien'.

4. M. Dahood, 'Hebrew-Ugaritic Lexicography ix', *Bib* 52 (1971), p. 348. See also Meyer, *Hebräische Grammatik*, §63.5d.

5. *Devenir*, p. 35.

6. *Exodus*, p. 3.

7. *The Torah: The Five Books of Moses: A New Translation of the Holy Scriptures according to the Masoretic Text* (Philadelphia: Jewish Publication Society, 2nd edn, 1967 [1962]). (This will henceforth be indicated by its standard abbreviation NJV.) Little help is given here in H.M. Orlinsky (ed.), *Notes on the New Translation of The Torah: A Systematic Account of the Labors and Reasoning of the Committee that Translated* The Torah (Philadelphia: Jewish Publication Society, 1969), p. 149.

Another suggests 'arise from the underworld, gain a resurrection'.[1] Both translations are anachronistic, since the Hebrews do not fall into hardship until this speech is acted on.

The other variation from the literal is 'gain ascendancy over the land',[2] a translation that chafes against the natural constraints of the lexical and narrative context. For עלה מן־הארץ is a stereotypical expression in Hebrew for the action of leaving Egypt, attested even in Egyptian.[3] Note especially that Joseph 'went up' to bury his father in the last moments of Genesis (Gen. 50.5-6, 9, 14). In Gen. 50.24 he predicted that God would 'bring [his family] up' later: והעלה מן־הארץ הזאת. In Exod. 3.8, God says he 'has come down... to bring them up out of that land'. Our work has begun to expose the close relation between these promises in Genesis and their realization in Exodus. Pharaoh is an unwitting instrument of this fulfilment; as we will see, his own speech is ironic, and, with the meaning 'go up from the land', this expression in his mouth is a first example.[4]

Verse 14b. את (no English equivalent). The function of this word here is a crux of biblical syntax. This translation deliberately does not render it, accepting with Hoftijzer that it is simply 'determinative'. Such uses of את are not necessarily emphatic.[5] Respect is due to Muroaka's argument that את is never used for emphasis even where

1. W.L. Holladay, ''*Ereṣ*—Underworld: Two More Suggestions', *VT* 19 (1969), pp. 123-24.

2. M. Lambert ('Notes Exégétiques III: Exode, I, 10 et Osée, II.2', *REJ* 39 (1899), p. 300), whose idea won the support of Eissfelt, Beer and Noth. See K. Rupprecht, 'עלה מן הארץ (Ex. 110 Hos. 22): "sich des Landes bemächtigen"?', *ZAW* 82 (1970), p. 443.

3. G. Wehmeier, עלה *'lh* hinaufgehen', *THAT*, II, p. 274; *HALAT*, III, pp. 783, 784; *ANET*, p. 258 n. 3; see Gen. 13.1; 45.25; Exod. 12.38; 13.18; Num. 32.11; Judg. 11.13, 16; 19.30 etc.

4. In its literal sense, and because of these parallels in Genesis and Exodus, Weimar (*Berufung*, p. 128) calls 1.10 a 'theologische Reflexion'.

5. J. Hoftijzer, 'Remarks Concerning the Use of the Particle *'et* in Classical Hebrew', *OTS* 14 (1965), pp. 27, 92-93; cf. p. 23. See also J. MacDonald, 'The Particle את in Classical Hebrew: Some New Data on its Use with the Nominative' (*VT* 14 [1964], pp. 264-75), who lists instances where the particle seems to introduce without emphasizing. T. Muraoka (*Emphatic Words and Structures in Biblical Hebrew* [Jerusalem: Magnes Press, 1985], p. 149) may be harsh with MacDonald in not recognizing that he is making this distinction.

awkwardly employed because of a 'Konstruktionsmischung'.[1] The stress in the sentence would more naturally seem to bear on the rare and repeated expression בפרך. Hence Houtman translates the sentence, 'All the work for which they conscripted them went together with mistreatment'.[2]

GKC (§117i, m) admits the possibility of את as introducing or emphasizing a nominative, but does not quote our text as an example. Joüon[3] hesitates between this position and an 'accusatif de limitation ou de spécification'.

Since A. Dillmann, many commentators have taken this את as the sign of the accusative, used by attraction under the influence of the verb in the following relative clause.[4]

But A.B. Ehrlich returns to the idea of the emphatic, objecting that this verb עבד is intransitive with the instrumental בהם, giving it a causal sense: את כל־עבדתם אשר־עבדו בהם, literally, 'all the work which they (had, arranged to have) worked by them'. And such phrases cannot take את as a *nota accusativum*.[5]

Cassuto translates it as the preposition, 'with' but does not explain its relation to the five instances of ב in vv. 13-14 that also carry that meaning.[6]

1. Muraoka, *Emphatic Words*, pp. 146-58. He denies that it is ever used with a 'genuine subject noun' (p. 158).

2. 'Al de arbeid, waarbij zij hen inzetten, ging gepaard met mishandeling' (*Exodus*, p. 237).

3. *Grammaire*, §125j.

4. A. Dillmann, *Exodus und Leviticus* (Kurzgefasstes exegetisches Handbuch zum Alten Testament, 12; Leipzig: Hirzel, 3rd edn, 1897), p. 14. J. Blau ('Zum angeblichen Gebrauch von *'t* vor dem Nominativ', *VT* 4 [1954], p. 11) is notable among those who agree with Dillman. Meyer (*Hebräische Grammatik*, §105, 1b, n. 1, p. 72) criticizes Blau for believing so. Meyer himself defends the emphatic use of the particle with the nominative.

5. A.B. Ehrlich, *Randglossen zur Hebräischen Bibel: Genesis und Exodus* (Leipzig: Hinrichs, 1908), I, p. 260. P.P. Saydon ('Meanings and Uses of the Particle את', *VT* 14 [1964], p. 201) also calls it 'a clear case of emphasis', but Muraoka (*Emphatic Words*, p. 151) accuses him of confusing emphasis and determinedness or definiteness.

6. *Commentary*, p. 12. Muraoka (*Emphatic Words*, p. 156 n. 136) rejects Joüon's view (*Grammaire*, §125j) that את can stand in apposition to another preposition.

2. *Delimitation*

We have already noted in the last chapter under this heading that Exod. 1.8-14 is marked by a פ as a פתוחא. It is narratively distinguished from the previous passage by the introduction of a new character, the king who did not know Joseph, and a new discoursive technique, direct speech.[1]

The passage begins and ends with mention of the antagonists, Egypt (vv. 8a, 13) and the Israelites (vv. 9c, 12c). Verses 13 and 14 conclude the episode by summarizing its action. The next pericope begins with the arrival on the scene of the Hebrew midwives and the change from monologue to dialogue.

3. *Narrative Structure*

Deep

The narrative scheme is complicated by the failure of Pharaoh's plan and his determination to continue the persecution. The formal pattern of Exod. 1.8-14 is of the type, 'problem–attempted solution–result'. The Israelites' growth is a blessing in itself. But Pharaoh presents it as a problem in a way that sets the train of the narrative. As one author has put it, 'The only crime of which the people Israel stands accused is that of existence. They dare to exist, to multiply, and to flourish.'[2]

Surface

Unlike 1.1-7, which, as we saw, had no independent arc of tension, 1.8-14 shares with many other biblical plots a simple 'dramatic structure'.[3] In this structure, the narrative builds up tension from an opening of relative calm. A sense of anxious uncertainty arises—a

1. Vriezen ('Exodusstudien', pp. 338-39) sees the same division of the first and second pericopes of Exodus, but makes a different link between them. He maintains that the verbs of vv. 6 and 8, וימת and ויקם, are a succession formula occurring also in Josh. 1.2 and Judg. 2.8-10 and linking them to Exod. 1.

2. D.E. Zeligs, *Moses: A Psychodynamic Study* (New York: Human Sciences Press, 1986), p. 42.

3. The expression is S. Bar-Efrat's ('Some Observations on the Analysis of Structure in Biblical Narrative', *VT* 30 [1980], p. 165). He outlines the theory of the pyramid pattern in pp. 165-66, and in *The Art of Narration in the Bible* (Tel Aviv: Sifriat Poalim, 2nd edn, 1984 [1979]), pp. 135-36 (Hebrew).

mixture of suspense and surprise blended in various proportions and ways according to the narrative in question.[1] It progresses to a turning point, that is, to the climax of the tension, when the future direction of the story is immediately in question and must be settled in one way or the other. A lessening of the suspense follows until the conclusion, which is usually but not always more or less tranquil.[2]

The opening verse quickly becomes alarming, because a new ruler who does not know the Hebrews' contribution to Egypt is liable to set off the cruelty predicted in Gen. 15.13-14: '"Know, yes, know that your descendants will be sojourners in a land that is not theirs, and will be slaves there and they will be oppressed for four hundred years"'. The tension mounts until v. 12a-12b: 'And the more they continued to oppress them, the more...' Until this point, we have not known the effect of the oppression on the Israelites. Do they suffer loss in proportion to their suffering? This is the climax, the moment of greatest anxiety when the future direction of the story is immediately in question and must be settled in one way or the other. It passes when we learn that in fact they are multiplying more than ever.

The tension diminishes somewhat after the climax, but it does not relax fully because the persecution goes on. We expect more danger soon; for the Egyptians now 'shudder in horror at the Sons of Israel'.

The concluding vv. 13-14 give details of the work imposed. Since the conflict is not resolved, the conclusion does not restore equilibrium to the relations of the characters. On the contrary, we suspect that Pharaoh will soon put forth a second plan.

4. *Point of View*

If for no other initial reason, our sympathies lie with the Israelites because they are the descendants of the patriarchs whom we already know, and they are the inheritors of God's promises to them. It is interesting therefore that the point of view here in no way favours these protagonists. The focalization remains external and unpersonified, close to the narrator.

But an outside focalizer can perceive an object either from without

1. S. Chatman, *Story and Discourse* (Ithaca, NY: Cornell University Press, 1978), pp. 59-62.

2. Coats ('Tale', p. 65), referring to Olrik; Licht, *Storytelling*, p. 26.

or within, 'In the first case, only the outward manifestations of the object (person or thing) are presented... In the second case, the external focalizer (narrator-focalizer) presents the focalized from within, penetrating his feelings and thoughts.'[1] Twice we see within characters in Exod. 1.8-14, but in each case they are the antagonists with whom we have no empathy. In v. 8b we learn that the new king did not know Joseph. In v. 12c the narrator-focalizer tells us that the Egyptians shuddered in horror at the Hebrews.

Two results come from this technique of focalization. First, our allegiance to the Israelites is not built on pathos. We are kept at a distance and the narrator does not emotionally exploit their predicament to secure our good will for them. Other aspects of the narration will establish the pericope's ideology.

Secondly, the focalization prevents us from undue arrogance in relation to Pharaoh. He does not know Joseph, but we do. That is normally what Sternberg (*Poetics*, p. 163) calls a 'reader-elevating' strategy of focalization, since it places us in a position superior to the character. But our advantage over him in this regard is balanced out by our ignorance of something else that he alone knows, his real motivation for persecuting the Hebrews. Houtman thinks he fears the submersion of Egyptian culture and the loss of the Hebrews' manpower.[2] J.S. Ackerman and E. Fox speculate that he is paranoid.[3] Another commentator writes that Pharaoh's attempt to destroy the Hebrews must be 'attributed to pure animosity or viewed as a metaphor for the cheapening of life through slavery'.[4] According to another, he was turning the Hebrews into scapegoats because he faced an undescribed threat to his authority from others. It was Egyptian xenophobia for Fox.[5]

As we will see in the section on rhetoric, the reasons he actually

1. Rimmon-Kenan, *Narrative Fiction*, p. 76; also G. Prince, *Narratology* (Janua Linguarum, Series Maior, 108; Berlin: Mouton, 1982), pp. 50-51.

2. *Exodus*, pp. 225, 231.

3. 'The Literary Context of the Moses Birth Story (Exodus 1–2)', in *Literary Interpretations of Biblical Narratives* (ed. K.R.R. Gros-Lewis, J.S. Ackerman *et al.*; New York: Abingdon Press, 1974), I, p. 81; *Names*, p. 12.

4. J. Nohrnberg, 'Moses', in *Images of God and Man* (ed. B.O. Long; Bible and Literature Series, 1; Sheffield: Almond Press, 1981), p. 50.

5. Fox, *Names*, p. 13, who cites the Egyptians' horror of eating with foreigners alluded to in Gen. 43.32.

gives are demagogic. From the text, we simply do not know the real motives behind Pharaoh's policy. As so often in Biblical narrative, the narrator-focalizer is even-handed, keeping the audience dependent on him by controlling our knowledge. At times we are admitted to the divine eyrie, looking out over history, but we are never allowed to tarry there and so forget our place in God's created order. We are put in mind of our human limitations which lower us beneath the narrator's and God's omniscience. We undergo the drama of discovery that is part of the experience of the Bible.[1]

5. *Narrative Symmetry*

The whole passage is set off by an inclusion of מצרים and בני ישראל (vv. 8-9, 13).

Pharaoh's speech has a peculiar syntax that will be studied later. In the observation of the narrative pattern here, one need only remark that it is embraced and set off by two series of *wayyiqtol* verbs (vv. 8a, 9a, 11a, 11b: ויקם, ויאמר, וישימו ויבן). This second series cuts off suddenly at the beginning of the climax to distinguish the rise in tension: וכאשר (v. 12a).

The conclusion has an unmistakeable symmetry—an inclusion of בפרך and two kinds of stark repetition. The eight-fold recurrence of the preposition ב is an epanaphora, intensive recourse to the same word at the beginning of successive phrases. Polyptoton is the term for the multiplication of a root in various forms, for example, עבד, which occurs five times here. These are blunt means to show the grinding down of the Israelites.

The general outline of the pericope is drawn broadly with two strokes: the speech of Pharaoh, and his audience's response in their oppression of the Hebrews. Note the four twinned verbs of motion that join these lines: literally, a new king 'arises upon' Egypt and the people 'set down overseers upon' the Hebrews (v. 8a: ויקם...על; v. 11a: וישימו...על). To prevent their 'going up from the land', they 'oppress' them, the latter a *piel* derivation of 'to bow down' (v. 10h:

1. Sternberg, *Poetics*, pp. 166-72. Some critics (e.g. Chatman, *Story*, pp. 116-26) hold that one may infer about a character beyond the information provided by the text. However legitimate this speculation, its advisability depends in part on the nature of the work. Hamlet or the biblical David are richer stuff for free questions than this skeletal portrait of an unnamed Pharaoh.

עלה מן; v. 11a: ענתו; v. 12a: יענו). The verbs give a physical accent to the turn in the destiny of the Hebrews that perhaps reflects the rigours of their labour.

6. *Rhetorical Analysis*

The first spoken words of the Book of Exodus are a piece of public discourse. Pharaoh's speech to his people is short, almost a telegraphic rendition of a leader's words, but it contains rich material for a rhetorical analysis.

The student's first task is to identify the rhetorical situation in terms of the persons, events, objects and relations involved.[1] This rhetorical state of affairs is different from political or personal problems.

These last are unclear and cannot form part of synchronic exegesis. We saw in Section 4 on point of view that we do not know Pharaoh's real and unexpressed motives for his persecution.

His rhetorical task, on the other hand, is plain: his speech tries to describe the proliferation of the Hebrews as a danger and to win the Egyptians to his side against them. According to the text, this exigence lies within Pharaoh himself; for the proliferation of the Hebrews in 1.1-7 is not described as an encroachment on the Egyptians, and nothing stated proves that they would not be valuable allies in case of an enemy attack. In C. Perelman's phrase, Pharaoh's biased presentation of the data endows the Hebrews' growth with rhetorical 'presence', an importance quite apart from its intrinsic value. This rhetorical presence is a psychological element.[2]

Rhetoricians distinguish three branches of the art: deliberative, to exhort or dissuade; judicial, to accuse or defend; and epideictic, to blame or commemorate.[3]

It is evident and noteworthy that Pharaoh's speech is deliberative, not judicial. He does not prove anything against the Israelites forensi-

1. The methodology of this section owes much to the suggestions of G.A. Kennedy (*New Testament Interpretation through Rhetorical Criticism* (Chapel Hill, NC: University of North Carolina Press, 1984), pp. 33-38). Kennedy incorporates here L.F. Bitzer's idea of the 'rhetorical situation'.

2. C. Perelman and L. Olbrechts-Tyteca, *Traité de l'argumentation: La nouvelle rhétorique* (Brussels: Editions de l'Université de Bruxelles, 1988 [1958]), pp. 155-56.

3. Lanham, *Handlist*, p. 106; Kennedy, *Interpretation*, pp. 19, 36.

cally, and cannot even draw inductively on past examples, as is common in other deliberative discourse.[1] Instead he speaks in the hypothetical, and, without himself suggesting a plan, calls on the Egyptians to deal wisely with the Hebrews, because in his rhetorical world they endanger the future.

Pharaoh's speech contains two elements of rhetorical structure: the proem or exordium, and the argumentation or confirmatio. The proem is rarely omitted because it seeks to obtain the attention and goodwill of the assembly.[2] It defines the speaker, the audience and the issue: 'Behold, the people of the Sons of Israel are too many and too mighty for us. Come, let us deal shrewdly with them lest they multiply' (vv. 9b-10c). We will examine later how the choice of words like הנה and הבה impels the audience. More important now is the rhetorical strategy: Pharaoh associates himself with his listeners by using the first-person plural. Aiming, as one does in a proem, most specifically at the disposition of the audience,[3] he is presenting himself as solidary with his people. This 'ethos' must persuade the audience to trust him, and it is especially necessary here because the threat must be created speculatively in the consciousness of the people.

Perelman notes that a proem should stress the qualities in the speaker that one might doubt.[4] Pharaoh's listeners might question his ability to identify with them, because he is an exalted person, because he is new, or for both of these reasons. Pharaoh's introduction (vv. 9b-10c) aims at conquering this doubt. He stands beside them against the conjectural danger of the Hebrew's growth—'too mighty for us'.[5] And he suggests the people can share with him the proverbial wisdom of the kings of Egypt: 'Let us deal shrewdly with them'.[6] The proem creates a community of values that both stimulates the egoism

1. Kennedy, *Interpretation*, p. 36.

2. Kennedy, *Interpretation*, pp. 23-24; Perelman, *Argumentation*, p. 657; H. Lausberg, *Handbuch der Literarischen Rhetorik* (2 vols.; Munich: Max Huebner, 2nd edn, 1970 [1960]), I, §263.

3. Perelman, *Argumentation*, p. 656.

4. *Argumentation*, p. 657.

5. This is the reason for the translation chosen. See above, 'Notes on the Literal Translation'.

6. About the wisdom ascribed to Pharaoh, see Ackerman, 'Literary Context', p. 80; J.A. Wilson, 'Pharaoh', *IDB*, III, p. 774; S.H. Blank, 'Wisdom', *IDB*, IV, p. 855.

of the audience and enhances the appeal of the speaker.

The second part of the speech is the argumentation proper. Pharaoh's rhetoric is quasi-logical, based on an enthymeme or abridged syllogism:

> whoever is רב ועצום ממנו is a threat
> they are רב ועצום ממנו
> therefore they are a threat.

The first, unspoken premise is faulty; numbers do not determine loyalty and, as already noted, nothing suggests the Hebrews had lost the tradition of Joseph's service to Egypt. The error of the argument is disguised by the ambiguous syntax of the middle term; רב ועצום ממנו can mean either 'too many and too mighty for us', an unproved proposition, or 'more numerous and mighty than we', perhaps a statistical truth, but inconclusive.[1]

That Pharaoh's argument is irrational does not mean it lacks cogency. The people's initial opinion of Pharaoh is not recorded, but their response to his speech is immediate. They act on his warning and place taskmasters over the Hebrews. According to the Masoretic text, it is 'they' who take action, either the people alone or the people and Pharaoh: וישמיו עליו שרי מסים (v. 11a). Since Pharaoh's speech does not mention a specific plan, the failure of this first scheme does not lose him his audience's favour. They confirm their allegiance by shuddering in horror at the Hebrews (v. 12c) and never questioning the demagogy. As Lausberg writes, half-quoting from classical vocabulary, 'Die *virtus* des *argumentum* ist in dem *credibile*'.[2] Valuable work by Perelman helps us understand how his speech succeeds with his own listeners, the Egyptians, but fails with us, the authorial audience.

Perelman distinguishes two basic kinds of argumentation:

> Arguments are sometimes given in the form of *liaison* which allows for the transference to the conclusion of the adherence accorded the premises,

1. Incidentally, רב ועצום is indicated as a Ugaritic and Hebrew word pair in L.R. Fisher (ed.), *Ras Shamra Parallels (AnOr*, 49; Rome: Pontificium Institutum Biblicum, 1972), I, p. 516. עצום is used only with collectives: J.W. Olley, '"The Many": How is Isa. 53.12a to be Understood?', *Bib* 68 (1987), p. 340.

2. *Handbuch*, I, §368.

> and at other times in the form of a *dissociation*, which aims at separating elements which language or a recognized tradition have previously tied together.[1]

Perelman outlines a process, almost ignored by traditional rhetorical theory. It seeks to reconcile logical incompatibilities by re-establishing a coherent vision of reality that separates ideas accepted together at the start.

We understand that an oar plunged into the water appears broken to our sight but straight when we touch it, because we distinguish between appearances that correspond to reality and those which do not and are deceptive.

> Hence appearance will have an equivocal status: sometimes it is the expression of reality, at other times only the source of error and illusion. Whereas appearance is given, immediate, the beginning of knowledge, reality which, when it is known, is normally known only through appearances, becomes the criterion that allows us to judge them. Reality will be 'term II', which will be normative in relation to 'term I', to the very extent that it confirms term I as the authentic expression of the real or disqualifies it as error and false appearance.[2]

Dissociation expresses a vision of the world, establishing hierarchies for which it seeks criteria. With the couple 'appearance/reality' as a prototype of notional dissociation, a plethora of philosophical couples can be isolated:[3]

means/end	multiplicity/unity
act/person	individual/universal
accident/essence	particular/general
occasion/cause	theory/practice
relative/absolute	language/thought
subjective/objective	letter/spirit

Couples need not be philosophical and can be antithetical (up/down; good/evil; just/unjust), or simply classificatory: the past may be divided into epochs, an area into regions, a genus into species.

1. C. Perelman, *The Realm of Rhetoric* (trans. W. Kluback; Notre Dame, IN: University of Notre Dame Press, 1982), p. 49.
2. Perelman, *Realm*, p. 127.
3. Cf. Perelman, *Realm*, p. 130; *Argumentation*, pp. 562-64.

> Term I corresponds to the apparent, to what occurs in the first instance, to what is actual, immediate and known directly. Term II, to the extent that it is distinguished from it, can be understood only by comparison with term I: it results from a dissociation effected within term I with the purpose of getting rid of the incompatibilities that may appear between different aspects of term I. Term II provides a criterion, a norm which allows us to distinguish those aspects of term I which are of value from those which are not; it is not simply a datum, it is a *construction* which, during the dissociation of term I, establishes a rule that makes it possible to classify the multiple aspects of term I in a hierarchy. It enables those that do not correspond to the rule which *reality* provides to be termed illusory, erroneous, or apparent (in the depreciatory sense of this word). In relation to term I, term II is both normative and explanatory. After the dissociation has been made, term II makes it possible to retain or to disqualify the various aspects under which term I is presented. It makes it possible to distinguish, out of a number of appearances of doubtful status, [t]hose which are mere appearances and those which represent reality.[1]

We have seen that the major premise of Pharaoh's argument is presupposed and undefended: 'whoever is רב ועצום ממנו constitutes a threat'. Rather than trying to relate a series of logical liaisons to this assumption, he works by the second process of argumentation just described, the technique of dissociation. He changes his countrymen's perception of appearance and reality by projecting before them a world of disturbing rhetorical couples: safety/danger; naivety/cunning; inaction/action; present/future; peace/war; weakness/power; Hebrews/ Egyptians.

A reconstitution of the rhetorical process notes first that, like the rower observing an oar in the water, Pharaoh has asked himself what is real and apparent in the first terms. Regardless of his personal, unknown motives in making the speech, behind his remarks are the questions: what are real and apparent safety, naivety, peace, weakness? What is the consequence of inaction, the true meaning of the present and the actual identity of the Hebrews? This is the initial dissociation effected within term I of which Perelman speaks. Imposing his own biased interpretation, Pharaoh makes the second terms normative, shedding light on these presupposed queries:

1. Perelman, *Realm*, p. 127.

the growth of the Hebrews is danger
accepting his analysis is cunning
action is needed
the future could be a scenario of war
the war could be against an alliance of enemies
power is a matter of controlling a people's numbers (and not, for example, assuring their loyalty)
the Egyptians are a threatened people

These representations of reality now allow him to return to the first members of the couples and distort them:

the safety that Egypt now seems to enjoy is deceptive
only the naive could disagree with him
inaction is dangerous
the present is threatening
true peace can come only through a solution to this crisis
doing nothing would be a sign of weakness
the Hebrews are a menace

The relationship between these couples of terms I and II is not logically rigorous. Most are inverse relations like peace and war which he superimposes by loose analogy on the basic couple 'appearance/reality'. These in turn imply a new distinction between the future and the present, and between the Egyptians and the Hebrews.[1] 'While the original status of what is presented as the starting point of the dissociation is unclear and undetermined, the dissociation into terms I and II will attach value to the aspects that correspond to terms II and will lower the value of the aspects that are in opposition to it.'[2] In any process of dissociation, term II is coherent; it has the substance of unicity and reality. The argument denigrates term I which is multifarious and deceptive.[3] With respect to the Egyptians, Pharaoh gains a double advantage here: by making rhetorical distinctions, his

1. Perelman (*Argumentation*, p. 566) says that the connection between couples often does not have to be explicit. It can be established by various means, like a direct liason between Term I of one couple and Term I of the other, a liason founded on the structure of reality. Or the liason can be between Term II of one couple and Term II of the other. Or can it be a quasi-logical argument, notably the affirmation of the identity of the couples. Most especially the liason can be analogical relations between couples.

2. Perelman, *Realm*, p. 128.

3. Perelman, *Argumentation*, p. 558.

discourse grows in both realism and value preference.

But the speech has two audiences, the immediate one within the narrative, and the second one that reads or listens to that account. The Egyptians, the narratorial audience, believe Pharaoh and turn against the Hebrews. We, the authorial audience, do not. Perelman points out that an unconvinced audience does not always reject the dissociations.[1] Here, for example, we maintain the distinction Pharaoh has made between the Hebrews' past in Egypt before the conflict and their situation now. We recognize that safety and danger are at stake and that a barrier has risen between the Hebrews and Egyptians. But we conceive of these pairs differently from Pharaoh. One of the ways that dissociations are refuted is by the reversal and transformation of the speaker's terms.

We do not find that Pharaoh's dealings are cunning, since his plan fails. That is, we detect an incompatability. And so we reverse the terms naivety/cunning established by Pharaoh. His term II, 'cunning', which he associates with his call to action, ('Let us deal cunningly with them'), is in fact not real or cohesive as he maintains. It becomes term I of a new version of the dissociation that we are to propose to ourselves: 'folly/wisdom'.

	Pharaoh's Version:	Our Reinterpretation:
Term I (related to unreality, error):	naivety	Pharaoh's folly
Term II (related to reality):	Pharaoh's cunning	wisdom

Likewise, we do not accept that the Egyptians are imperilled, and we do not evaluate the Hebrews as a disguised threat under term I's categories of illusion and error. We reverse the formula, define the Egyptians as term I, and his dissociation 'dangerous Hebrews/ imperilled Egyptians' becomes for us 'Egyptian oppressors/oppressed Hebrews'.[2]

1. *Argumentation*, p. 570.

2. Perelman (*Argumentation*, p. 570) writes that a change in terminology almost always indicates a loss of value ('devaluation') in the notion that becomes Term I and a gain in value ('valorisation') in the one that becomes Term II. The change indicates that this reversal is part of another vision of the particular situation, or of the world.

	Pharaoh's Version:	Our Reinterpretation:
Term I (related to unreality, error):	dangerous Hebrews	Egyptian oppressors
Term II (related to reality):	imperilled Egyptians	oppressed Hebrews

By analogy we can make new dissociations as well. 'Folly/wisdom' evokes 'Pharaoh/Joseph', because 'there is no one so perceptive and wise as [Joseph]' (Gen. 41.39). We remember Joseph, but this Pharaoh does not know him—'his ignorance/our knowledge'. We understand that God himself had promised to multiply the Hebrews, and, as the next section will show, the speech reminds us by using the vocabulary of Genesis. Pharaoh is thus opposing God's will: 'Pharaoh/God' and 'evil/good'.

Pharaoh's series of dissociations has three effects on the two audiences. As he intended, it rallies the Egyptians around him. At the same time, it both distances us from him and draws us closer to the Hebrews. Our empathy with the Hebrews is strengthened in the measure that Pharaoh's dissociations are self-convicting.

Already quoted in the introduction, Frye believes that one of the revolutionary innovations of the Book of Exodus is the dialectical turn of mind that divides the world into allies and enemies.[1] Our rhetorical analysis shows that Pharaoh is the one who introduces it into the relations among the characters and the audiences. God himself will sanction the rift between the Egyptians and the Israelites. As he says through Moses to Pharaoh, 'I will set redemption [or division] between my people and your people. By tomorrow this sign will be' (Exod. 8.19).

Pharaoh's speech is profoundly paradoxical. It succeeds in its goals, but fails in its effects. The wise king makes himself foolish. The powerful are thwarted by the weak. He wins one audience but loses another. And he deceives the Egyptians while calling them to awaken to reality. This last incongruity is a matter of irony, the perception of gulf between pretense and reality.[2] In the contradictions of its rhetoric, the Egyptians' oppression is the vehicle of its own rebuttal,

1. *The Great Code*, p. 114.

2. E.M. Good, *Irony in the Old Testament* (Bible and Literature Series, 3; Sheffield: Almond Press, 2nd edn, 1981 [1965]), p. 14.

just as, in the plot, the rigours of their forced labour are self-defeating, stimulating the proliferation that they were intended to ruin.

7. *Vocabulary*

The vocabulary of Exod. 1.8-14 sharpens the authorial audience's response to Pharaoh's rhetoric; it points to the nature of the violence he unleashes, and it sets the whole pericope in the context of past and future events.

All the fields except the last appeared already in 1.1-7. 'Perception' will become more important in later pericopes.[1]

Fertile Life: רב, עצום, רבה (2×), פרץ, חיים
Nationality: מלך, מצרים (2×), עם (2×), בני ישראל (2×), ארץ, פרעה
Affliction: מלחמה, שנאינו, לחם (*niph.*), שים על, קוץ, שרי מסים, ענה (*pi.*),
סבלת, בנה, ערי מסכנות, בפרך (2×), לבנים, חמר, עבד
(5×), מרר (*pi.*), קשה, שדה
Motion: קום, עלה
Perception: הנה, ידע, התחכם
Communication: אמר

אמר qualifies for a semantic field by itself, because it introduces the speech that is two verses long and is key to the development of the plot. The field of communication will grow in importance in later pericopes.

הנה is listed as a word of perception in its quality as a deictic interjection,[2] crudely but adequately translated here as 'Behold!'[3] S. Kogut concludes that הנה grasps and directs the reader's attention.[4] It usually

1. For the notion of perception to group together such fields as knowing and seeing, I am grateful to G. Fischer, who used the term 'Wahrnehmen' in his discussion of the field of 'Sehen' in *Jahwe unser Gott: Sprache, Aufbau und Erzähltechnik in der Berufung des Mose* (*Ex 3–4*) (OBO, 91; Freiburg: Universitätsverlag, 1989), p. 69. According to him, the field of seeing is dominant in Exod. 3.1-9. See also my comments in 'Vocabulary', Chapter 4.

2. *HALAT*, I, p. 242; Brockelmann, *Hebräische Syntax*, §§159a, 164b; Niccacci, *Syntax*, §66; C.J. Labuschagne, 'The Particles הן and הנה', *OTS* 18 (1973), p. 1.

3. Compare for imprecise elegance Houtman, *Exodus*, p. 211: '"Ik heb geconstateerd dat. . . "'.

4. S. Kogut, 'On the Meaning and Syntactical Status of הנה in Biblical Hebrew', in *Studies in Bible 1986* (ed. S. Japhet; Scripta Hierosolymitana, 31; Jerusalem: Magnes Press, 1986), pp. 138, 149; Muraoka, *Emphatic Words*, p. 140. It often

carries 'an overtone of feeling' and always keeps its connection with verbs of perception.[1] Pharaoh uses it to begin the exordium of his speech on a note of some urgency in preparation for his rhetorical ploys.

Certain words define the relation between the categories of vocabulary and also the conflict between the Hebrews and the Egyptians.

First, Pharaoh uses roots that the narrator in 1.1-7 himself repeated from Genesis: רב ועצום and רבה (vv. 9b, 10c, 12b; cf. v. 7).[2] These refer the reader to the previous passage that we know is a fulfilment of the divine promises to the patriarchs. Since Pharaoh is ignorant of Joseph and his family history, his derivative diction here like his argumentation is ironic at his expense. It belittles Pharaoh by reminding us that if he objects to the Hebrew's fertility, his opponent will be the God of the promises.

The second key word is עם. The narrator calls the Egyptians the 'people' of Pharaoh, עמו (v. 9a), and Pharaoh speaks to them about 'the people of the Sons of Israel', the first time they are so called (עם בני ישראל, v. 9c).[3] The issue is thus between two peoples, defined by Pharaoh as a conflict because of their difference in strength (רב ועצום ממנו).[4] One is interested and not surprised therefore to find similarities between this pericope and the biblical origin of diversity among peoples, the Tower of Babel story (Gen. 11.1-9). Many words are shared: הבה, פן, כן, בנה, לבנים, חמר, עיר, בנים, ארץ, הן־הנה, and of course עם.[5] Both stories put emphasis on 'human ingenuity'[6]

marks the beginning of dialogue, as here, according to Niccacci (*Syntax*, §66) and W. Schneider (referred to in H. Katsumura, 'Zur Funktion von *hinneh* [sic] und *w^ehinnēh* in der biblischen Erzählung', *Annual of the Japanese Biblical Institute* 13 [1987], p. 8).

1. D.J. McCarthy, 'The Uses of *w^ehinnēh* in Biblical Hebrew', *Bib* 61 (1980), p. 331.

2. See the Appendix.

3. The phrase is a stylistic link between 1.8-14 and the description of this growth in 1.1-7, which is itself an allusion to Genesis, as we have seen. Greenberg (*Understanding Exodus*, p. 35) says the same thing about פרץ which he calls a telescoping of פרה and שרץ used in 1.1-7.

4. The expression implies strength from large numbers according to A. Berlin, 'On the Meaning of *rb*', *JBL* 100 (1981), p. 91.

5. הבה with the cohortative and פן occurs only here and in Gen. 11.4, according to Kikawada, 'Literary Convention', p. 14.

6. Ackerman, 'Literary Context', p. 81.

conveyed by the cohortative modal form (Gen. 11.3, 4: 'let us make bricks...let us build'; Exod. 1.10: 'let us deal shrewdly'). The fragmentation of the human family into peoples in Genesis is a precondition of Pharaoh's divisive conniving in Exodus.[1]

Finally, a third set of key words helps define the relation between the categories of diction and the antagonists. It is a string of three words that suggests this national conflict between the Hebrews and Egyptians is also a matter of injustice. All vocabulary studies in Biblical Hebrew are subject to the circumscriptions of the corpus.[2] But within its range, ענה (*pi.*), פרך and the interjection הבה belong to the realm of right and wrong.

Daube, the scholar of civil law and the Bible, writes that the verb ענה (*pi.*) means 'to afflict a dependent', and that it has its origin in the area of social rights and duties. Similarly, E.S. Gerstenberger sees a juridical character in the word. J. Pons adds that this oppression is an act against both the physical and moral aspect of the person.[3]

The word פרך is used twice here, but elsewhere in Scripture only in Lev. 25.43, 46, 53 and Ezek. 34.4, and always with the preposition ב. Both other passages are about questions of iniquity. Leviticus says that masters may not rule over their 'brothers, the people of Israel, with rigour'; Ezekiel prophesies against the 'shepherds of Israel' because they have ruled 'with force and rigour'.

1. Ackerman ('Literary Context', pp. 81-82) points out as well that God 'comes down' in Gen. 11. He will do so later in Exodus (3.8).

2. B. Kedar, *Biblische Semantik: Eine Einführung* (Stuttgart: Kohlhammer, 1981), p. 50; C.R. Taber, 'Semantics', *IDBSup*, pp. 801-802. For a detailed list of the dangers of careless word studies, see D.A. Carson, *Exegetical Fallacies* (Grand Rapids: Baker, 1984), pp. 25-66.

3. Daube, *Exodus Pattern*, pp. 26-27:

> [This origin] is assured by the fact that it appears not only in the Book of the Covenant, 'Ye shall not afflict any widow or fatherless child' etc. (Exod. 22.21 [22] E), but also in two incidents from the lives of the patriarchs with a distinctly legal flavour. 'And Sarai afflicted Hagar', we are told, 'and she fled' (Gen. 16.6 J); and in the course of the treaty between Jacob and Laban the latter declares, '"If thou shalt afflict my daughters and if thou shalt take wives besides my daughters. . . see God is witness"' (Gen. 31.50 J).

E.S. Gerstenberger, 'ענה II *'ānāh*', *ThWAT*, VI, p. 259; J. Pons, *L'Oppression dans l'Ancien Testament* (Paris: Letouzey et Ané, 1981), p. 100. In almost half the occurrences, the oppressor is foreign. The idea of humiliation, submission and labour—not poverty—predominates (pp. 101, 104, 123).

More by context than meaning, הבה too implies wrongdoing. It is an interjection, the *qal* imperative emphatic of יהב, 'to give'.[1] There are only four other times out of 31 occurrences of the imperative where this root means not literally, 'Give!', but something like 'Come now!'. These instances occur in the Tower of Babel story (Gen. 11.3, 4, 7) and in the encounter of Tamar and Judah (Gen. 38.16). The builders of the Tower, the father-in-law of the widow Tamar and Pharaoh all abuse their rights and power. The culprits in Genesis fail; can Pharaoh hope to succeed?

In varying degrees, then, ענה (*pi.*), פרך and הבה all indicate that the people of Israel in Exodus not only suffer—they are wronged. Here and in other pericopes in Exodus 1–2, their situation is described with a lexicon of juridical words.[2] Injustice such as this calls for a judge, and the next words we will study direct us to him.

We remark first that the new king does not 'know of Joseph'. Even in passages like here where the word means a kind of historical awareness, F. Gaboriau concludes that ידע means a personal relation, clearly affective in character, founded on an action.[3] Also, W. Schottroff surveys other studies and concludes that the word means something richer than a theoretical, connative act of thought. The knowledge to which it alludes is the fruit of a practical rapport with its object.[4] H.B. Huffmon and S.B. Parker have proposed that ידע could have parallels to Hittite treaty passages and so mean 'recognize by covenant'. Hence the new king might not have acknowledged officially a covenant or another legal arrangement between Joseph and his predecessor. If this theory is true and applicable here, it would mean another, even stronger association between the Pharaoh and Joseph.[5]

1. Meyer, *Hebräische Grammatik*, §89.2; BDB, p. 396; GKC, §§69b, 105; Joüon, *Grammaire*, §§75k, 105e.

2. For other reflections on the juridical vocabulary of Exod. 1–2, read the sections on vocabulary in Chapters 4, 5, 6 and 7, as well as 'Vocabulary' and 'Thematic Synthesis: Justice' in the Conclusion.

3. F. Gaboriau, *Le thème de la connaissance: Etude d'une racine* (Paris: Desclée, 1969), pp. 48, 38.

4. W. Schottroff ('ידע *jd'* erkennen', *THAT*, I, pp. 689-90) summarizes Pedersen, Wolff, Gaboriau and Botterweck.

5. H.B. Huffmon, 'The Treaty Background of Hebrew YĀDA'', *BASOR* 181 (1966), pp. 34-35; H.B. Huffmon and S.B. Parker, 'A Further Note on the Treaty

God had made Joseph a father to the earlier Pharaoh (Gen. 45.8), equal to him in all but the throne (Gen. 41.40). When Jacob died, Pharaoh's household mourned (Gen. 50.7-8). Such is the bond as described in the text that the new king's ignorance changes.

The occurrence of ידע here also prefigures later passages of Exodus, where it becomes an expression of God's self-revelation. Pharaoh refuses Moses' petition, scoffing that he 'does not know the Lord' (5.2). Again and again during the plagues, God declares that by his powerful deeds, Pharaoh and the Egyptians will come to 'know' that he is the Almighty (7.5, 17; 8.6, 18; 9.14; 14.4, 18) and that the earth is his (9.29). The Hebrews too must 'know' that he, the Lord, is God (6.7; 10.2; 16.12), that it was he who brought them out (16.6). They must 'know' his statutes and decisions (18.16) and the upright way (18.20). God himself intervenes when he himself 'knows' (2.25).[1]

The pattern of the verb ידע in Exodus makes clear that God himself will reverse the loss of freedom, an injustice that begins in ignorance.

The root עבד tells us more about the nature of this oppression. It becomes dominant in the conclusion of the passage (vv. 13-14).[2] Meaning 'to work' and 'to serve', it both describes the form of the subjection here and points ahead to the reason for which God will stop it later.

It indicates the new brutalized state of affairs between the Egyptians and the Hebrews.[3] Meaning 'to work', עבד signifies the occupation assigned to or forced on one person by another. It pertains to personal

Background of Hebrew YĀDA'', *BASOR* 184 (1966), p. 36. See also Durham, *Exodus*, p. 7.

1. The particular importance of this verb to the plague account is noted by Childs, *Exodus*, p. 136, and Isbell, 'Exodus 1–2', p. 55.

2. Isbell ('Exodus 1–2', pp. 43, 58) cites and agrees with Ackerman and Cassuto that עבד is the key word of the entire passage 1.8-14.

3. According to D. Kellermann ('סבל *sāḇal*', *ThWAT*, V, p. 747), סבלות occurs only in the plural and only in Exod. 1.11; 2.11; 5.4, 5; 6.6, 7, where it means 'forced work'. He cites Mettinger, for whom מס and סבלת are synonyms, while for Noth and Rainey סבלת means the transport of goods necessary for the construction work and מס is the general term for forced work on the construction project. Similarly, J.A. Wainwright ('Zoser's Pyramid and Solomon's Temple', *ExpTim* 91 (1978–80), p. 139) believes that מס is 'unskilled labour'. Pons (*L'oppression*, p. 130) holds that סבלות is certainly social oppression, but when it is too heavy it also carries a clearly political character. מס is a synonym of סבלות for R. North ('מס *mas* סבל *sæḇæl*', *ThWAT*, IV, p. 1007).

relations.[1] The Egyptians and the Hebrew remain bound to one another, though now by constraint, and not by mutual respect, as previously.

Later in Exodus God will use the word עבד for the association he wants with the people he liberates and calls to know him. When God intervenes, he instructs Moses to tell Pharaoh to let 'my son [Israel] go, that he may serve me' (Exod. 4.23). 'Thus says the Lord, "Send my people that they may serve me"' (Exod. 7.26; 9.1, 13; 8.16; 10.3; also 7.16; 9.14; 10.26). Pharaoh falsely promises to let the Hebrews leave: 'Go, serve your God' (10.8, 11, 24; 12.31; also 10.7). Moses is God's servant (4.10, 31). The Hebrews should 'keep this service' (12.25; 13.5). In the wilderness they wonder if it would not be better to serve Pharaoh (14.12). One of the key questions of Exodus, the first elements of which are here, is whom Israel will serve, Pharaoh or YHWH.[2]

The vocabulary of the pericope thus tells us that the Hebrews' wretchedness constitutes oppression, and oppression is unjust because it depreciates human relations. True liberation through God's intervention will therefore be more than the mere cessation of cruelty. It must bring true justice, that is, a deeper bond between God and the Israelites, restoring the value of knowledge (ידע) and service (עבד) by directing them to him.

This covenantal implication of the passage's vocabulary is confirmed by the occurrence of a number of its important words in Gen. 15.12-21, a passage that might be called the programme of the conflict in Exodus between Israel and Egypt. God makes a covenant with Abram, predicting their enslavement and using words found here in Exod. 1.8-14: 'Know, yes, know (ידע) that your descendants will be sojourners in a land (ארץ) not theirs. They will work (עבד); and they will oppress (ענה [*pi.*]) them for four hundred years.' Foreseeing the judi-

1. I. Riesener (*Der Stamm* עבד *im Alten Testament* [BZAW, 149; Berlin: de Gruyter, 1979], p. 49) writes that this verb indicates an act that is in some way occasioned by another person, either by a direct order or request, or as required by a certain kind of conduct or behaviour.

2. D.M. Gunn, 'The "Hardening of Pharaoh's Heart": Plot, Character and Theology in Exodus 1–14', in *Art and Meaning*, p. 81; Isbell, 'Exodus 1–2', pp. 45, 58, citing Waldman and Ahuviah; Fox, *Names*, p. xxxiv; G. Auzou, *De la servitude au service: Etude du livre de l'exode* (Connaissance de la Bible, 3; Paris: L'Orante, 1961), p. 79; M. Goldberg, 'Exodus 1.13-14', *Int* 37 (1983), p. 391.

cial nature of the conflict, God continues, 'But on the nation for which they work, I will bring judgment'. Pharaoh's plan must fail; for God promises, 'And afterwards, they will go out with great possessions'.[1]

A number of commentators have pointed out the pun between פן ירבה (v. 10c), the preoccupation of Pharaoh that the Hebrews might increase, and כן ירבה (v. 12b), the actual reaction to the Egyptians' plan.[2] To these words, one might also add other looser aural associations: ויבן, בני (ישראל) (vv. 9c; 12c) and מפני (v. 12c), the method of the oppression, its object and result.

The expression שרי מסים may be a play on the Hebrews' former occupation in Egypt before their oppression. They were the heads of flocks: שרי מקנה (Gen. 47.6).[3]

More word play associates 'Joseph', יוסף (v. 8b), with '[and] join', ונוסף (v. 10d). Since Pharaoh does not know the first, he fears the second. The audience is aware of the etymology of Joseph's name because Genesis says that his mother Rachel named him with the root יסף in mind, 'So she named him Joseph, saying "May the Lord add (יוסף) to me another son!"' (Gen. 30.24).[4]

Pharaoh's use of the expression נוסף על is a rhetorical ploy. The preposition על is used with that verb when new members join a group already formed.[5] Here it heightens the sense of danger by implying that some dark conspiracy already threatens Egypt and that the Hebrews could make it more powerful.

The presence and absence of names in Exodus 1–2 strikes the reader/listener. Pharaoh is not named, but the store-cities Raamses and

1. Moses will name his son Gershom because '"A sojourner have I been (גר הייתי) in a foreign land"' (2.22). See the discussion on this strange phrase in Chapter 6, 'Vocabulary and Characterization'.

2. Cassuto, *Commentary*, p. 11; Greenberg, *Understanding Exodus*, pp. 32-33.

3. J. van der Ploeg, 'Les chefs du peuple d'Israël et leurs titres', *RB* 57 (1950), p. 41.

4. Ackerman ('Literary Context', p. 80) notes this pun, but not the etymology of the name in Genesis. This oversight perhaps explains why his analysis goes far astray. He calls Joseph 'the one who adds, increases', that is, he brought prosperity to Egypt. The new king does not want the Hebrews to 'be added' ('Josephed') to those who hate them. He is a 'subtractor, a decreaser', who could have brought continued prosperity to Egypt. Instead he diminishes Egypt through his anti-Hebrew activity. According to Gen. 30.24, however, Joseph's name is based on the root יסף because of Rachel's wish for more children, not because of Joseph's skill.

5. Brockelmann, *Hebräische Syntax*, §110g.

Pithom are, as the midwives will be later. The phenomenon is noted here and will be studied more fully in Chapter 3.

8. *Conclusions*

The suffering of the Hebrews is a matter of oppression beginning in ignorance and advanced by Pharaoh's rhetorical reinterpretation of Egypt's situation as an array of polarities. The oppression is unjust because it disorders human relations established with God's blessing, a distortion of God's world that he himself will repair by centring knowledge and service on himself.

EXCURSUS: WOMEN IN EXODUS 1–2

The title of this section is contradictory, as though women were an adjunct to the action of the chapters. In fact they are central but illusive. Three daughters, a sister and two midwives are important in Moses' early life, a large number in such a small cast of characters. The Israelite women are fertile and healthy (1.19). The women give life not just as mothers but also as plotters. With both their wombs and their intelligence, they cooperate with God's providence. They are tricksters, but nowhere are they condemned for their subterfuge.[1] Their powers, though deceptive, are not conferred on them by men.[2] Nor are they only warriors in the battle of the sexes—the sister's deception is aimed against another woman, the princess. Modern sensibilities may be offended by women who have wiles but no political rights. But perhaps it is precisely because the Hebrews in Egypt—men and women—had no rights that women can work as agents of change. The importance of women in Exodus 1–2 may be a correlative of the Hebrews' vulnerability. But it is also a testament to their ingenuity.

1. E. Fuchs ('Who is Hiding the Truth? Deceptive Women and Biblical Anthropocentrism', in *Feminist Perspectives on Biblical Scholarship* [ed. A.Y. Collins; SBL Biblical Scholarship in North America, 10; Chico, CA: Scholars Press, 1985], p. 140) notes that the deceptive woman in the Bible is normally condemned when her behaviour gains her something for herself alone.

2. J.A. Hackett ('Women's Studies and the Hebrew Bible', in *The Future of Biblical Studies: The Hebrew Scriptures* [ed. R.E. Friedman and H.G.M. Williamson; SBL Semeia Studies, 16; Atlanta, GA: Scholars Press, 1987], p. 153) says that men usually give women whatever power they have in the Bible.

Chapter 3

EXODUS 1.15-22

1. *Literal Translation*

15a Then the king of Egypt spoke to the Hebrew midwives,
15b one whose name was Shifrah
15c and the second whose name was Puah,
16a and said,
16b 'When midwifing the Hebrew women,
16c look at the stones.
16d If it is a son,
16e put him to death,
16f but if it is a daughter,
16g she shall live.'
17a But the midwives feared God
17b and did not do
17c as the king of Egypt had told them,
17d but let the male children live.
18a The king of Egypt called the midwives
18b and said to them,
18c 'Why have you done this thing
18d and let the male children live?'
19a The midwives spoke to Pharaoh,
19b 'For the Hebrewesses are not like the Egyptian women
19c because they are lively.
19d Before the midwife comes to them,
19e they have given birth.'
20a God dealt well with the midwives;
20b the people multiplied
20c and grew very powerful.
21a And since the midwives feared God,
21b he made them descendants.
22a Then Pharaoh ordered all his people,
22b 'Every son that is born, into the river you shall throw him,
22c but every daughter you shall let live'.

Notes on the Literal Translation

Verse 15a. למילדת העברית: 'to the Hebrew midwives'. This translation reflects the MT and its vocalization. The construction as it stands is a substantive participle and a modifying adjective, both preceded by the definite adjective. Other translations, such as 'those midwifing the Hebrews', solve some but not all the logical inconsistencies in the story by presenting the women as either Hebrew or Egyptian. However, these renderings require that the first word be repointed *limᵉyallᵉdot*, a participle in a construct phrase or an elliptical phrase without את, where העברית is a direct substantive complement and not a qualifying adjective.[1]

Verse 16c. האבנים: *hā'obnayim*, 'the two stones'. The translation chosen here is the point of departure for other proposed translations: 'birthstool' and 'genitals'.[2] The only other occurrence is in Jer. 18.3, where it is usually rendered 'potter's wheel'. This sense could also be an expansion of this basic meaning. If the two stones do in fact refer to an Egyptian chair for delivery, then this literal rendition perhaps suffices to express it, since the Egyptian phrase 'to sit on the brick' meant to give birth.[3] 'The two stones' is also

1. Michaeli, *Livre*, p. 32 n. 2. Josephus took them for Egyptians, as have later commentators: Holzinger, Beer, Stalker (cited by Michaeli, *Livre*, p. 32), and Ehrlich (*Randglossen*, p. 260). Dillman (*Exodus und Leviticus*, p. 14) is gullible to take the midwives' statement in v. 19b literally and conclude that they must have been Egyptian because the Hebrews did not need help delivering. Noth (*Exodus*, p. 23) is correct but surely oversimplifying the question when he says they are called Hebrew women expressly.

2. Houtman (*Exodus*, p. 243) follows the same line, but renders the literal 'stones' as 'women's sexual organs'. For more on the proposal 'birthstool', see e.g. W. Spiegelberg, *Aegyptologische Randglossen zum Alten Testament* (Leipzig: Hinrichs, 1904), pp. 19-25. For arguments in favour of the translation 'genitals', see e.g. Ehrlich, *Randglossen*, p. 261. See also J. Döller, '"Obnajim" Ex 1,16', *BZ* 7 (1909), p. 259.

3. A. Niccacci, 'Sullo sfondo egiziano di Esodo 1–15', *Liber Annuus* 36 (1986), p. 12. The newborn was often placed on a second brick stool, similar to the mother's, while incantations and gifts were offered for his or her protection. H.A. Brongers agrees (in H.A. Brongers and A.S. van der Woude, 'Wat is de betekenis van 'ābnāyîm in Exodus 1:16?', *NedTTs* 20 [1965–66], p. 249). N.M. Sarna (*Exploring Exodus* [New York: Schocken Books, 1986], p. 24) quotes the line of an Egyptian hymn, 'I sat upon bricks like the woman in labor'. It is

accurate according to the consonantal text.

But its disadvantages are two: the exact meaning of the stones remains uncertain, and the translation is at odds with the vocalization of the MT. The word אבן is a segholate from a primordial **qatl* (GKC, §84^{a}a; 93g). The dual אבנים seems to be from a **qutl*, after the pattern of **mutn* → **mōten* → *motnayim*.[1] Despite these faults, it is the rendition given by a number of other translations from the original.[2]

Fortunately, the meaning of the sentence as a whole is clear and narrative analysis in no way depends on the translation of this word.

Verse 19c. כי חיות: *ḥāyot*, 'because they are lively'. Vocalized as in the MT, the word חיות is a hapax legomenon. Some emend the pointing to *ḥayyôt*, 'animals', indicating that the Hebrew women are animals who do not need help delivering.[3] Making too rigid a distinction between poetry and prose, Schmidt[4] and Driver[5] reject this interpretation because, they claim, the prose would have a כ, 'like animals'.

Y. Kutscher associates חיות with the broad meaning of חי, 'living'.[6] In the Targum Onkelos, Galiliean Aramaic and Syriac, midwives and delivering mothers are called 'living' because, he suggests, חי and its equivalent in these sources connote expeditiousness and even wisdom. The expression is something like 'quick' in English, 'lebhaft' in German, or, as one might add about wisdom, 'sage-femme' in French.

reproduced in *ANET*, p. 381. See also D. Cole, 'Obstetrics for the Women of Ancient Egypt', *Discussions in Egyptology* 5 (1986), p. 31; C. Fontinoy, 'La naissance de l'enfant chez les Israélites de l'Ancien Testament', in *L'enfant dans les civilisations orientales* (ed. A. Théodoridès *et al.*; Acta Orientalia Belgica, 2; Leuven: Peeters, 1980), p. 115, referring to D. Schapiro.

1. Joüon, *Grammaire*, §96Ag; Schmidt, *Exodus*, p. 5; *HALAT*, I, p. 8.

2. Lacocque, *Devenir*, p. 42; *Jerusalem Bible*: *Esodo* (trans. B.B. Boschi; Nuovissima Versione della Bibbia dai Testi Originali, 2; Rome: Edizioni Paoline, 1978); *Noms* (trans. A. Chouraqui; La Bible, 2; Bruges: Desclée de Brouwer, 1974); Durham, *Exodus*, pp. 11-12.

3. J.E. Hogg, 'A New Version of Exod 1,19', *AJSL* 43 (1926–27), pp. 297-99; Ehrlich, *Randglossen*, p. 261; Houtman, *Exodus*, p. 245. Houtman suggests that the pointing of the MT was changed to hide this unflattering description of the Hebrew women.

4. *Exodus*, p. 6.

5. G.R. Driver, 'Hebrew Mothers (Exodus i 19)', *ZAW* 67 (1955), p. 247.

6. Y. Kutscher, 'For a Biblical Dictionary: Exod. 1.19', *Leš* 21 (1956–57), pp. 251-52 (Hebrew).

The Hebrew women did not need midwives because they delivered speedily or they knew enough to deliver alone. But his short article ignores the difference in pointing between חיות and חי, and it lacks specific references to the Targumic texts. Schmidt mentions that this middle-Hebrew link between midwives and 'living' may account for the ancient translations.[1]

None of the commentators mentions that one reason for their dispute is the polyvalence of כי. It can mean 'when', and fits a rendition like 'when they are in labour', but it can also mean 'for', or 'because', as in 'because they are lively'.[2] It can also simply introduce direct discourse, as Schmidt suggests for its first occurrence in v. 19b.[3] The end of 'Vocabulary' will explain why the word is translated twice in the causal sense here.

In conclusion, no argument precludes חיות as a hapax legomenon, correctly vocalized and preserved in our text, or suggests a convincing substitute.

Verse 20b-c. וירב העם ויעצמו מאד: 'the people multiplied and grew very powerful'. The translation here is literal for the purposes of narrative analysis. However, a freer rendition could treat the two verbs as a hendiadys: 'the people increased very mightily'. They are not listed as a standard semitic word-pair.[4]

Verse 21b. להם בתים: '[made] them descendants'. The first word refers to the midwives despite the masculine gender, not for euphony

1. *Exodus*, p. 6; 'They give birth' (LXX similarly Theod.); 'they are prolific', or 'women in child-birth' (Aquila); 'they are midwives' (Symm.); 'they know about delivering' (Vulg.; similarly Targum Onkelos, Pseudo-Jonathan). See Hogg, 'Exod. 1.19', p. 297, and Driver, 'Hebrew Mothers', p. 247, who cites them as support for his hypothesis that, repointed to *ḥayyôt*, the word is an Aramaism for '[when they are women] in labour'.

2. A. Schoors, 'The Particle כי' *OTS* 21 (1981), pp. 264, 267; A. Aejmelaeus, 'Function and Interpretation of כי in Biblical Hebrew', *JBL* 105 (1986), p. 196.

3. *Exodus*, p. 6.

4. Y. Avishur, *Stylistic Studies of Word-Pairs in Biblical and Ancient Semitic Literatures* (AOAT, 210; Neukirchen–Vluyn: Neukirchener Verlag, 1984); L.R. Fisher (ed.), *Ras Shamra Parallels: The Texts from Ugarit and the Hebrew Bible*, I (AnOr, 49; Rome: Pontificium Institutum Biblicum, 1972); II (AnOr, 50; Rome: Pontificium Institutum Biblicum, 1975); S. Rummel (ed.), III (AnOr, 51; Rome: Pontificium Institutum Biblicum, 1981).

between the labials ב and מ,[1] but simply by virtue of the Hebrew idiom of anomalous grammatical concord.[2] בתים is metonymical. In the sense of 'clans' or 'households', it means here 'Nachkommen', 'family of descendants, descendants as an organized body'.[3] Houtman reverses the sense and reads 'made them into ancestresses'.[4]

J.E. Hogg suggests that the sentence from v. 21a should read: 'and it came to pass that the midwives were God-fearing and they [the midwives] established families for them [the people]'.[5] He follows the Septuagint in making the women the subject of the verb ויעש, a case of irregular accord. להם would refer to העם in v. 20b and ויהי כי in v. 21a would be 'and it came to pass that'. However, Hogg cites no other passage in which ויהי כי has his suggested meaning. And a study of the concordance brings none to light.[6]

Verse 22b. תשליכהו: 'you shall throw him'. M. Cogan suggests that שלך (*hiph.*) should at times be translated 'to leave, abandon, expose', referring to something with which one cannot or does not want to deal.[7] Certainly it is more natural that a child would be 'exposed' rather than 'thrown' upon a field (Ezek. 16.5) or under a bush (Gen. 21.15), especially by a person like Hagar, who abandoned her child reluctantly. The translation here keeps 'throw' only because it is possible with 'into the River', and a literal rendering is best for close narrative analysis.

2. *Delimitation*

This passage is marked off by the introduction and departure of new

1. Cassuto, *Commentary*, p. 15; Lacocque, *Devenir*, p. 46.
2. Brockelmann, *Hebräische Syntax*, §124b; GKC, §135o.
3. Bullinger, *Figures of Speech*, p. 538, citing this verse: 'Metonomy (of the subject) is when the subject is put for something pertaining to it'. Cf. *HALAT*, I, p. 120; BDB, p. 109. See Exod. 2.1; 2 Sam. 7.11-12; 1 Kgs 2.24; Ruth 4.11, 12.
4. 'maakte hij hen tot stammoeders' (*Exodus*, p. 247).
5. J.E. Hogg, 'Exod 1.21: "He made them houses"', *AJSL* 41 (1924–25), pp. 267-71.
6. Schoors ('The Particle כי, p. 268) classifies ויהי כי only as a temporal phrase, literally something like 'and it came to pass when'. Aejmelaeus ('Function', p. 198) writes that the 'great majority' of circumstantial cases of כי are introduced by ויהי, but she says nothing about the phrase in Hogg's sense.
7. M. Cogan, 'A Technical Term for Exposure', *JNES* 27 (1968), pp. 133-35. Also F. Stolz, 'שלך *šlk* hi. werfen', *THAT*, I, p. 917.

characters, the midwives. It brings dialogue to the book for the first time. In v. 16 and v. 22, Pharaoh's two commands, each with בן, בת and חיה, embrace the pericope. It is an episode in the continuing story of Pharaoh's plan against the Hebrews.

3. *Narrative Structure*

Deep

Consistent with its function as a dependent part of a larger whole describing the subjugation of the Hebrews, the basic plot outline of 1.15-22 is the same as the previous section's: '(problem)–attempted solution–result'. The 'problem' is inherited from 1.8-14, and is Pharaoh's perception of a threat in the Israelites' growth.

Surface

Told over several episodes in Exodus 1–2, the full story of the Hebrews' suffering is growing in narrative complexity.

We saw that 1.1-7 had no plot tension. Then verses 1.8-14 had a simple dramatic structure: ominous beginning, a climax, relief, and a suspenseful conclusion.

The opening of the last episode was already taut because a new ruler who does not know the Hebrews' contribution to Egypt is liable to set off the cruelty predicted in Gen. 15.13-14. The moment of greatest anxiety was v. 12a-12b, 'And the more they continued to oppress them, the more...' The tension unwound somewhat when we learned that the Hebrews were not expiring, but growing in proportion to their mistreatment. It mounted again at the concluding description of the rigorous work (vv. 13-14).

Now, in 1.15-22, the opening is also foreboding. Once Pharaoh has set his face against the Hebrews, he cannot mean them good when he speaks to the women who care for their newborn. But instead of a single swell and ebb of tension between the introduction and conclusion as before, the body of this pericope has two waves, cresting at v. 16g and v. 19e. After the first, the midwives react to the order by fearing God and disobeying. We relax momentarily, but we know that Pharaoh must complain. He calls them, they explain, we wait for his answer. Just then the narrative shifts, and God relieves the suspense—he deals well with the midwives. As in 1.8-14, it rises again at the conclusion in preparation for the next episode. But proportionally the final suspense is greater here than in the last pericope. All the Egyptians must now throw every Hebrew son into the Nile.[1]

The narrative unity of the whole chapter is maintained not only by the sequential plot, but also by the pattern that every mention of the proliferation of the Hebrews is followed by a new rise in tension. Hence, in v. 7 'the Sons of Israel bore fruit, they teemed...'; suddenly the new king appeared (v. 8). In v. 12 they increased and spread despite the oppression; then we are told how their life was made bitter (vv. 13-14). Now, thanks to the midwives, the people 'multiplied and grew very powerful' (v. 20), so Pharaoh gives a new order to all his people (v. 22).

4. *Point of View*

The focalization here is of the same type as in the previous episode: an external narrator-focalizer who twice focuses within a character. In 1.8-14 we received a brief interior view of the king who 'did not know Joseph' and of the Egyptians who 'shuddered in horror at' the Hebrews. Here we learn (v. 17a) and are reminded (v. 21a) that the midwives 'feared God'.

The focalization has thus shifted its internal angle from the Egyptians and their king to the midwives. It has not broadened it to show both groups' thoughts and feelings together, as one might expect in a dialogue. This restraint in the point of view reflects their degraded relations and the limitations of their exchange.

The interior view of the focalization sets this estrangement in relief, and it encourages our subsequent allegiance to the Hebrews because it gives us intelligence about the midwives that we never had concerning Pharaoh: we know their true motives, never his.

We saw that the last pericope showed a balance between ideological preference and access to information. We discovered less about the Hebrews' thoughts than about those of their enemies. And we knew the limits of Pharaoh's knowledge but not the innermost reasons for his action.[2] The story now abolishes this equilibrium, and the point of

1. On biblical narratives with two climactic points, see Bar-Efrat, 'Structure', p. 166, whose examples are Isaac's blessing in Gen. 27 and Job's trial in Job 1–2 and 42.

2. See 'Point of View' and 'Rhetoric' in Chapter 2, where it is remarked that the reasons he states are unsound.

view fully favours the protagonist. In doing so, it follows the change in the dynamic of the plot. For, by the end of the story, it is the midwives who have taken the initiative, and Pharaoh is reacting to them.

Also, by telling us most about the people we are meant to support, the point of view has a common-sense logic that contrasts with the folly of the king in the plot. We gain a symmetry of insight and empathy just at the moment when Pharaoh takes a step further in a scheme with no coherence or rationale.

5. *Narrative Symmetry*

The beginning and end of the pericope are marked by Pharaoh's two commands each with בן, בת and חיה, obvious inclusions already mentioned under the heading 'Delimitation'. The section is joined to the earlier stories as these are to Genesis by the vocabulary of proliferation, here רבה, עצם and מאד (v. 20).

J.C. Exum sees a chiastic structure:[1]

A '. . . if it is a son, you shall kill him; but if it is a daughter, she may live'.
B But the midwives feared God
C and they did not do (עשׂ) as the king of Egypt commanded (דבר) them, but let the male infants live.
C^1 'Why have you done (עשׂיתן) this thing (הדבר) and let the male infants live?'
B^1 And because the midwives feared God. . .
A^1 'Every son that is born you shall expose on the Nile, but every daughter you shall let live.'

However, she overlooks vital elements. First, her scheme suppresses any sign of the narrative technique of dialogue, new here to the chapter, because it omits the response of the midwives to Pharaoh. Secondly, it does injustice to the level of conceptual content by omitting the important verses about God's beneficence to the women and the continued increase of the people. Thus, and thirdly, in her legitimate concern to promote our awareness of Biblical women, she seems to disregard a careful distinction made by the text. The text itself avoids implying that the intention of the characters is necessary for

1. J.C. Exum, '"You Shall Let Every Daughter Live": A Study of Exodus 1:8–2:10', *Semeia* 28 (1983), p. 71.

the implementation of God's will.[1] Her readers lose one of the chief benefits of a chiastic analysis, the clearer discernment of the theme.[2]

Another design, by D.W. Wicke, respects more of the pericope's thematic imperatives:[3]

A^1 Pharaoh's directive to the midwives (vv. 15-16)
B^1 The midwives' fear of God—civil disobedience (v. 17)
C The king's charge against the midwives and their response (vv. 18-19) (v. 20 a gloss)
B^2 The midwives' fear of God—reward (v. 21)
A^2 Pharaoh's command to all his people (v. 22)

His outline is a useful study tool. It is attentive to the dialogue; in fact it is the centre-piece of his construction. But, like Exum, he overlooks the theme of proliferation and dismisses v. 20 as a gloss, a marginal comment that has crept into the text (p. 102). This conclusion demonstrates the risks attending redactional criticism by structural models.[4] He overtrusts the objectivity of his chiasm and has not considered its implications.[5] By dismissing v. 20 as an addendum, he detaches the pericope from the vocabulary of proliferation, its verbal link to the unfolding story that gives it sense. And although he recognizes that the conflict in this unit is between God's plan and Pharaoh's (p. 103), he does not plot this opposition schematically.

Adapting Wicke's chiasm, one might suggest:

1. On this point, Schmidt (*Exodus*, p. 44) speculates that the *piel* of חיה in v. 17d, of which the midwives are the subject, is to be related to the *hiphil* of Gen. 50.20, in which God meant the evil actions of Joseph's brothers 'to keep alive' many people.

2. J. Breck, 'Biblical Chiasmus: Exploring Structure for Meaning', *BTB* 17 (1987), p. 71.

3. D.W. Wicke, 'The Literary Structure of Exodus 1.2–2.10', *JSOT* 24 (1982), p. 101.

4. For a brilliant attack on this kind of methodological error, see Kugel, 'On the Bible and Literary Criticism', pp. 224-25. His remarks and mine do not deny that the study of chiastic patterns can help in text and redaction criticism. See, for example, the section on 'The Value of Recognizing the A:B::B:A Word Pattern' in Ceresko, 'Chiastic Word Pattern', pp. 306-308, and the chapter, 'Textual Emendations Based on Word Pairs', in Avishur, *Stylistic Studies*, pp. 669-98.

5. B.W. Kovacs addresses the problem of subjectivity in structuralist analysis in his 'Structure and Narrative Rhetoric in Genesis 2–3: Reflections on the Problem of Non-convergent Structuralist Exegetical Methodologies', *Semeia* 18 (1980), pp. 139-47, especially p. 140.

A Pharaoh's directive to the midwives (vv. 15-16)
B The midwives' fear of God—their refusal to obey (v. 17)
C Pharaoh's reaction to their refusal—the midwives' response (vv. 18-19)
C[1] God's reaction to their refusal—the effect on the people (v. 20)
B[1] The midwives' fear of God—their reward (v. 21)
A[1] Pharaoh's command to all his people (v. 22)

The royal accusation and women's reply are noted but made ancillary to the distinction between God and Pharaoh. The women's non-action (B) is symmetrical with God's action (B[1]).[1] So is the dialogue (C) with God's favour to the midwives and the effect of his brief intervention (C[1]): the people multiply and become very strong (v. 20). The clear meaning of this structural parallel is that one does not make retorts to God as the women do to the monarch. God acts and things simply happen. The contrast invalidates any pharaonic claims to divinity.[2]

6. *Vocabulary*

Fertile Life and Family: ילד (verb: 2×; noun: 2×; participial noun: 7×; derived form: 1×), בן (2×), בת (2×), חיה (*pi.*: 3×; derived forms: 2×), רבה, עצם, בתים
Nationality: מלך (3×), מצרים (3×), עברי (3×), פרעה (2×), מצרי, עם (2×)
Affliction: מות (*hiph.*), שלך (*hiph.*)
Communication: אמר (5×), דבר (*pi.*), קרא, צוה (*pi.*)
Perception: ראה, ירא (2×)

The most obvious feature of the diction in 1.15-22 is the preponderance of words in the semantic field of 'Fertile Life and Family'. Fertility counters affliction in the vocabulary, like the midwives and Pharaoh in the dialogue, God and Pharaoh in the narrative structure, and Pharaoh's orders to spare the girls but kill the boys.[3]

The root ילד in its various forms here is an addition to the field of

1. Houtman, *Exodus*, p. 247.
2. J.A. Wilson, 'Pharaoh', *IDB*, III, p. 773; 'Egypt', *IDB*, II, p. 56.
3. P. Weimar (*Untersuchungen zur Redaktionsgeschichte des Pentateuch* [BZAW, 146; Berlin: de Gruyter, 1977], p. 30) sees this contrast between life and death as one of the main points of contact between this pericope and Gen. 12.10-20, Abram's deception about Sarai. Other resemblances are the dialogue, the accusing question and the verb יטב (*hiph.*).

'Fertile Life and Family'. Greenberg[1] remarks that repetition is the simplest indication of a dominant theme. The renewed victory of life over the now deadly threat is conveyed by the expanded range of the semantic field of 'Fertile Life and Family': this root (12×), together with חיה (5×), בן (2×), בת (2×) and בתים, is joined to רבה and עצם (v. 20), which are continued from the previous pericopes.

The appellation 'Hebrew' intensifies these distinctions. In Gen. 14.13, Abram is called העברי. The term is also used five times in the Joseph story, never by the Israelites as a description of themselves. The setting is always a confrontation of Joseph or his brothers with the Egyptians, where it either describes them as seen from the Egyptians' side or is the name by which the Egyptians call them.[2] In Genesis, the word thus connotes God-given dignity, by reference to Abraham who is divinely favoured, and separateness in the context of the Joseph cycle. When addressing Pharaoh, Moses will speak of the demands of 'the God of the Hebrews' (Exod. 3.18; 5.3; 7.16; 9.1; 10.3).

Since life prevails here through the action of the midwives, we can best understand the polarity between death and life by studying the description of the women's motives. The conflicts set out in the dialogue between them and Pharaoh and the narrative structure between Pharaoh and God will also become more intelligible.

'But the midwives feared God and did not do as the king of Egypt had told them, but let the male children live' (v. 17). The courage of the midwives is set against the fear of the Egyptians, who 'shudder in horror' at the Hebrews. The verb קוץ implies an element of fear as well as disgust.[3]

1. *Understanding Exodus*, p. 32.

2. Gen. 39.14, 17; 40.15; 41.12; 43.32. N.P. Lemche, '"Hebrew" as a National Name for Israel', *ST* 33 (1979), pp. 12, 20. Lacocque (*Devenir*, pp. 41, 44) says they are called עברי when oppressed; Durham (*Exodus*, p. 19) says that it is an 'uncomfortable' designation.

3. According to B. Costacurta (*La Vita minacciata: Il tema della paura nella Bibbia Ebraica* [AnBib, 119; Rome: Pontificium Institutum Biblicum, 1988], pp. 78-79 nn. 274, 276), קוץ ב means 'to be disgusted or tired of', while קוץ מפני is 'to be afraid of'; but a certain ambiguity plays between the meanings, notably in this verse. The Egyptians are tired and disgusted of Israel and its growth, she writes. But, for Costacurta, the accent should above all be placed on their fear, as made explicit in Pharraoh's speech. For the growth of the Israelites is preceived as a threat.

Commentators agree that ירא here envelops a moral concept,[1] for 'fear of God' includes an ethical stance in all Semitic languages.[2] This semantic precision applies especially when the verb ירא is used with the direct accusative, as here, instead of with the prepositions מן, מפני or מלפני.[3]

Further, the midwives stand as prefigurements, anticipated examples, of the conduct that Israel will learn in the Exodus. J.-L. Ska has noted that the Israelites will undergo a transformation when they reach the Reed Sea.[4] In 14.10-12 they fear Pharaoh and complain in vocabulary reminiscent of Exodus 1: 'It would have been better (יטב *hiph.*) for us to serve (עבד) the Egyptians than to die in the wilderness'. Moses calls on them to be brave: 'Do not fear, stand firm, and see YHWH's salvation, which he will work for you today'. Indeed at the Reed Sea, 'Israel saw the great work which YHWH did against the Egyptians, and the people feared YHWH; and they believed in YHWH and in his servant Moses' (Exod. 14.31).[5]

But terror before the army of Pharaoh is not simply superseded by the same emotion with respect to God. Rather ירא changes from fright to veneration, from panic before the danger of death to reverence before the source of life.[6] The expression 'to fear God' never sheds all its concreteness. It holds out to the imagination the powerful image of God as the *mysterium tremendum*, the source of fear as over-

1. S. Plath, *Furcht Gottes: Der Begriff* ירא *im Alten Testament* (Arbeiten zur Theologie, 2.2; Stuttgart: Calwer Verlag, 1963), p. 45; J. Becker, *Gottesfurcht im Alten Testament* (AnBib, 25; Rome: Pontificium Institutum Biblicum, 1965), p. 193; Schmidt, *Exodus*, p. 43; Houtman, *Exodus*, p. 243.

2. When physical fear lessens, fear of God becomes the equivalent to religion and piety; that is, fear of God becomes a synonym for the honour, service and obedience shown to God, according to H.F. Fuhs ('ירא *jāre'*', *ThWAT*, III, p. 878).

3. Becker, *Gottesfurcht*, p. 59.

4. J.-L. Ska, *Le passage de la Mer: Etude de la construction, du style et de la symbolique d'Ex 14,1-31* (AnBib, 109; Rome: Pontificium Institutum Biblicum, 1986), pp. 136-43.

5. Note also the wordplay between ירא and ראה. Its role in our passage will be noted later.

6. Costacurta (*La vita*, pp. 271, 276) writes that the life of a person, constantly marked by threats and fear, is destined for a definitive liberation from this reality of death. Thus fear can give way to transcendence and it can become a locus of truth for humans, and of the possibility of an intervention on God's part.

whelming awe.[1] The phrase has a fullness of reality that elicits a broader observation about its application to the midwives. The women are engaged in a struggle with Pharaoh that has physical as well as moral import for them.

The fates of Pharaoh's chief butler and baker in Gen. 40.1-23 dramatize the arbitrary omnipotence of Egypt's ruler. Nevertheless the midwives dare to defy him. In other words, they do not fear Pharaoh, but only God. They are both physically fearless and morally God-fearing.

The implied contrast is yet another blackening of Pharaoh to God's advantage, like the parallel C // C[1] in the narrative structure.[2] But, as so often in this chapter, the full range of the meaning is best seen by looking more closely through the prism of Genesis and Exodus.

Jacob should not be afraid to go down to Egypt; for God will be with him there (Gen. 46.3-4). When God promises descendants to Abram in Gen. 15.1 and Isaac in Gen. 26.24, he begins with אל־תירא, even before any mention that the men are afraid. Reviewing several passages, Ska concludes that the instruction not to fear is not an attempt to re-establish the calm that preceded, but rather a call to overcome obstacles, to move on. In the case of a theophany, it amounts to entering into the divine plan.[3] The midwive's courageous attitude, like their life-saving action, is thus part of their full obedience to the will of God expressed to the patriarchs in these apparitions.[4] The midwives' freedom from physical fear recalls this divine

1. S. Terrien, 'Fear', *IDB*, II, p. 258: 'Although many commentators and historians have fallen into this error during the past hundred years, the fear of the Lord is not merely to be equated with reverence, piety, or religion because it is impossible today to revaluate and again charge these terms with their ancient—but now largely lost—connotation of awesomeness'. Plath (*Furcht Gottes*, p. 49) issues the same warning with specific reference to this passage of Exodus.

2. Pharaoh's reaction to their refusal—the midwives' response // God's reaction to their refusal—the effect on the people.

3. *Passage*, p. 139.

4. Becker, *Exodus*, p. 205; Schmidt, *Exodus*, p. 44. Interestingly, in Genesis, all the occurrences of אל־תירא in all grammatical persons are injunctions to depend on the help of God, who is spoken of in the same verse. Only in Gen. 35.17 is God not specifically mentioned. There a midwife tells Rachel not to be afraid because she is about to give birth to a boy, implying Gen. 35.10-12, where God had promised this progeny to Jacob.

exhortation, the first words of God's liberating message.[1]

Thus in Genesis and Exodus ירא can imply, and the midwives adopt, a stance before God and the dangers of the world that is physically and morally coherent. The correlation between fearlessness and fear of God is best summarized in Exod. 20.20: 'Do not fear; for God has come to prove you, and that the fear of him may be before you, that you may not sin'.

Parts of the Joseph cycle are also valuable for the study of ירא and other words in our passage.[2] Joseph tests his brothers, telling them, 'Do this and you will live; for I fear God' (Gen. 42.18). Later he says, 'And God sent me before you to place for you a remnant on earth, and to keep alive for you a great deliverance' (Gen. 45.7). At the end of the story, his brothers say to him,

> 'forgive the transgression of the servants of the God of your father... behold we are your servants'. But Joseph said to them, 'Fear not [אל־תיראו], for am I in the place of God? As for you, you meant evil against me; but God meant it for good, to bring it about that many people should be kept alive, as they are today. So do not fear' (Gen. 50.17-20).

These verses share the following words with Exod. 1.15-22: ירא, יטב (*hiph.*), עם, חיה and למען.[3] Joseph works for God in the preservation of the Hebrews, those who fear God honour his life-giving project. The midwives continue Joseph's cooperation; as it were, they remember the man whom this Pharaoh does not know. At the same time, they foreshow the future deeper relation between the Lord and the Israelites, announced too by the vocabulary of the previous pericope, in which he will restore the value of knowledge and service by directing them to himself.[4] As W. Eichrodt writes, the fear of God is our response to his holiness and covenant.[5]

1. Any distinction between the negative particles אל and לא would not seem to affect this interpretation. Meyer (*Hebräische Grammatik*, §100e) lists only אל as the usual particle of negation for the imperative. GKC §107o adds, 'The imperfect with לא represents a more emphatic form of prohibition than the jussive with אל־... [which] is rather a simple warning, *do not that*!'

2. Weimar, *Untersuchungen*, p. 29.

3. In addition, of course, 'servants' (עבדים) brings to mind the repeated use of עבד just previously in Exod. 1.8-14.

4. In Chapter 2, see 'Conclusions', and the end of 'Vocabulary'.

5. W. Eichrodt, *Theologie des Alten Testament*. II.3. *Gott und Mensch* (Stuttgart: Ehrenfried Klotz, 4th edn, 1961), p. 184. This link between the fear of

Pharaoh and most of his servants 'do not yet fear the Lord God' (Exod. 9.30; see also 9.20). They will be taught to do so at their cost. He puts himself 'in the place of God' by spreading fear and death. The choice of life or death belongs only to the Creator who gave life (Gen. 2.7) and can take it back (Gen. 7.4).[1] Disobedience to Pharaoh is thus religious reverence. And, as this story presents it, the first grounds of resistance to oppression lie in one's awe before God and cooperation with him in his gift of life.

The diction of the prelude (Exod. 1.1-7) showed God's willingness to operate through human history. Then the words in the last episode (Exod. 1.8-14) defined the Hebrews' plight as a case of injustice and so implied the question of who would do the judging. The vocabulary of Exod. 1.15-22 now answers why God will intervene: not only are the people he has blessed under attack, but the prerogatives of his own divinity are offended. The integrity and resolution of the midwives set forth the holiness with which the Israelites should respond to God's impending restoration of his inexorable supremacy.

Scholars have long debated why the text names the midwives and why there are only two of them. Greenberg, for example, says that we know their names the better to remember them for their virtue.[2] Their names apparently mean 'Beauty', and 'Splendour' or 'Maiden'.[3] They may have been introduced because they are typical for Israelite

God and the Covenant reinforces, but does not prove, the perception of the midwives as Hebrews rather than Egyptians.

1. Examining the numerous other references to God and life, H. Ringgren ('חיה *ḥājāh*' *ThWAT*, II, p. 890) sums up that it is self-evident that YHWH is the Lord of life and death.

2. *Understanding Exodus*, p. 30.

3. J.J. Stamm, 'Hebräische Frauennamen', in *Hebräische Wortforschung* (Festschrift W. Baumgartner; ed. B. Hartmann *et al.*; VTSup, 16; Leiden: Brill, 1967), pp. 323-27, citing Noth and Gordon. 'Shifrah' would be from שפר and 'Puah' from יפע (*hiph.*) or related to the Ugaritic name *pġt* meaning 'maiden'. O. Odelain and R. Séguineau (*Dictionnaire des noms propres de la Bible* [Paris: Editions du Cerf, 1978], pp. 305, 353), Schmidt (*Exodus*, p. 42) and Greenberg (*Understanding Exodus*, p. 27) all agree, against Cassuto (*Commentary*, p. 14). Driver ('Hebrew Mothers', p. 246 n. 1) proposes 'beauty', 'dawn', or perhaps 'flattery' for the first and 'fragrance' for the second. Lacocque (*Devenir*, p. 41) wants to relate Puah to a transitive verb 'to speak in a loud voice', but adduces 'Exod 42, 12' [*sic*].

women.[1] But we cannot know this for certain from the limited corpus of Hebrew literature. The effect of the names can be discussed more readily than the original reason for them. Set with the mention of the store cities Raamses and Pithom in 1.11, and set against the omission of the Pharaoh's name, they offer another view of history: the most noteworthy people are not the mighty, but those who suffer and do God's will. And the names reveal nothing of the character of the women. The sense of their existence is conveyed in action unencumbered by personal details.

Schmidt says that pairs are common in sagas.[2] Perhaps they are a couple here especially because in this way they better represent all the Israelites, acting as they do now with the qualities to which God's self-communication and the Exodus will soon call the community as a whole.

The second ויאמר in v. 16a is not grammatically necessary, but serves several stylistic purposes. It slows down narration time and thus conveys something of the solemnity of Pharaoh's office. But it is an ironic comment on the limits to his power when he opposes God's plan. For in this passage, as in the last, all Pharaoh does is talk. The midwives and God take action and so make his words empty.

Many have remarked on the word play between וראיתן (v. 16c) and ותיראן (v. 17a).[3] Instead of 'looking' at the stones as ordered, the women 'fear' God. The difference is set off in a chiastic structure:

A בילדכן
B וראיתן
C אם
C[1] אם
B[1] ותיראן
A[1] המילדת

This illustrates well a point made by Kogut about chiastic structures in general. A chiasm simultaneously associates and distances its

1. R.E. Clements, *Exodus* (Cambridge Bible Commentary; Cambridge: Cambridge University Press, 1972), p. 14.

2. *Exodus*, p. 42.

3. Lacocque, *Devenir*, p. 43; Weimar, *Untersuchungen*, p. 28. Costacurta, (*La vita*, p. 35) speaks of the frequency of the phenomenon. I.M. Casanowicz (*Paronomasia in the Old Testament* [dissertation, Boston, 1894], p. 42) and Hogg ('Exod.1.21', p. 269) call it paronomasia; Schmidt (*Exodus*, p. 14) and Houtman (*Exodus*, p. 244) label it an anagram.

members.[1] Their fear of God is indeed related to Pharaoh's order (C // C[1]), but as an incitement to disobedience.

There are stylistic advantages to Pharaoh's use of בן and בת in v. 16d, f instead of other possibilities like ילד or ילדה to match the plural ילדים in vv. 17 and 18. The word בן keeps continuity with the rest of the chapter: the sons of Jacob–Israel became the בני ישׂראל, the Israelites, who were first oppressed in 1.8-14, and whose sons are now threatened.

A chiastic pattern ties בן, בת and ילדים together:

A	בן־בת (v. 16)
B	הילדים (v. 17)
B[1]	הילדים (v. 18)
A[1]	בן־בת (v. 22)

In v. 18c-d one can feel the balance of the clause: מדוע עשׂיתן הדבר הזה. The sounds *d, a* and *'* dominate its four words.

Its ringing syllables amplify its formalized nature as a legal accusation. In a study of legal language in the Hebrew Bible, H.J. Boecker has determined that it is a 'Beschuldigungsformel', the initiation of a process of juridical interrogation.[2] In this way the clause is an extension of the judicial motif we found in Exod. 1.8-14, and it serves the same purpose of showing that the oppression of the Hebrews is a matter of injustice. The situation demands a true judge. Pharaoh is an unfit adjudicator since the injustice is his own misdeed. Moreover, he is impotent because his inquiry is cut short.

The narrator reports that they did not do (ולא עשׂו) as Pharaoh had said (דבר), but allowed the male children to live (ותחיין את־הילדים). However, Pharaoh accuses them in, respectively, the affirmative and the concrete forms of the same roots, and he repeats verbatim the final phrase: 'Why did you do (עשׂיתן) this thing (הדבר) and let the male children live (ותחיין את־הילדים)?' Pharaoh has relinquished the initiative in his language by talking like the narrator, just as he has lost the lead in the plot by having to respond to the midwives' refusal.

1. S. Kogut, 'On Chiasm and its Role in Exegesis', *Šnaton* 2 (1977), p. 197 (Hebrew).

2. H.J. Boecker, *Redeformen des Rechtslebens im Alten Testament* (WMANT, 14; Neukirchen–Vluyn: Neukirchener Verlag, 1964), pp. 30-31, 67 n. 3, aided by the work of I. Lande. The identifying elements are מדוע and הדבר הזה followed by a relative clause. Similar examples are 1 Kgs 1.6; 2 Sam. 16.10.

Until this verse, the passage has referred to the opponent as 'the king of Egypt' (vv. 15a, 18a). From the moment of the women's answer to the end, he is called 'Pharaoh' (vv. 19a, 22a), from the Egyptian title meaning 'Great House'.[1] Adopting the Egyptian word brings a touch of verisimilitude to accompany the dialogue. It may also be mildly ironic: the title evokes the tremendous power of the Egyptian throne just when Pharaoh loses control of the situation. A comparison might be a French author making subtle fun of an English aristocrat by calling him 'un milord'.

Alliteration also colours the women's response: כי לא כנשים המצרית העברית כי־חיות הנה. Almost all the sounds are repeated at least once: *k*, *y*, *h*, *ḥ*, *t*, *a*, *n* and *m*. In this opening remark, the midwives match or even surpass the solemnity of Pharaoh's accusation and this tone displays their quiet courage. Since the midwives are not developed as full characters, the reader/listener appreciates all the more this aural dimension to their presence in the passage.

Under 'Notes on the Literal Translation', we noted the various translations possible for the two occurrences of כי in this verse. They have been rendered 'for' and 'because' here to emphasize the motive, since the statement is a response to a juridical inquiry.

The decision of the midwives not to 'do' (עשׂו) what Pharaoh 'said' (דבר) moves God to 'make' them (ויעשׂ) descendants (v. 21). The use of the same verb suggests their cooperation. Similarly, by treating the sons like the daughters (בת), they win בתים. Pharaoh, the man of words, is again contrasted with God, the one who takes action: Pharaoh called their disobedience a 'deed' (דבר), but God responds to it with a deed. The midwives answer back to Pharaoh with the fabricated excuse: כי...כי (v. 19). God sees to the heart of the matter and acts on their true reverence using the same conjunction: ויהי כי־יראו המילדת את־האלהים.

Every son is to be thrown into the river. The effect of this universal penalty is to stress that now the conflict is total just as, before, the trust between Joseph and his master was perfect: the repetition of כל here reminds the reader of its threefold use in 1.1-7, where 'all the offspring of Jacob' came, and 'all his brothers and all that generation died'.[2] Like Childs,[3] one can follow the Samaritan Pentateuch, the

1. J.A. Wilson, 'Pharaoh', *IDB*, III, p. 773.
2. B. Chiesa ('Sull'utilizzazione dell'*Aggadah* per la restituzione del testo

LXX and the Targum in reading contextually that 'every son' here means every Hebrew male.

7. *Narrative Speeds and Order*

Each with particular vocabulary, scholars distinguish between two scales of time or speed in a narration, 'the time it takes to peruse a discourse...and the duration of the purported events in the discourse'.[1] One kind of relation between the two is ellipsis, in which 'no part of the narrative corresponds to a particular event that took time'.[2] In Chatman's terms, 'the discourse halts, though time continues to pass in the story', where 'story' is the events, characters and setting, and 'discourse' the expression or means by which that content is communicated.[3]

We saw in 'Narrative Structure' that v. 20 brought an extinction of the suspense when God saved the midwives. In v. 19 the midwives answer Pharaoh's question. We then expect either more interrogation or a word from the narrator that Pharaoh judged them. Instead, abruptly, 'God dealt well with the midwives', and 'the people multiplied'. The rescue is not a sudden miracle or feat of derring-do. Instead the narrator brings the women out of danger by advancing the pace and changing the scene. One minute they are standing before the king. Then suddenly the narrative speeds up and attention pivots to God and the Hebrews. Pharaoh's confrontation with the midwives is not resolved or stopped; it is elided and he is simply left behind. For just a moment, narrative technique gains control of the plot, and the

ebraico in *Esodo* 1,22', *Henoch* 1 [1979], p. 349) cites an ancient tradition recorded in *Exod. R.*, according to which Pharaoh ordered even Egyptian babies to be killed because astrologers told him that the saviour of Israel was to be born, but did not say if he was to be Egyptian or Israelite.

3. *Exodus*, p. 17.

1. Chatman, *Story*, p. 62. He credits G. Muller with the well-known German terms Erzählzeit and Erzähltezeit and lists other designations (n. 23). G. Genette (*Figures III* [Paris: Editions du Seuil, 1972], p. 122) called the phenomenon 'durée', but later suggested 'vitesse' or better 'vitesses' in his *Nouveau Discours du Récit* (Paris: Editions du Seuil, 1983), p. 23. 'Speed' had already been used by Prince, *Narratology*, p. 54.

2. Prince, *Narratology*, p. 55.

3. *Story*, p. 70, cf. p. 19.

midwives escape, as it were, through the overlay of form and content. Narration becomes the event.

This ellipsis affects our evaluation of the characters. God's momentary conspicuousness here confirms all the chapter's allusions to his beneficence, and this is an example of what Sternberg calls the Bible's 'foolproof composition'.[1] The audience might under-read Exodus 1 and miss its many vocabulary and plot references to God's blessings in Genesis. But it cannot 'counter-read' the chapter's intention, now that God openly joins the story.

Verse 20 also invites us to compare Pharaoh and God as actors in the plot. First, in 1.8-14 Pharaoh ruled by words not deeds. He simply spoke and the Egyptians took the oppressive measures for him. These failed. By contrast, God now works effectively and by action without words. Secondly, Pharaoh distorted a projected image of reality through his rhetorical skill. God now alters the real situation itself.

Further, the rescue is an act of collaboration between the narrator and God as super-agents to the advantage of both. The first accelerates the narrative and the second gives the midwives descendants. They operate together, as do the midwives with God, in that they perform his will.[2] Pharaoh, whose speech was twice approved by his audience in 1.8-14, has now been both strategically and narratively isolated.

We have witnessed the omniscience of the narrator in the internally-directed focalization that has so far made known to us the thoughts of Pharaoh (v. 8), the Egyptians (v. 12) and the midwives (vv. 17, 21). Now we see his omnipotence too, and we can compare the narrator and Pharaoh as well as God and Pharaoh.[3] The failure of the king's plot stands out in the stark light of these two comparisons.

God, the omniscient, benefits from any display of this quality in the narrator through the 'rhetoric of glorification'.[4] 'The narrator's access to the whole truth within the discourse enables him to bring home God's unique privilege within the world.'[5] (We have seen in

1. *Poetics*, p. 50.

2. Schmidt, *Exodus*, p. 44.

3. About the control of time as proof of a narrator's omnipotence, see G. Cordesse, 'Narration et Focalisation', *Poétique* 76 (1988), p. 490.

4. Sternberg, *Poetics*, p. 91. It was already mentioned in Chapter 1, 'Repetition and Narrative Gaps'. The idea was that the narrator's summarized repetition of the end of Genesis enhanced his authority.

5. Sternberg, *Poetics*, p. 93.

Chapter 2, for example, how the narrator's information that Pharaoh did not know Joseph inversely prefigures later passages of Exodus in which ידע becomes an expression of God's self-revelation and bond with his people.)

The juxtaposition here of the narrator's omniscience in the focalization and his omnipotence in the narrative speed might seem to affront God's supremacy rather than celebrate it. Lest we doubt that this power and knowledge are only reflections of God's, the narrator uses his authority precisely to transport God into the story. He chooses God of all the subjects he could have raised when he cuts short the interrogation in v. 20.

The very termination of the suspense also magnifies God's ascendancy. Undue suspense in a tale 'militates against our sense of the divine control of history', by requiring us to 'form hypotheses and calculate probabilities by reference to general laws' rather than divine command.[1] It was remarked under 'Narrative Structure' that 1.15-22 has two waves of suspense. This one breaks abruptly in a kind of narrative obeisance to God.

The readers are kept in their place within the ranking of those who control and understand. We are reminded of our inferiority because v. 20 opens up for us an 'informational gap'[2] or 'paralipsis'.[3] That is, we never learn what Pharaoh would have done to the midwives. The rescue removes any anxiety. But our curiosity is never satisfied.

This quick spell of divine action precedes God's full engagement in the story, which is to be formally heralded at the Burning Bush: 'I know their sufferings, and I have come down to deliver them' (3.7-8). His favour and reward here anticipate this great entrance on the stage. They are proleptic, where prolepsis is any narrative manoeuvre that consists in recounting or evoking in advance an event to come.[4]

In literary styles more self-consciously artful than those in the Bible,[5] prolepsis is usually an announcement by the narrator, such as Crusoe's description of an early warning against sea-life as 'prophetic', or the passing mention of a character whom 'we will meet

1. Sternberg, *Poetics*, p. 267.
2. Sternberg, *Poetics*, p. 250.
3. Genette, *Figures*, p. 93.
4. Genette, *Figures*, p. 82.
5. See Sternberg, *Poetics*, p. 65, on the anonymity of biblical narration.

later'.[1] God instead foreshadows his salvation here by actively working in the plot.

At the risk of excessive jargon, we can therefore conclude that in v. 20 ellipsis, prolepsis and paralipsis in readjust the speed and order of the narrative to promote a value hierarchy among the characters.

8. *Conclusions*

The pericope continues the contrasted themes of the proliferation of the Hebrews as a blessing and their oppression as an injustice. It adds to them an evaluation of the characters in relation to God: to save the children, the midwives cooperate with him with bravery and reverence. These traits prefigure the new life awaiting the Israelites beyond the Reed Sea. On the other hand, Pharaoh usurps God's dominion over life and death, and so loses his sway over events. The comparison of Pharaoh and the midwives makes clear that the first grounds for resistance to oppression here lie in serving God and honouring his gift of life.

1. Genette, *Figures*, pp. 106, 111.

Chapter 4

EXODUS 2.1-10

1. *Literal Translation*

Exposition:

1a	A man from the House of Levi went
1b	and took [as wife] the daughter of Levi.
2a	The woman conceived
2b	and bore a son.

Complication:

2c	When she saw him
2d	—that he was goodly—
2e	she hid him for three months.
3a	But when she could no longer hide him,
3b	she took for him a basket of bulrushes,
3c	loamed it with loam and with pitch,
3d	put the child in it,
3e	and put [it] among the reeds at the River's bank.
4a	His sister positioned herself far off,
4b	to know
4c	what would be done to him.
5a	The daughter of Pharaoh came down
5b	to wash at the River,
5c	while her attendants walked beside the River.
5d	She saw the basket amidst the reeds,
5e	sent her maid,
5f	took it,
6a	opened it,
6b	saw him, the child,

Turning Point:

6c	and, behold, a boy crying!

Denouement:

6d	She took pity on him,
6e	thinking,

6f 'One of the Hebrews' children is this'.
7a His sister said to Pharaoh's daughter,
7b 'Shall I go
7c and call a nursing woman from the Hebrewesses for you,
7d to nurse the child for you?'
8a Pharaoh's daughter said to her,
8b 'Go!'
8c The young woman went
8d and called the child's mother,
9a and Pharaoh's daughter said to her,
9b 'Have this child go
9c and nurse it for me,
9d and I myself will give you your wages'.
9e The woman took the child
9f and nursed him.
10a The child grew.
10b She brought him to Pharaoh's daughter.
10c He became as a son to her.

Conclusion:
10d And she called his name Moses,
10e for, she said,
10f 'Since from the water I drew him'.

Notes on the Literal Translation
Verse 1b. את־בת־לוי: 'the daughter of Levi'. GKC §117d argues for the definite article in translation, but does allow for exceptional occurrences of את with undetermined nouns. F.E. König and Houtman[1] allow the phrase as it stands through association with Exod. 6.18, 20 and Num. 26.59, where Moses' mother is named.[2] Brockelmann[3] and Michaeli[4] raise the possibility that a proper name has dropped out of the text.

Verse 2c-d. ותרא אותו כי־טוב הוא: 'When she saw him—that he was goodly'. This literal translation contrasts with the suggestions of J.L. Kugel, who argues for an adverbial use of כי טוב such that a sentence similar to ours, Gen. 1.4, וירא אלהים את־האור כי־טוב, would

1. *Exodus*, p. 258.
2. F.E. König, *Historisch-Comparative Syntax der Hebräischen Sprache* (Leipzig: Hinrichs, 1897), §304a.
3. *Hebräische Syntax*, §96.
4. *Livre*, p. 33 n. 1.

be construed 'and God was very pleased with the light'. And Gen. 49.15 should be 'and he was very pleased with [the] place'. The expression would thus be much like the archaic English 'to look pleasingly upon'. His argument rests on the position that כי is 'well known [to have] the force of an intensifier or asserverative'.[1] Aejmalaeus argues forcefully, however, that this function of כי is much more limited than generally perceived.[2] The few examples of it that she cites do not resemble this sentence.[3] J.G. Janzen accuses Kugel of applying principles derived from more ambiguous phrases to those like Exod. 2.2 and Gen. 1.4, where the referents of כי טוב are clear.[4]

W.F. Albright held that as a refrain in Genesis כי טוב originally meant 'how good' or 'very good'.[5] But W.H. Schmidt responds that at least in Gen. 3.6 ('the woman saw that the tree was good for food'), 'how good' would not apply, since that is a conclusion about the tree that she could make only after having tasted its fruit.[6]

Verse 6b. ותראהו את־הילד: 'saw him, the child'. The RSV omits this apposition, but others admit the possibility, unless 'the child' is a late gloss.[7]

Verse 9b. היליכי: 'make [this child] go'. The verb היליכי should probably be הוליכי, a regular *hiphil* of הלך. The mistake may be a confused association with the following verb, והינקהו.[8] For Brockelmann,[9] it

1. J.L. Kugel, 'The Adverbial Use of *kî ṭôb*', *JBL* 99 (1980), p. 433.
2. 'כי', p. 208.
3. Gen. 18.20; 1 Sam. 26.16; Isa. 7.9.
4. J.G. Janzen, 'Kugel's Adverbial *kî ṭôb*: An Assessment', *JBL* 102 (1983), pp. 105-106.
5. W.F. Albright, 'The Refrain "and God saw ki tob" in Genesis', in *Mélanges Bibliques* (Festschrift A. Robert; Travaux de l'institut catholique de Paris, 4; Paris: Blond & Gay, 1957), p. 26.
6. W.H. Schmidt, *Die Schöpfungsgeschichte der Priesterschrift* (WMANT, 17; Neukirchen–Vluyn: Neukirchener Verlag, 1964), pp. 59-60 n. 2.
7. Brockelmann, *Hebräische Syntax*, §68b; Joüon, *Grammaire*, §146e; GKC §131m and R.J. Williams, *Hebrew Syntax: An Outline* (Toronto: University of Toronto Press, 2nd edn, 1976), §71.
8. So argue Schmidt, *Exodus*, p. 51, GKC §69x, and F.E. König, *Historisch-Kritisches Lehrgebäude der Hebräischen Sprache* (Leipzig: Hinrichs, 1881), I, p. 416.
9. *Hebräische Syntax*, §4.

should read הא לך, 'Behold, for you' (the Syriac is *h' lki*). Childs is of the same mind, and asks further if it is an adoption formula.[1] This is unlikely, since the speaker, the princess, is herself about to adopt the child. Ehrlich,[2] supported by Lacocque,[3] considers anachronistic a *hiphil* of הלך in the sense of 'to bring [an object that is not self-propelling]'. He proposes the word as an overlay of הוליכי and הא לך, but does not explain why הוליכי should lie behind the conflation if it is anachronistic. Offering a radical solution, Joüon emends it to קחי לי to match the לקח in v. 9e-f: 'The woman took the child and nursed him'.[4]

Verse 10e. ותקרא...ותאמר: 'she called him... for, she said...' In the second of two coordinate *wayyiqtol* verbs, the ו can have an explicative value as here in the attribution of a name.[5]

2. *Delimitation*

בת, בן, בית and יטב (*hiph.*) / טוב are 'linking words' between this pericope and the previous one, reinforced by a chiastic distribution of two of them: בן...בת...בת...בן.[6] A conventional birth description is divided here between the opening and closing verses of the pericope.[7] It will be examined in detail in the vocabulary analysis. Verse 1 introduces to the story a new complement of characters: the man, his wife and the boy. Between the end of the pericope in v. 10 and the beginning of the next, there is a significant spread of time as Moses grows up. The ס before v. 1 marks it as a סתומא.

3. *Narrative Structure*

Deep

After two pericopes in which the deep structure was 'problem–

1. 'Birth', p. 113 n. 23.
2. *Randglossen*, pp. 264-65.
3. *Devenir*, p. 58.
4. Joüon, 'Notes de critique textuelle (AT): Exode, 2.9', *MUSJ* 5 (1911–12), p. 453.
5. Joüon, *Grammaire*, §118j; GKC §111d.
6. Houtman, *Exodus*, p. 257. About 'linking words', see 'Delimitation' in Chapter 1.
7. Bar-Efrat, *Art*, p. 113: the account of a birth or death often delimits a unit.

attempted solution–result', the narrative returns to the functions noted in the first unit, Exod. 1.1-7: 'danger–escape from danger'.

Surface

Our work on the last unit, 1.15-22, laid bare a graduated complication in the narrative structure of Exodus 1–2.[1] The first pericope showed no plot tension; the second moved in a simple climactic curve; the third had two moments of suspense. Now for the first time in Exodus a pericope unfolds dramatically in five stages.

The parts roughly match the time-honoured pyramidal construction first proposed by Gustav Freytag, in which dramatic action moves from an introduction through a 'rise' to the summit, then a 'fall' and the conclusion.[2] This correlation does not imply, however, that a narrative without these developments is atypical or sub-standard. Nor is Freytag's outline flawless even where applicable.

Hypothesized as a universal formula, Freytag's idea is not only too rigid, but also too static, especially in its location of expositional material.[3] Many narratives omit this background initially, and begin *in medias res*. Or an artist will sometimes leave the opening explanation incomplete, holding back some circumstantial details until later in the story where they have a more telling effect.

> What [Freytag] really describes is not the movement of the action but the structure of the conflict. He divorces this from the actual temporal movement of the action, presenting a structure that is viewed by the reader only when he retrospectively looks back on the action and rearranges or reassembles it chronologically in his mind. What Freytag and his followers fail to take into account is that the chronological order in which events happen need not necessarily coincide with the order in which they are imparted to the reader.[4]

Although not a generic standard, Freytag's model is fit for the study of certain single pericopes. But it must be adjusted for each piece to which it is applied.

1. Chapter 3, 'Narrative Structure'.
2. G. Freytag, *Technique of the Drama* (trans. E.J. MacEwan; Chicago, 1908 [1863]), quoted in M. Sternberg, *Expositional Modes and Temporal Ordering in Fiction* (Baltimore: Johns Hopkins University Press, 1978), p. 5. See also Abrams, *Glossary*, p. 130.
3. Sternberg, *Modes*, p. 8.
4. Sternberg, *Modes*, p. 8.

Preliminary Exposition (vv. 1a-2b). This first stage is the weakest in Freytag's theory and the one least suited to this passage. According to a generalization in the style of Freytag by G.W. Coats, the exposition introduces the elements necessary for the storyteller's craft, that is, it gives 'a definition of the principal characters in the narrative, and, in some cases, a brief presentation of the situation that holds these characters together in an interesting and significant combination of events'.[1]

However, these verses do not bring out all the main characters.[2] Pharaoh's daughter is absent here. Nor does Moses' sister come on stage until v. 4a when the action is well under way. The value of a study within a five-step dramatic frame is precisely to alert us to these extraneous elements of distributed exposition that heighten the suspense.

Verses 1a-2b should therefore be called the 'Preliminary Exposition'. It is a description of the parents' marriage, and of Moses' conception and birth. The verses are typical of expositional material: they are summary, rather formulaic,[3] and antecedent to the specific action of the complication that will distinguish this story from others of its kind.[4]

Complication (vv. 2c-6b). In Sternberg's words, expository material ends when the text makes 'the scenic launch', when action becomes 'discriminated' and 'fully dramatized'.[5]

In Chapter 3, we noted that narrative speeds can vary.[6] The speed became infinite when an ellipsis omitted the end of Pharaoh's interrogation of the midwives. By contrast, here narration time is braked and specified during the complication. Sternberg's term is 'represented time', that is, 'the duration of a projected period in the life of the characters', as opposed to 'representational time', 'the time that it takes the reader, by the clock, to peruse that part of the text projecting

1. G.W. Coats, 'Tale', in *Saga, Legend, Tale, Novella, Fable: Narrative Forms in Old Testament Literature* (ed. G.W. Coats; JSOTSup, 35; Sheffield: JSOT Press, 1985), p. 64.

2. A common feature of biblical expositions is the delaying of information; cf. Bar-Efrat, *Art*, p. 130; Alter, *Narrative*, pp. 80-81.

3. The section 'Vocabulary' will discuss the conventional language used to tell of the birth.

4. Sternberg, *Modes*, pp. 23-30.

5. *Modes*, pp. 30, 28.

6. Chapter 3, under 'Narrative Speeds and Order'.

this fictive period'. The ratio between the two changes when a cursory scene of exposition gives way to the more elaborated 'action proper'.[1] Indeed, time does become quantified here: the mother hides the baby for three months.[2] And it is slowed: the narrative lingers on her preparation of the basket.[3]

Freytag wrote of 'the entrance of exciting forces' to describe the charging of intensity as relations and events clash.[4] This inciting moment here is v. 2c-d, when the mother sees that the infant is clean-limbed and decides to hide him from Pharaoh's sentence. The princess tautens the suspense to its critical degree by spotting the basket, opening it and finding the child.

Turning Point (v. 6c). This is the zenith of the suspense: 'And, behold, a boy crying!' H. Katsumura had found that והנה often interrupts the 'syntagmic narrative chain' with a new reality.[5] Here, for the good or ill of the protagonist, the story is on the verge of some kind of resolution of the problem in the plot. The princess must now react to the discovery, and her response will lay the path for the rest of the plot. She can save the child or order its death.[6]

Denouement (vv. 6d-10c). The princess has pity on the child, giving us hope that he will survive. Tension then mounts again when she notices that he is a Hebrew. Will she follow her emotions and spare

1. *Modes*, p. 14.

2. Margalit ('Studies in Several Biblical Expressions for Time', *Beth Mikra*, 89–90 [1982], p. 212 [Hebrew]) cautions, however, that months and years do not seem closely calculated in Scripture.

3. M. Duvshani ('Time in Biblical Narrative', *Beth Mikra* 73 [1978], p. 225 [Hebrew]) devotes some attention to the disparity between narration time and narrated time as a device of emphasis. He cites as contrasting examples the brief visit of the angels to Abraham, which is narrated over 16 verses (Gen. 18.1-16), almost half a chapter, and the story of Judah and Tamar, which lasted at least 20 years, but is sketched in a single chapter, Gen. 38.

4. Cited by Sternberg, *Modes*, p. 5.

5. H. Katsumura, 'Zur Funktion von *hinneh* [*sic*] und *w^ehinnēh* in der biblischen Erzählung', *Annual of the Japanese Biblical Institute* 13 (1987), p. 10.

6. Coats's five-part scheme marks slightly different graduations on the same arc of tension ('Tale', p. 65). His third division is the 'resolution', the moment that the tension breaks. The 'turning point' here immediately precedes and causes that dramatic relief.

him, or her father's orders and have him killed? The demonstrative זה keeps the perspective closely fixed on the infant and the person with him during this new moment of danger.

In v. 7a we are surprised that the person speaking is the sister. As in v. 3a, narration time has quickened and the sister is suddenly beside the princess. We might have expected the maidservant whom she had sent. But the sister completely replaces the נערת and the אמה as the princess's company. The same verb הלך refers to her and them. In the servants' case it suggested some kind of aimless strolling. They walked back and forth beside the River (v. 5c). The sister, however, uses it to introduce her clever plan that will persuade the princess and begin once again to relax the narrative tension.

Like the midwives in Chapter 1, the sister is an ironic contrast to the Pharaoh who boasted of dealing shrewdly with the Hebrews (1.10).[1] A simple girl outsmarts the ruler whose court was the paradigm of wisdom in Middle Eastern tradition.[2] We are finally assured of Moses' well-being only when the princess agrees to the sister's plan.

Conclusion (v. 10d-e). The naming of Moses by his adoptive mother completes the conventional description of a birth and brings the action of the pericope to a close.

These five narrative stages are framed by the broader plot and tension concerning all the Hebrews' fate, but they are fixed on only one family and its son. That is, the complexity of the narrative structure here is in inverse proportion to its scope. They have brought Moses through two passages: from the threat of death to the assurance of life, and from the circle of his Hebrew parents to the court of his Egyptian guardian.

4. *Point of View and Narrative Gaps*

Twice the narrator's eye shifts in rhythm with the dramatic development. In the introduction, the point of view is universal and external. Then verse 2c-d, which interrupts the birth description and begins the complication, records the mother's thoughts in another example of

1. R.B. Lawton, 'Irony in Early Exodus', *ZAW* 97 (1985), p. 414.
2. For references to Pharaoh's wisdom, see the footnote in 'Rhetorical Analysis', Chapter 2.

external focalization directed within: 'When she saw him—that he was goodly...'[1]

The narrator immediately withdraws until v. 6c, the turning point. Here again the focalization penetrates a character, this time the princess. It presents the event as she herself experiences it: 'And, behold, a boy crying!'

And so, at the complication and the turning point, these junctures in both the drama and perspective, the real and the adoptive mother each discover an interest in the boy. Their emotion is compared and accented by the same shift in the point of view.

Two other remarks about the focalization prompt larger thoughts. We never glimpse within the mind of the sister. Instead we stand beside her, as it were. From 'far off' (v. 4a), we too watch the daughter of Pharaoh come down to the river and find the basket. We share her point of view, as well as her sympathy for the child. Suddenly she is with the princess and a narrative gap opens between us and her: how did she get past the maids to the princess's side? She proposes her plan, and soon its success shows a second gap, this one temporary. Unknown to us, she intended her mother to be the boy's nursemaid. Our relation to the sister is thus a careful balance. A common concern and perspective draw us to her. But we are also separated by a disparity regarding information that the story reserves for her alone.

An identical dynamic plays between us and the princess. The appearance of the oppressor's daughter is not welcome. But this distrust is tempered by intimacy: the focalization scans internally letting us share her thoughts. And these thoughts are those we hoped to hear: 'She took pity on him' (v. 6d). The narrative moves between reserve and affinity, a counterpoint whose climax, like that of the dramatic stages, is at the turning point. For v. 6c is cast in free indirect discourse, which creates both 'ironic distancing' and 'empathetic identification':[2] 'And, behold, a boy crying'. Free indirect discourse achieves this twin result by cutting across direct and indirect discourse. No reporting verbs like 'she thought' or 'she exclaimed' are used, as they would be in indirect speech. But free indirect discourse retains the deictic elements of direct quotation, such as vocatives and

1. Previous instances have been 1.8b (a new king 'did not know of Joseph'); 1.12c (the Egyptians 'shuddered in horror at the Hebrews'); 1.17a and 1.21a (the midwives 'feared God').

2. Rimmon-Kenan, *Narrative Fiction*, p. 114.

interjections: 'behold!'[1] It 'indexes mimesis' while being evidently artful.[2] The language is clearly that of the character, though not attributed to her, because Moses is נער with no article before the noun: the sentence is conceived in the princess's mind where the discovery has no antecedent.[3] In Rémi Lack's image, the narrator gives the word to the character while also keeping hold of it.[4]

The play of reader- and character-elevating strategies works to the same balanced end. We are superior to the princess in comprehension in that we know already what is in the basket. But once she opens it, only she knows until v. 6d that she has pity on the child.

Both the sister and the princess are thus presented to the reader as though nearby but behind a veil. We keep our sympathies for the Hebrews, of course, but the perspective and gapping do not direct us in that preference as in 1.15-22, where the focus went within the midwives but not Pharaoh. Earlier, at the beginning of the oppression (1.8-14), we found a similar objectivity of perspective that held us back from emotional indulgence in the predicament of the Hebrews. It has the same effect now, and more.

We have seen that Exodus 1–2 has an interest in the theme of knowledge. The Hebrews' oppression is born of ignorance and promoted by Pharaoh's manipulation of his people's understanding. God will correct the skewing of human relations that results by centring knowledge and service on himself. Already in the midwives scene (1.15-22) God's intervention shows that the narrator's omniscience, like his omnipotence, is here only a reflection of divine limitless

1. Consult Chatman, *Story*, p. 202, about the aptness of exclamations in free indirect discourse. Covert narrators are hard put to use them because of the undue attention they draw to the narrator.

2. Rimmon-Kenan, *Narrative Fiction*, p. 114. M. Ron, 'Free Indirect Discourse, Mimetic Language Games and the Subject of Fiction', *Poetics Today* 2.2 (1981), p. 17: 'FID can be meaningful only within literary mimesis and its limits may be taken to mark some of the limits of the mimetic powers of language'.

3. It is interesting to remark in passing that, just before he commissions Moses, God speaks a sentence that regroups the same semantic elements as here: 'crying' or 'calling out', 'child' or 'sons', 'seeing' and the same particle הנה. 'And now, behold, the cry of the people of Israel has come to me and I have seen the oppression with which the Egyptians oppress them' (3.9).

4. R. Lack, *Letture strutturaliste dell'Antico Testamento* (Rome: Borla, 1978), p. 73.

power. Now we learn the accompanying lesson: our human perception is imperfect.

Since the new Pharaoh began his plot, we have been clear about the matters at stake. The oppression is unjust. Characters have knowingly striven for or against it, and it has been easy to judge their actions ethically. But now the narrative makes a nice distinction. The conflict still cuts sharply between right and wrong. But the characters' actions and their outcome are not so unambiguous.

Is the princess's pity for the boy as good morally as the midwives' fear of God? Does she adopt him because she opposes her father's measures absolutely, or is it only in the case of this child who has moved her? More important, how does Moses' rescue help his suffering brothers and sisters? We know from 1.1-7 that the present is predicated on the past in these chapters. And so how will Moses' origins here affect his future as an adult? He is nursed by his mother, named by the princess; he is adopted by the second but not abandoned by the first. His future is mysterious because he is still passive. For the time being, both the Hebrew and Egyptian worlds act on him. Which world will he eventually choose? And which one do we want for him? Moral imponderables coexist with moral imperatives. This pericope confronts us with the complexity that adheres to any matter of justice.

The reversion to an impartial focalization just when the oppression has reached its pitch, and the gaps that keep us at the same distance from the sister and the princess are signs of a reality in this text: the conflict entails dilemmas of understanding and judgment. They point to the limits of our own faculties and so implicitly direct our attention beyond, back to God himself, who has already intervened once and by his omnipotence shown that he alone can perceive absolutely—as we will soon read, 'And God knew' (Exod. 2.25).

On a technical note, one remarks the return of a short but evocative word that sharpens the interiority of the focalization at the turning point in v. 6c: 'behold, a boy crying'. The הנה and participle בכה signal that the narrator has shortened his focal distance.[1] As

1. F.I. Andersen (*The Sentence in Biblical Hebrew* [Janua Linguarum, Series Practica, 231; The Hague: Mouton, 1974], pp. 94-95) calls this verse a 'surprise clause' from the 'participant perspective'. According to A. Berlin ('Point of View in Biblical Narrative', in *A Sense of Text: The Art of Language in the Study of Biblical Literature* [*JQR* Supplement; Winona Lake, IN: Eisenbrauns, 1982], pp. 92-93), with reference to Andersen (*Sentence*, p. 82), when the הנה clause is a nominal

J.P. Fokkelman notes about the same structure in another text, the narrator moves to 'a subordinate position behind' the princess and records what her eyes see.

> There is no longer a narrator who looks back to a past; there is only the present as [the character] experiences it. . . This past of what [the character] saw forces itself so strongly upon the narrator that it becomes present. It sweeps away the distance-in-time which is included in narratives; the narrator unites, as it were, with [the character]. . . The particle *hinnē* features in this process, thanks to its deictic power; it is partly pre- or para-lingual, it goes with a lifted arm, an open mouth.[1]

Opening the denouement, v. 6d continues this narrative solidarity with the princess by revealing to us that she has pity on the child. Cassuto suggests that the ותאמר in v. 6e should be translated 'she thought'.[2] Such a reading is possible lexically[3] and would continue the same interior focus. But without the support of a modifying phrase such as אל לבה, it could also mean simply 'she said' and mark the beginning of speech, a semantic field distinctive of the fourth and fifth stages in the story. In v. 7a she addresses the sister; indisputably now the focalization is again external.

5. *Perspective*

Focalization is about the subject of perception and the question of who orients it. But the object of interest is also important in this passage. A characteristic feature of the pericope is that, from the complication on, the perspective usually rests on the child and the person with him. Moses lies at the centre of the other characters' attention and of the narrative's focus. After the introduction, the Hebrew woman and girl are generally designated by their relation to him: 'his sister' (vv. 4a,

construction while the verbs in the main clause and surrounding narration are in the 'perfect tense', the Hebrew is showing synchrony; but it may also serve the poetic purpose of indicating point of view. It 'internalizes the viewpoint' (p. 91) in much the same way as other kinds of interior monologue.

1. J.P. Fokkelman, *Narrative Art in Genesis* (The Biblical Seminar; Sheffield: JSOT Press, 2nd edn, 1991 [1st edn Assen: Van Gorcum, 1975]), pp. 51-52. L. Alonso-Schökel ('Nota estilistica sobre la partícula הנה', *Bib* 37 [1956], p. 74) also speaks of its deictic function. The effect is quite the opposite of Durham's weak translation here: 'understandably' (*Exodus*, p. 14).
2. *Commentary*, p. 19.
3. BDB, p. 56; *HALAT*, I, p. 64.

7a), and 'the child's mother' (v. 8d). When Moses is with his mother, the reader follows her actions as she hides him, then makes and places the basket. As the complication moves towards the turning point, each successive verb brings the narrative camera closer to the contents of the basket. The princess sees it, sends for it, takes it, opens it. Literally, she 'saw him, the child, and behold, a boy crying' (v. 6b-c). The narrative eye stays fixed on the princess and the child until v. 8c, being strengthened by the demonstrative pronoun זה in v. 6f, and later by the adjective הזה in v. 9b. In v. 8c-d we do follow the girl for a short while as she calls the mother, but Moses is never far from mind; for even though her own daughter fetches her, the woman is called אם הילד, his mother, not hers. We might expect the subject of the verbal phrase ותאמר לה in v. 9a to be the girl. Instead the narrator has already returned to the princess with the child. The girl has executed her task with respect to the child and, like her father earlier, makes her exit from the stage. In the same way, we know nothing of the princess while the Hebrew woman is nursing the boy (vv. 9e-10a), nor of the latter once the Egyptian has taken him on (v. 10b-e).

This intense narrative concentration on the boy solves the literary problem he poses as an important but inactive character. It may also announce the nature of his future greatness. Just as in his infancy here he is quiescent but central, so later he is chosen not by merit but by grace to be the chief servant of the Lord: 'Who am I that I should go to Pharaoh, and bring the Israelites out of Egypt?' (Exod. 3.11).[1]

In the complication especially, the narrator is mindful of location, of where characters and objects are: 'among the reeds at the River's brink' (v. 3), 'far off' (v. 4), 'at the River', 'beside the River', 'among the reeds' (v. 5). In addition to stressing the river, and thus the water symbolism to be discussed hereafter, this attention increases the suspense by defining the perspective. It will progressively narrow around the basket in the princess's hands as the plot reaches its climax.

1. Weimar (*Berufung*, p. 222) notes that Moses is also passive in Exod. 3 at the Burning Bush. In both instances, his attitude allows him to develop a special affinity, first with the princess, then with God. Oddly, however, Weimar calls these relations Moses' goal.

6. *Narrative Symmetry*

The pericope knits a chiastic pattern:

A	The parents' marriage; the birth of Moses (vv. 1a-2b)
B	The mother hides him; puts him in the basket (vv. 2c-3e)
C	The sister positions herself (v. 4)
D	The princess finds him (vv. 5-6)
C[1]	The sister makes a proposal (vv. 7-8)
B[1]	The princess gives him to his mother to be nursed (vv. 9a-10b)
A[1]	The adoption and naming of Moses (v. 10c-f)

Parts A and A[1] are the description of the birth and adoption, and they set Moses in his Hebrew and Egyptian families. B and B[1] are about the mother, then the mother and the princess, that is, the natural and adoptive parents. The sister dominates C and C[1]. (She deals with the princess in C[1], but the princess says only one word during these verses: לכי). The axial verses D include the turning point and speak of the princess and the child. The only unevenness in the length of the corresponding sections is in C[1], which is longer than C because the sister has changed from an observer to a participant in the action.

D.W. Wicke has reflected on the relations between this pericope and the first two passages in our study, which stretch from 1.1 to 1.14. The words שם and בוא form an inclusio around the entire piece (1.1 and 2.10b, d). 'At the beginning of the unit the sons of Israel are separated from the promised land, and they go down to the land of Egypt. At the end of the unit, Moses is separated from his people and is brought to the palace of Pharaoh.'[1]

Some of the parallels he finds show that the relation between 1.1-14 and 2.1-10 is that of the general to the specific. Instead of the twelve sons of Jacob, we concentrate now on one son. The Hebrews built store-cities with mortar (1.14: בחמר *b*[e]*ḥomer*); the mother daubs the basket with pitch (2.3: חמר *ḥēmār*).

Other parallels indicate opposition according to Wicke. In 1.6 the death of Joseph and all that generation prepares for the confrontation between the sons of Israel and Egypt. In 2.1-10 it is a birth that sets the stage for an encounter with Pharaoh's daughter. In 1.8 a new king arose who did not 'know' of Joseph; the sister hides so that she might 'know' Moses' fate. The Egyptians 'shuddered in horror' at the

1. Wicke, 'Literary Structure', p. 99.

Hebrews (1.12); Pharaoh's daughter 'has compassion' on the child.

Wicke draws another contrast that is less persuasive. 'In 1.14', he writes, 'the sons of Israel lose their identity. At the beginning of the narrative they are named. At the end they are a nameless mass of slaves. In 2.10 the nameless child received his identity.'[1]

In fact, narrative clues reveal that the opposite is true. Analysis of the narrative symmetry of 1.1-7 has demonstrated that that passage shifts from the static to the dynamic as Israel's sons become a people. If they are not named individually at the end, it is simply because they are too many. Rather than losing an identity, they have gained one as a nation: by 1.7 בני ישׂראל means 'the Israelites'. They are no longer just a family, as Pharaoh himself confirms by calling them עם בני ישׂראל in 1.9. The princess, on the other hand, gives Moses a name, but that puts at risk any self-awareness as a Hebrew. His birth is in contrast to that of the nation. The Israelites gained the status of a people despite a threat. On the contrary, Moses' future identity becomes uncertain exactly because of the way in which the immediate danger against him is removed. Both the difference and the bond between Moses and his fellow Israelites are underscored by their all being called בן, but in his case it is meant once again in the genealogical sense.

Read together, the pericopes are making a broader statement that follows the conclusion already noted, that human understanding is described here as imperfect.[2] Circumstances brought the Israelites to nationhood, but other events can obscure their awareness of it. Only a force above the currents of happenstance can set the seal on their identity as a people. As with the focalization of this passage, we again remember the display of omnipotence in God's intervention for the midwives, and that refers us further back to his promises to the patriarchs. Not history alone, but God in history must be the guarantor of the Israelites' sense of the body corporate. The past shapes the present, according to 1.1-7. But that continuum yields meaning and stimulates loyalty only if its interpretation, like all knowledge, is oriented to the Lord of history whose identity is alone self-sufficient and unchanging: 'I AM WHO I AM' (Exod. 3.13). We are applying here the lesson of

1. 'Literary Structure', p. 100. J. Barr ('The Symbolism of Names in the Old Testament', *BJRL* 52 [1969–70], pp. 11-29) warns of attempts to see exaggerated meaning in Biblical names and their bestowal. One might add by extension attempts to see an assurance of identity in a name.

2. Refer to 'Point of View and Narrative Gaps'.

1.8-14. To know themselves, the Israelites and Moses must know God.

The motif of knowledge in Exodus 1–2 is a thematic mirror to the story of the Fall. In that disaster were born freedom, however abused, and human consciousness, however dimmed. It inaugurated our capacity to choose, and to respect or disrespect the God-given distinctions between appetite and value.[1] The failure of the couple was the first breach of humanity's association with God. Soon, in a new and covenantal way, God himself will repair these relations. To assuage that archetypical Fall God now prepares the model of all redemptions[2]—the Exodus of his people, the outbreak of responsible freedom, the construction of their national consciousness.

To return to the formal, the text 2.1-10 is shaped by a number of elements. The preliminary exposition (vv. 1a-2b) is a stylistic unit marked by nominal parrallelisms:

וילך	איש	
ויקח		את־בת־לוי
ותהר		האשה
ותלד	בן	

Note also:

A	איש
B	בית לוי
B[1]	בת־לוי
A[1]	האשה

The nouns איש and בן designating males are parallel, as are בת and האשה. The disposition and phonetic resemblance of איש... בית לוי... אשה... בת־לוי form a chiastic pattern.

A chiastic structure links vv. 2d and 3a:

ותצפנהו	שלשה ירחים
עוד	הצפינו

1. S.J. de Vries, 'The Fall', *IDB*, II, pp. 236-37.

2. A. Spreafico (*Esodo: Memoria e Promessa: Interpretazioni profetiche* [Supplementi *RivB*, 14; Bologna: Associazione biblica italiana, 1985], p. 152) calls the Exodus a salvific model that describes and announces the intervention of God in the history of Israel. Read also Frye, *The Great Code*, pp. 171, 176.

The components are the two occurrences of the verb צפן and the two temporal expressions עוד and שלשה ירחים. The chiastic pattern stresses the precision in narration time that we studied under 'Surface Structure' as one of the features of the complication.

Besides the recurrence of בן already noted throughout 1.1–2.25 as a thematic conductor, together with בת here it braces this pericope as an inclusion (vv. 1.2, 10). Generally the two words advance the motif of proliferation begun in Exodus 1, and specifically they shape the question of Moses' identity. To the same effect, the conventional language of conception and childbirth that was discussed above is split between the beginning and the end, the Hebrew parents and the Egyptian guardian. The structure of the passage thus hangs from the motifs of propagation and provenance, and so reinforces the question of where Moses' adult loyalties will lie after his Hebrew birth and Egyptian adoption.

The actions of the mother and of the princess correspond. The beginning and end of Moses' passage through the water are stylistically matched:

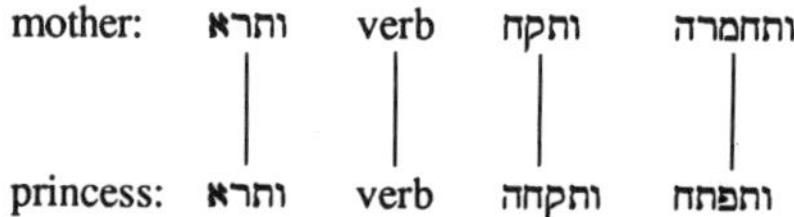

The second verbs are the ones that do not match: they are neither identical (לקח, ראה) nor opposite (פתח חמר). In the mother's case, the verb is 'hide/cannot hide [her son]'. In the princess's, it is 'send [her maid]'. These differing verbs point to the disparity between the social positions of the two women and thus to the radical nature of the passage that Moses is about to make from Hebrew degradation to Egyptian aristocracy.

A chiastic structure stretches from v. 9b to v. 10b:

A	הילכי את־הילד הזה
B	והינקהו לי
C	ואני אתן. . .ותקח
B^1	ותניקהו
A^1	ליגדל הילד. . .ותבאהו

That is,

$A–A^1$ =	'make go' + ילד // ילד + 'make come'
$B–B^1$ =	ינק (*hiph.*) + suffix הו־
C =	give // take

The transposition of the internal elements in v. 9b and v. 10a-b forms a second chiastic structure within and at the limits of the larger symmetry: הילד...ותבאהו // היליכי את־הילד הזה.

As in the scheme above for v. 3, the style here links the natural and the adoptive mother. The association is appropriate, since they are about to engage in business.

The sister and the daughter of Pharaoh are also introduced in parallel sentence patterns:

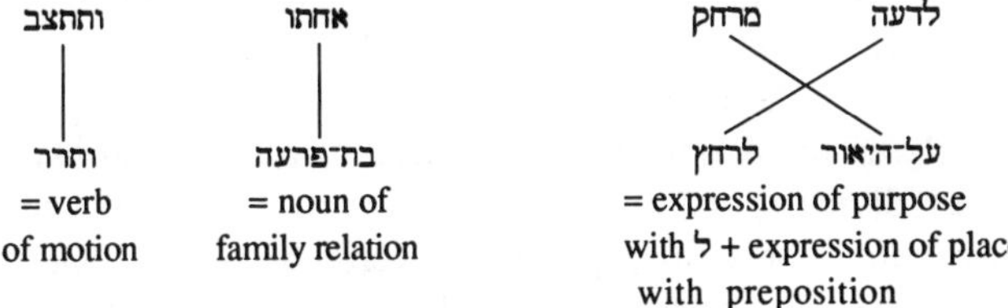

These two ordered presentations of events and characters belie the risk of the women's plan and perhaps hint at a mysterious purposefulness in the adventures of the infant Moses.

The sister wants to 'know what would be done to him', לו (v. 4). She heightens the suspense by asking herself the same question as we the readers or listeners.

The last recurrence of לו, 'to' or 'for him' was v. 3b; unable to hide the infant, the mother took a papyrus basket for him, or, in the rendition of Cassuto, 'unto him'.[1] Once she has placed the basket on the water and the sister is posted to observe, she has done all she can. She is now utterly powerless, just as the newborn is. The two uses of the word form an inclusion and define the limits of the mother's ability to save him.

A chiastic structure in vv. 5c-6b closes the complication and accents three quick verbs:

A	ונערתיה		הולכת
B	ותרא		את־תבה
C	...ותשלח	...ותקחה	ותפתח
B^1	ותראהו		את־הילד
A^1	והנה־נער		בכה

1. *Commentary*, p. 17.

That is,

A–A[1] = ו + נערת / נער + participle
B–B[1] = ראה + object with את

The participles here are the only ones in the pericope. They help build the suspense to its climax by stressing the durative aspect of the actions described.[1] To the same effect, the three verbs within the chiastic structure, 'send', 'take' and 'open', form an auxesis, a series of 'words or clauses placed in climactic order'.[2] The princess sends (שלח) the maid into the water to fetch the basket, thus saving the boy. The verb may be a pun on שלך in Pharaoh's order to kill the boys by throwing them in the water (1.22).

The verbs in the narrative can be traced to a pattern in two ways. First, they divide roughly by kind into verbs of action, which are dominant before the turning point, and verbs of diction. The second type begins in v. 6c, when action and diction combine: Moses cries. It is his only 'action' in the whole narrative, and it is also the first utterance of any character. In the latter half of the pericope, the verbs of action and diction mix in a way best described by turning first to the other general point of symmetry among the verbs.

The form of the verbs in the pericope also takes on a rough pattern. Basically, the narrative is a succession of *wayyiqtol* broken tidily in three measured places. Except for v. 3a, the first interruption begins at the word לדעה (v. 4b), exactly halfway through the complication, and runs to v. 5c with two infinitives,[3] a future-*yiqtol* and a participle. This morphological change coincides with the introduction of the sister and helps inflate the surprise attending her appearance.

The second set of variations from the *wayyiqtol* is at the turning point, v. 6c, in the very middle of the narrative. Moses' crying is recounted with a participle, and from then until v. 8b the *wayyiqtol* verbs of action, hitherto usual, yield to a rash of *wayyiqtol* verbs of speech, an imperative, a future-*yiqtol* and two *w^eqatalti* in a direct question. This grammatical shift gives acuity to the turning point as

1. Joüon, *Grammaire*, §166h. The complete pattern in both instances (v. 5a-5c and v. 6b-6c) is *wayyiqtol*. . . ו. . . *qotel*. The first action is instantaneous, the second circumstantial and durative.

2. Lanham, *Handlist*, p. 124.

3. *HALAT*, II, p. 373; I, p. 219, lists דעה as an infinitive. GKC §69c, m calls it a rare form of *qal* infinitive construct with a feminine ending.

the critical angle of the narrative setting a new direction for the plot.

The third break in the string of *wayyiqtol* verbs is at another midpoint, this time the centre of the denouement. In v. 9 the princess uses other forms: an imperative, a *w^{e}qatalti* and a future-*yiqtol*. Meanwhile in the plot she is unknowingly striking a remarkable deal with Moses' mother: the mother's enemies, the Egyptians, restore to her the child she herself abandoned. Pharaoh's daughter appoints her as nurse to feed one of the Hebrew boys that her father ordered killed. And, to boot, the mother will be paid for her trouble. The daughter of Pharaoh stresses that she herself will give the mother her wages (v. 9d: ואני אתן). She is not only betraying her father's campaign against the Hebrews; she is paying a Hebrew to help in the operation. The change in the pattern of verb forms underwrites this extraordinary development in the plot.

7. *Vocabulary*

Fertile Life and Family: בית, בת (6×), הרה, ילד (noun: 8×; verb: 1×), בן (2×), אחות (2×), נער, ינק (*hiph.*, 4×), גדל (verb), קרא שם, היה ל...ל...
Nationality: עברי (2×)
Affliction: צפן (*qal* 1×; *hiph.* 1×), בכה
Construction: תבה (2×), גמא, חמר, חמר (*ḥēmār*), זפת
Giving, Taking, Motion: לקח (4×), שים (2×), שלח, נתן, בוא (*hiph.*), משה (2×), יצב (*hithp.*), ירד, הלך (6×)
Perception: ראה (3×), ידע, הנה
Communication: אמר (5×), קרא (2×)

The vocabulary of the pericope moors it between the past and the future, the stories in Genesis and the rest of Exodus.

For example, one notices immediately some important words from the last book, כי טוב and תבה. The meaning of כי טוב has already been discussed under 'Notes on the Literal Translation'. It reminds the reader or listener of Genesis 1, and we can justly ask if the Creation story is the taproot of Moses' birth story by direct connection with those of its verses using כי טוב (Gen. 1.4, 10, 12, 18, 21, 25). It is not, for three reasons.

The narrative is unlikely to cast Moses' mother in any role previously played by God, as though her son were her own handiwork. Children come from God's bounty, and even a hint otherwise would be no introduction to the Exodus where God alone is victorious: 'Who is like you, YHWH, among the gods?' (Exod. 15.11).

Also, the expression is not limited to Genesis 1 and Exodus 2. It occurs elsewhere in the Pentateuch in instances that have nothing to do with brave beginnings. On the contrary, later in Exodus the Hebrews complain about their new life in the desert: 'For it would have been better for us (כי טוב לנו) to serve the Egyptians than to die in the wilderness' (Exod. 14.12). Deut. 15.16 contains laws about a bondman who wishes to remain in service because 'he fares well (כי טוב לו). Isaac worries about Rebekah, כי־טובת מראה היא (Gen. 26.7).

One might object that this construct chain in Genesis 26 and כי טוב ל in Exodus 14 and Deuteronomy 15 are not the same expressions as כי טוב. But exegetical judgments are made through the convergence of evidence. We must also consider a conclusion from the reading of 1.1-7, that Exodus 1–2 looks back not to one or two moments in the Hebrews' past, but to their entire history as it fashions their emerging nation. Like the words of proliferation, the expression כי טוב is one thread among many tying this pericope to the broad fabric of Genesis, but it does not bind it to any single episode.

The same is true for תבה, here the 'basket', and used elsewhere only for the 'ark' of Noah. Ackerman sees a direct parallel: 'through Noah man was saved from extinction, partially purged of the corruption which had engulfed the world. Through Moses... Israel was to be delivered from the spiritual death of bondage and oppression.'[1] But Ackerman himself admits that the lines of resemblance are uneven. The condemnation here is pharaonic and not divine, and the intended victims are the Hebrews, not the whole human race. He might have added that the Hebrews did not deserve their suffering, as the human race did its punishment. And Noah was spared because he was righteous and 'walked with God' (Gen. 6.9), whereas Moses is an unproved baby.

It is overstated to call the recurrence of תבה here a direct allusion. It is at most another reverberation from Genesis in the echo-chamber of history where the story of Exodus 1–2 is told. It recalls suggestively rather than emphatically, and the object is not its close context, but the two chapters' whole reflection on the nature and purpose of the past within God's plan of history.

As mentioned under 'Delimitation' and 'Narrative Symmetry',

1. *Literary Context*, p. 91.

Moses' birth is told in conventional language split between the preliminary exposition and conclusion. No one pattern describes births in Scripture. Rather, each instance draws freely from a broad stock of diction: לקח לאשה, בוא אל, הרה, ילד, קרא שם and a reason for the name given.[1] הרה and ילד are a particularly common word pair.[2] Not all pericopes record the name of the newborn, but Exod. 2.1-10 is the only one that does so after such a long interval. The delay in laying out expositional material helps us to see the birth as special and the adoption as its continuation.[3]

Other words and phrases in Exodus 1–2 also add significantly to the address of its argument. The phrase just before the turning point literally translates, 'And she opened and she saw him, the child'. The *BHS* lists textual variants that add an object to the first verb and omit the pronominal suffix from the second. However, of the latter part, Cassuto writes that the repeated object is emphatic and can be found in

1. R.W. Ramsey ('Is Name-Giving an Act of Domination in Genesis 2:23 and Elsewhere?', *CBQ* 50 [1988], p. 26, citing P. Trible) says that קרא שם is especially important. Houtman, *Exodus*, p. 300: either the father or the mother can give the name, as Moses does to Gershom (2.22).

2. Cf. Avishur, *Stylistic Studies*, pp. 559-60; Fisher, *Ras Shamra*, I, p. 173; W.R. Watters, *Formula Criticism and the Poetry of the Old Testament* (BZAW, 138; Berlin: de Gruyter, 1976), p. 61; and Avishur, *Stylistic Studies*, p. 13 n. 6, about the pair as common to Akkadian, Ugaritic and Hebrew.

3. A. Lacocque postulates that the mother's exclamation was over the infant's circumcision, a version of the Egyptian myth that Seth closed Osiris in a basket and threw him on the Nile where his phallus was eaten by fish. Greenberg (*Understanding Exodus*, p. 40) also compares the Egyptian story. But, as T.L. Thompson and D. Irvin make clear, the motif of the child hidden in the floating basket is international and cannot be identified as specifically Egyptian simply on the basis of Egyptian parallels. D.B. Redford agrees in his research into the motif of the exposed child in world mythology. He uncovers 32 versions of the story. The closest parallel to the birth of Moses is the much-discussed Sargon legend quoted in *ANET*, p. 119, but whether this is the parent of the Moses story or whether the motif enjoyed autonomous popularity among West-semitic peoples is virtually impossible to decide. Coats (*Moses*, pp. 46-47) explains the detailed differences between the birth of Sargon and of Moses. References are to A. Lacocque, 'L'idée directrice de l'Exode I à IV', *VT* 15 (1965), pp. 348-49; T.L. Thompson and D. Irvin, 'The Joseph and Moses Narratives', in *Israelite and Judaean History* (ed. J.H. Hayes and J.M. Miller; London: SCM Press, 1977), p. 155; D.B. Redford, 'The Literary Motif of the Exposed Child (cf. Ex. ii 1-10)', *Numen* 14 (1967), pp. 224-25, 227.

Phoenician too.[1] Certainly the narrative and stylistic structures underscore the sentence, and a syntactical emphasis on the object of the verb would not be out of place.

Appropriately, the largest semantic field is of fertile life and family. This diction corroborates the narrative's continuing concern with life and proliferation in general, and now Moses' own safety in particular.

Another cluster of words involves motion, giving and taking. Moses' birth and survival are due to three instances of לקח. His father 'took the daughter of Levi' (v. 1b); his mother 'took for him a basket of papyrus' (v. 3b); and the daughter of Pharaoh 'took' the basket and opened it (v. 5f). Verse 3, parts b and d, contains a chiastic structure where לקח and שׂים are parallel:

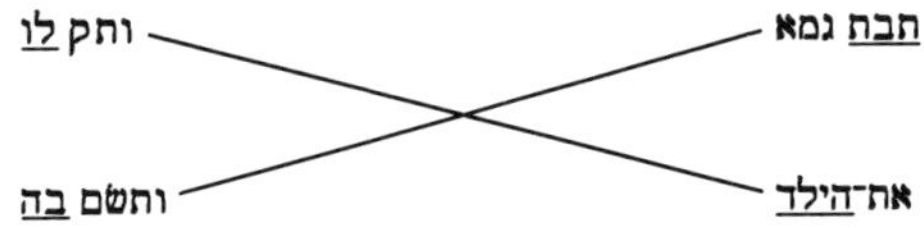

On the other hand, the princess agrees to 'give' (נתן) wages to the mother (v. 9d). And with a repetition of the verb השׂים,[2] the mother places the infant in the basket and the basket among the reeds. שׂים contrasts with the *hiphil* of שׁלך in Pharaoh's order (1.22). Ironically, of course, the mother is obeying the letter but not the spirit of this command.[3] This semantic field lends the pericope a character of busy enterprise, in contrast to Moses, who is often the object of these verbs but never their subject. And the chiastic structure sets the middle phrase in some relief: 'she loamed it with loam and with pitch'. Exum[4] sees the conjunction here of the verb חמר and חמר (*hēmār*) as an allusion to the forced work with חמר (*ḥōmer*) in 1.14. That was an act of slavery, this a 'labor of love'.[5]

When the princess 'goes down' to the Nile (v. 5a), she sets off a

1. *Commentary*, p. 19.

2. Cassuto (*Commentary*, p. 18) suggests that this implies great care, and Lacocque (*Devenir*, p. 53) suggests honour.

3. Durham, *Exodus*, p. 16.

4. 'Daughter', pp. 76-77.

5. As cited in 'Narrative Symmetry', D.W. Wicke notes the same correlation. While the three words are most likely related according to BDB, p. 330, H. Ringgren ('חמר *ḥmr*', *THWAT*, III, p. 1) has doubts about חמר (*ḥomer*), and *HALAT*, I, p. 317, relates it to a different חמר root. The most one can remark with certainty is a close aural similarity.

series of motion verbs: ירד is used once and הלך six times. The idioms 'to take away' (v. 9b) and 'to bring' (v. 10b) are likely to be *hiphil* forms of הלך and בוא, as reflected in the literal translation of the first.

If in fact היליכי is from הלך in v. 9b,[1] the narrative is coherent in repeating this root: הלך and ינק (*hiph.*) were the crucial words in the sister's suggestion to the princess. The princess has now wholly taken on both the vocabulary and the proposal of the slave-girl. How ironic then that the princess believes she is ordering the mother for her own sake, לי. She is simply parrotting the girl who just said לך.

The verb ראה in the third-person feminine singular marks the beginning and the end of the complication (vv. 2c, 6b). It also recurs before a swift succession of verbs that builds the suspense to the moment of highest tension (vv. 5d-6b). After the turning point, this semantic field of sight leaves off and another begins. In the denouement and conclusion, אמר is used five times and קרא twice in the literal sense.[2] The field of communication has been gaining importance since its introduction in 1.9. Visual recognition now gives way to vocal exchange.

To understand the importance of these semantic fields, we must look ahead in the Book of Exodus. God does not 'remember' his covenant' and 'know' until 2.24-25. But when he does move to save them, three of the semantic fields just studied will reappear: perception, communication and motion, giving and taking.[3]

He 'sees' them and answers their 'call' (2.23, 25; also 3.16) by 'coming down' to deliver them (3.8; also 3.7, 9, 16). The angel of the Lord 'appears' (3.2: וירא) to Moses who 'looks' and goes to 'see the great sight' (המראה), then is afraid to 'look at God' (3.6). God 'sends' him to Pharaoh or the Israelites (3.10, 13, 14, 15; also 'to go': 3.18). Pharaoh is to 'let them go', and 'when [they] go, [they] will not go empty' (3.18, 21). Moses 'answered' God that the people will not 'listen' to him; 'for they will say, "YHWH will not appear to you"' (4.1; also 4.5, 9). 'I am slow of speech and of tongue' (4.10). But the Lord said to him, 'Now therefore go, and I will...teach you what you shall speak' (4.12). Aaron will 'speak' for him to the people

1. See 'Notes on the Literal Translation'.

2. And once in the idiom 'to name', classified as 'Fertile Life and Family'.

3. Refer again to Fischer, *Jahwe unser Gott*, pp. 69-72, about the semantic field of seeing in Exod. 3.1-9; cf. pp. 72-76 about that of sending in Exod. 3.10-22; cf. pp. 79-81 about that of speaking in Exod. 4.10-17. A chart is on his p. 82.

(4.15). Jethro allows him to 'go' in peace (4.18). God tells Aaron to 'go' to meet Moses (4.27) and together they 'speak' before the elders (4.29).

From 2.23, when God remembers his covenant, to 4.31, just before Moses and Aaron appear before Pharaoh for the first time, the three semantic fields can be tabulated thus:

> *Communication*: אמר 43×, דבר (*pi.* and noun) 14×, פה 7×, קל 5×, זעק 3×, קרא 2×, אנה 1×, נאק 1×, שוע 1×, לשון 1×, נגד 1×, ענה 1×, שאל 1×, בקש (*pi.*) 2×, בי 1×, צוה (*pi.*) 1×, ירה (*hiph.*) 1×, צעקה 1×.
> *Perception*: ראה 16×, נבט (*hiph.*) 1×, שמע 7×, אלם (*'illēm*) 1×, חרש (*ḥērēš*) 1×, עור (*'iwwēr*) 1×, פקח (*piqqēaḥ*) 1×, הנה *hnh* 1×.
> *Motion, Giving, Taking*: הלך 16×, יצא 6×, קרב 3×, עלה 2×, ירד 1×, בוא 6×, שלח 15×, שוב (*hiph.* and *qal*) 8×, סור 2×, הלום 1×, קרב 1×, דרך 1×, שלך 2×, נוס 1×, נתן 2×, לקח 6×, אסף 2×, שים 4×, רפה 1×.[1]

Thus his new salvific plan will soon be announced in the terms that already dominate Moses' infancy narrative. The vocabulary here plays the proleptic role of the words about knowledge and service in 1.8-14 and of the fearless midwives in 1.15-22. Meanwhile God's abiding love for his people, already shown by his brief intervention in 1.20-21, is again hinted at in Moses' very birth; for in Scripture every birth is a token of the people's fruitfulness which is always a divine blessing.[2]

These narrative signs of God's coming salvation seem confirmed by the choice of three particular words, צפן, יצב (*hithp.*) and to a lesser extent חמל.

The mother 'hides' the boy (v. 2e: ותצפנהו) until she can no longer do so (v. 3a: הצפינו).[3] Exodus 2 is one of the very few passages in which צפן means hiding a person or thing, and the only one without an explicit moral or religious tone to the action.

The verb צפן recurs 33 times in Hebrew Scripture, always within

1. Ackerman ('Literary Context', p. 92) notices as well that God protects Moses who is placed as a child among the reeds (סוף); he will be with the Hebrews when Moses leads them across the Reed Sea (Exod. 13.18, ים־סוף). Houtman (*Exodus*, p. 266) remarks about ירד used here in v. 5a that it is usual in describing Moses' descent from Mount Sinai.

2. R. de Vaux, *Les institutions de l'Ancien Testament* (Paris: Editions du Cerf, 2nd edn, 1961 [1957]), I, p. 71.

3. Whatever the original reason for the dageš forte dirimens (GKC §20h), its aural effect now is emphatic.

the psalter and the canon of the sapiential and prophetic books except for our passage and Josh. 2.4. God is the most common subject (14×). And the context is always moralistic or 'theological', in the broad sense of speaking about God: God 'shelters' the just, for example (Pss. 31.20; 27.5). Or the wicked 'ambush' the innocent (Prov. 1.11) in 'hiding places' (Ps. 10.8). One 'lays up' knowledge (Prov. 10.14) or the words of the Lord (Job 23.12).

Only six times is a material thing or a person hidden, and, in the four cases outside our passage, the motivation and background is, as above, altruistic or devout.[1]

The sister 'stations herself far off to see what will be done to [Moses]' (v. 4a-b). For the standard lexicographers and grammarians, the word ותתצב is an anomalous form of the root יצב (*hithp.*).[2] In Biblical Hebrew, it is exceptional here for the verb יצב (*hithp.*) to apply to a mundane event like a young girl's hiding by a river; it most generally applies to an encounter with God or a divinely elected leader.

The verb יצב occurs 46 times in the Hebrew Bible all in *hithpael*. Seven times it means 'to take one's position' in open battle. It is never metaphorical in this sense in Scripture, and thus it can scarcely apply to Exodus 2. Most commonly (26×), it means 'to stand before' God, or the subject is God himself who comes among his people. Eight times the person is in the presence of a leader of the people who is chosen by God.[3] What the girl sees is the princess going down (ירד) to

1. Prov. 13.22: the 'inheritance' of a 'good man' is hidden; Josh. 2.4: Rahab 'hides' the Israelite scouts because '[she] knows the Lord had given [them] the land' (v. 9); Cant. 7.14: 'I have laid up [choice fruits] for you, O my beloved'; less clear is the corrupt text of Prov. 27.16: 'to restrain [a contentious woman] is to restrain the wind'.

For a statistical approach to this verb that is different but not contradictory, see S.E. Balentine, 'A Description of the Semantic Field of Hebrew Words for "Hide"', *VT* 30 (1980), pp. 137-53, especially pp. 139-40. He has a broad category 'hiding/man', as distinct from 'hiding/God', but some of its members are subsumed in our 'theological/moralistic' category. S. Wagner ('צפן *ṣpn*' *ThWAT*, VI, p. 1109) remarks on its frequency in wisdom literature.

2. BDB, p. 426; *HALAT*, II, p. 408; GKC, §71; König, *Lehrgebäude*, I, p. 429.

3. The only exception here is Exod. 8.16; 9.13, a strict reversal of the norm where God commissions Moses to stand before Pharaoh. There are just five exceptions to these usages, and only two of these are in the Pentateuch and the historical books. The two exceptions in the historical books are 2 Sam. 21.5, 'we

the river. Ackerman writes that ירד applies to God's movement in history, as in the Babel story (Gen. 11.7) and later in Exodus (3.8).[1] The implication of יצב (*hithp.*) with ירד here might be that Moses is a future leader of his people chosen by God, that the girl is witness to the works of God, or both of these.

When the daughter of Pharaoh beholds the infant in the basket, she 'has pity on him' (v. 6d). More than רחם, חמל concentrates on the moment of the decision to spare someone.[2] Lacocque says that it is not maudlin sympathy, but connotes a sense of responsibility.[3] He does not substantiate this interesting point. More concrete, if not too conclusive in itself, is the fact that God is the most common subject.[4] Any conclusion about חמל here must be the sum of contextual factors, including its proximity to צפן and יצב (*hithp.*).

Concluding strictly from the Biblical occurrences, then, צפן and יצב (*hithp.*), amplified somewhat by חמל, seem to intimate God's presence, although he is absent from the plot. And three semantic fields of the passage—communication, perception and motion, giving and taking—might be announcing already the form of his imminent intervention.

Once the mother decides to set Moses on the water, he is no longer called בן but ילד or נער. He will not be called 'son' again until v. 10c, when he has been adopted by the princess. S. Ben-Reuven has studied the word בן in relation to ילד and נער, and concludes that it conveys greater intimacy. In Scripture when a mother must separate from her child, as here, she uses the other two terms.[5]

A נער is dependent and in a condition of service.[6] A book-length study of the word by H.-P. Stähli decides that a נער is an unmarried male under the protection and authority of his father or the father's

should have no place in all the territory of Israel', and 2 Sam. 18.13, 'if I had dealt treacherously against his life. . . then you yourself would have stood aloof'. The exceptions in other books are Ps. 36.5; Prov. 22.29 and Job 38.14, where *BHS* emends the MT.

1. 'Literary Context', p. 92.
2. H.J. Stoebe, 'רחם *rḥm* pi. sich erbarmen', *THAT*, II, p. 764.
3. *Devenir*, p. 56.
4. 21 out of 41 occurrences. M. Tsevat ('חמל *ḥāmal*', *ThWAT*, II, p. 1044) warns that the theological content of the word itself is slight.
5. S. Ben-Reuven, 'בן in Contrast to ילד and נער in the Bible', *Beth Mikra* 93 (2) (January–March) (1983), pp. 147-49 (Hebrew).
6. H.F. Fuhs, 'נער *na'ar*' *ThWAT*, V, p. 514.

representative. The word refers to a status in law.[1] The word here therefore sharpens the implications of the crisis. This foundling seems to have no father to extend it protection and legal status. What will the princess do to it? There are already נערות attending her (v. 5c). Might she herself become the boy's juridical guardian?

Yes. Literally he 'becomes to her as a son' (v. 10c). B.S. Childs has written that היה ל...ל... was an adoption formula with a good number of Near Eastern parallels. He cites an Aramaic adoption contract, a Ugaritic legend and the Code of Hammarapi.[2] This evidence fits with the juridical nature of the word נער and the arrangement between the princess and the mother that was a business deal, perhaps even a legal contract.[3]

Hence the pericope has a juridical flavour that matches the language of 1.8-14 (ענה [*pi.*], פרך, הבה). Specifically it shows that the princess's decision is not just an act of personal infidelity; she is attacking the very legal complex of her country. More broadly, it means that this tale is not a folkloric excursus from the developing themes. As much as the previous pericopes, it treats injustice and the consequent questions of moral obligations.

The exchange between the sister and the princess is widely discussed in the commentaries.[4] For narrative analysis, the conversation is important because paradoxical. The daughter of Pharaoh never acknowledges that she is following the girl's suggestion, simply saying

1. H.-P. Stähli, *Knabe-Jüngling-Knecht: Untersuchungen zum Begriff* נער *im Alten Testament* (Beiträge zur biblischen Exegese und Theologie, 7; Frankfurt am Main: Peter Lang, 1978), pp. 99-100. J. Macdonald, 'The Status and Role of the Na'ar in Israelite Society' (*JNES* 35 [1976], pp. 156-57), is another shorter study. It concentrates on the high birth of the נער, a conclusion less enlightening for our purposes, since we already know that Moses is of the house of Levi.

2. B.S. Childs, 'The Birth of Moses', *JBL* 84 (1965), p. 114 n. 27.

3. Childs ('Birth', p. 111) has studied the deal in the light of Sumerian-Akkadian legal texts about foundlings. He cannot prove an interrelation, but concludes that 'at most the case can be defended that the sequence of the Moses story reflects a pattern which originally had a legal provenance'.

4. Cassuto (*Commentary*, p. 20) remarks that there would have been many nursing Hebrews whose children had just been killed. According to Ackerman ('Literary Context', p. 93), the princess agrees to a Hebrew wetnurse rather than an Egyptian lest her father discover her subversion. In *Exod. R.* 1.25 the point is that Moses was kept from the pollution of idolatry even in the milk that he drank.

to her, 'Go!'[1] Pharaoh is doubly defeated, and the irony is several layers deep. Pharaoh had allowed the Hebrew daughters to live (1.22). Now one of them is advancing a plan that overthrows his order against the newborn sons. The mother had literally followed his decree of infanticide and put the child on the water, but in order to save, not kill it. She lost her child to recover it. That is, the Egyptians who condemned the Hebrew woman's child are now paying her to care for it. The rescue is completed by Pharaoh's own daughter, so that Moses is saved by means of Egypt here. Later, Israel under Moses will be saved from the hands of Egypt.

The princess's one-word command is set against the blustering and irrational orders of her father in 1.8-14. In a single breath, she undoes her father's authority and contributes indispensably to a movement of rebellion that will eventually bring the destruction of the whole Egyptian army. When Pharaoh is finally forced to release the Hebrews in Exod. 12.31-32, he will use the same imperative twice in the plural: 'go, serve YHWH, as you said. Take your flocks and your herds, as you have said, and go'.

'And she went'. The sister immediately obeys Pharaoh's daughter, in contrast to the midwives, who defy her father and disregard his words. The life-saving effect, however, is the same. Cassuto checks Gen. 12.1-4, sees the same structure—הלך in the imperative then in the indicative—and argues that it implies speedy execution.[2] That is no doubt true. However, more significantly, the girl is hurrying to perform a commission that she herself has proposed. The princess has adopted her idea as her own, just as she will soon take on the infant as her son. The language here reflects the success of the Hebrews' plan.

Scholars have written much about the name the princess chooses, for emphasis the only one in the story.[3] The chief narrative point about משה is not its similarity to Egyptian roots,[4] but its construction

1. Fox's observation is the most germane: biblical Hebrew had no word for 'yes' ('Names', p. 17).

2. *Commentary*, p. 20.

3. Fox, *Names*, p. 15.

4. Noth (*Exodus*, p. 26) speculates that the whole story might have arisen as an aetiology of the name. Childs ('Birth', p. 114) reports that a general consensus attributes to the name an Egyptian origin from the root *ms*(*w*), 'to beget'. 'It is a hypocoristic form of a theophoric name built on the pattern of "Thutmose."' Odelain and Séguineau (*Dictionaire*, p. 261) concur. R. Beaud, former Egyptologist of the Ecole Biblique, remarked privately that a simpler solution is more likely—it is a

as an active participle. Moses means 'the drawer', not 'the one drawn', despite what the princess says. The confusion suggests the ambivalence in which Moses will now live. Throughout the pericope, he has been a central but passive figure. Now the active mode of his name may be announcing a future activity.[1] Moses' rescue ends with the giving of a name; in 3.14 Israel's salvation will begin with the telling of the Divine Name. Both the fact and the form of Moses' name may thus be announcing the Exodus.

8. *Symbolism*

The repeated mention of water in the passage (vv. 3e; 5c; 10f) invites associations, and one easily asks whether it could have symbolic meaning here. N. Frie writes that such a question may be answered in at least three ways:

> the connection between symbol and thing symbolized may be made explicit in the work. . . [t]he image may be presented in such a way as to discourage a merely literal interpretation. . . [Or] the pressure of implicit association may be so great as to demand a symbolic interpretation.[2]

He cautions that 'an image in a work is not symbolic unless a literal interpretation fails to do it justice' (p. 834).

His first point quoted is clearly inapplicable. The second raises the delicate matter of what might have seemed logical or plausible to the biblical authors and audience. (The notion of saving a baby by floating it away in a basket seems far-fetched to us and may have been so to

Hebraicized form of a very common Egyptian male name meaning 'son' and based on the root quoted above, but with no divine connotations.

1. Cassuto (*Commentary*, p. 21) draws a first conclusion similar to Beaud's, then adds that the name may encapsulate his destiny as deliverer, as in the image in Isa. 63.11. So too M. Buber, *Moïse* (trans. A. Kohn; Heidelberg: L. Schneider, 2nd edn, 1952 [Paris: Presses Universitaires, 1957]), p. 39. But Moses' present ambivalence may be more important for his name than his future greatness; according to Ramsey ('Name Giving', p. 34), biblical name-giving is more prophetic by current circumstances than determinant of what is to come.

2. N. Frie, 'Symbol', *Princeton Encyclopedia of Poetry and Poetics* (ed. A. Preminger *et al.*; Princeton: Princeton University Press, 2nd [enlarged] edn, 1974 [1965]), p. 833. O.F. Bollnow ('Die Welt der Symbole', in *Leben und Tod in den Religionen: Symbol und Wirklichkeit* [ed. G. Stephenson; Darmstadt: Wissenschaftliche Buchgesellschaft, 1985], p. 5) makes the same point that the first task is to decide if an element is a symbol.

them, but we today cannot know their minds.) More profitable for us is the question of implicit association.

Attention has been given throughout this work to the function of Exodus 1–2 as a hinge opening out both to Genesis and to the rest of the Book of Exodus. The weight of this evidence from various aspects of the narrative itself impels us to note the importance of water throughout the first two books, and to ask if these other recurrences do not bear on a close reading 2.1-10.

Water is prominent in the Creation stories (Gen.1–2) and the Flood (Gen. 6–7). It accompanies Moses' whole career: the drawing of the well-water in 2.15-22; the turning of the Nile to blood (Exod. 7); the crossing of the Sea (Exod. 14–15); the sweetening of the bitter water (Exod. 15), and the striking of the rock at Horeb (Exod. 17).

The next step is to decide whether a symbolic interpretation of the water in 2.1-10 would allow us to associate these other occurrences from the broad context, and so find a fuller meaning and function for water here that is appropriate and can be corroborated by the other narrative elements we have already analysed.

As a natural phenomenon, indispensable but dangerous, water brings both death and life.[1] In biblical cosmogony it also represents the primaeval chaos conquered by God at Creation but 'always restive and eager to reclaim dominion'.[2] Water is perfect indistinction,[3] the adversary of the Creator who separated light and darkness, earth and sea.[4] As such, it is both the enemy of order and the antithesis of the widening distinction between the Egyptians and the Israelites that God will consecrate in Exod. 8.19.[5]

According to M. Eliade, immersion is equivalent, on the human plane, to death, and on the cosmic plane, to catastrophe, as in the

1. R.E. Clements and H.-J. Fabry, 'מים *majim*', *ThWAT*, IV, p. 862; M. Lurker, 'Wasser', in *idem*, *Wörterbuch biblischer Bilder und Symbole* (Munich: Kusel, 1973), p. 338 (his 1987 edn was unavailable to me); P. Reymond, *L'eau, sa vie et sa signification dans l'Ancien Testament* (VTSup, 6; Leiden: Brill, 1958), p. 241; Fox, *Names*, p. xxxv.

2. R. Luyster, 'Wind and Water: Cosmogonic Symbolism in the Old Testament', *ZAW* 93 (1981), p. 1.

3. O. Reigbeder, *La Symbolique* (Que Sais-je?, 749; Paris: Editions du Seuil, 5th edn, 1981 [1957]), p. 27.

4. J.P. Fokkelman, 'Exodus', in *The Literary Guide to the Bible* (ed. R. Alter and F. Kermode; Cambridge, MA: Harvard University Press, 1987), p. 60.

5. See the end of 'Rhetorical Analysis' in Chapter 2.

Flood, which periodically dissolves the world in the primordial ocean.[1]

The great example of immersion in water in Exodus is, of course, the crossing of the Reed Sea. In his analysis of Exodus 14, Ska concludes that Israel has consented to risk its existence in the sea, the place of death, in order to escape Egypt and find true life.[2] It is this risk that opens the path for them: 'and the people feared YHWH; and they believed in YHWH and in his servant Moses' (14.31). This new world into which Israel emerges is that already bodied forth by the God-fearing midwives in 1.15-22. Moses' short but dangerous voyage on the river may be a foreshadowing of Israel's epic immersion, a fractured mirror-image in which he escapes death, as will Israel at the Sea, but by going to Egypt rather than escaping from it. He gains a new life now simply by surviving. After the theophany at the Burning Bush, Israel's renewal can come only from its covenant with God.

A symbolic reading of the water in Exod. 2.1-10 thus gives depth to the issues raised by the narrative otherwise. It solemnizes the passage that Moses makes from danger to safety, and from Israel to Egypt. It clarifies the meaning of the decision that Israel will soon make through Moses: to serve God and not Egypt is to choose life over death and integration over chaos. The symbolism materializes and amplifies the narrative.

9. *Conclusions*

From the efforts of the mother and sister, like those of the midwives, we see that rescue from oppression involves cooperation with God and so recognition of his omnipotence. It also involves conceding the limits and potential of our comprehension in the face of the moral complexity inevitably adhering to any situation of injustice. Liberation is thus a matter not just of power, but also of knowledge. In this, the Exodus thematically evokes the Fall. The story in Exodus 1–2 continues to evaluate the characters in relation to God, but now more introspectively. The question, 'Whom will we serve, God or Pharaoh?', can be recast in terms of historical self-understanding: 'Who are the Israelites in the light of their past?' The answer that Israel will give is a choice between creation and destruction, integration and chaos.

1. M. Eliade, *Traité de l'histoire des religions* (Paris: Payot, 1949), p. 173.
2. *Passage*, p. 130.

Chapter 5

EXODUS 2.11-15

1. *Literal Translation*

11a And in those days,
11b when Moses had grown up,
11c he went out to his brothers
11d and saw their burdens at first hand.
11e He saw an Egyptian man
11f hitting a Hebrew man from among his brothers.
12a He turned this way and that,
12b [and] seeing that there was no one,
12c hit the Egyptian
12d and hid him in the sand.
13a When he went out the next day,
13b and, behold, two Hebrew men quarrelling!
13c He said to the one who was in the wrong,
13d 'Why are you hitting your fellow?'
14a He said,
14b 'Who put you as ruler and judge over us?
14c Do you think to kill me as you killed the Egyptian?'
14d Moses was afraid,
14e and he thought,
14f 'Surely, the deed is known'.
15a When Pharaoh heard of this deed,
15b he sought to kill Moses.
15c But Moses fled from Pharaoh,
15d and settled in the land of Midian,
15e and sat down by a well.

Notes on the Literal Translation

Verse 11d. וירא בסבלתם: 'he saw their burdens at first hand'. This translation moves beyond literalness, using 'saw' to make transparent the passage's three-fold repetition of ראה. 'At first hand', Durham's coinage,[1] expresses the 'positive or negative interest' implicit in this verb with the preposition ב.[2]

Verse 14b. לאיש שר ושפט: 'as prince and judge'. At issue here are the meaning and function of לאיש. One common analysis says that איש with a word following in apposition is a sign of a profession or occupation.[3] A variation by Joüon (§13b) sees it and שר in apposition, the first word an index of genre, the second a 'nom d'espèce'.

M. Dahood demurred, calling the ל a sign of the vocative and finding new irony in the Hebrew's question: 'Who appointed you, O mortal, prince and judge over us?'[4] He admitted that other translations are possible, especially since שים ל is also found in Gen. 45.8-9, while Esth. 7.6 reads איש צר ואויב.[5] B. Couroyer answered Dahood's Ugaritic parallels with Egyptian ones.[6] For him, Joüon is correct, since איש can designate a parsonage of dignity, the master of a country (Gen. 42.3) or a prince (Est. 7.7 [sic]).[7]

Another challenging voice, R. Gelio's, complains that the absence of a second ל before שר disqualifies attempts to find a ל vocative or apposition.[8] Instead, he parses איש as a relative and שר as an alternative form of the participle from שרר, 'to the leader'. Hence the whole means, 'Who appointed you to be chief and judge over us?'

He is straining the suppleness of Hebrew. In apposition, prepositions

1. Durham, *Exodus*, p. 18. Less successful in capturing the subjective force of the preposition are Michaeli's 'il fut témoin de leurs travaux forcés' (*Livre*, p. 37), and Houtman's 'Hij was getuige van het zware werk dat zij moesten verzetten' (*Exodus*, p. 282).

2. König, *Syntax*, §212b; also *HALAT*, I, p. 100; III, p. 1080; BDB, pp. 90, 907-908; Daube, *Exodus Pattern*, p. 33; Fox, *Names*, p. 19.

3. *HALAT*, I, p. 42; N.P. Bratsiotis, 'איש', *ThWAT*, I, pp. 239-40; J. Kühlewein, 'איש *'īš* Mann', *THAT*, I, p. 134; H. Niehr, *Herrschen und Richten: Die Wurzel* špṭ *im alten Orient und im Alten Testament* (FzB, 54; Würzburg: Echter Verlag, 1986), p. 135 n. 43; Schmidt, *Exodus*, p. 92.

4. M. Dahood, 'Vocative *lamedh* in Exodus 2,14 und [*sic*] Merismus in 34, 21', *Bib* 62 (1981), p. 414.

5. It is not, as Dahood says, איש שר ואויב.

6. B. Couroyer, 'A Propos d'Exode, II, 14', *RB* 89 (1982), p. 49.

7. 'Exode, II, 14', pp. 50-51.

8. R. Gelio, 'È possible un איש relativo/dimostrativo in ebraico biblico?', *RivB* 31 (1983), p. 433.

are normally repeated, but not always.[1] The grammars do mention the contamination of geminates by hollow verbs.[2] This confusion could in theory produce שׂר instead of שׂורר, although that is the normal form for participles from stative geminate verbs, on the model of *qal* from *qll*. It would be the only occurrence for the root שׂרר, and generally the influence of hollow verbs on geminates is in the perfect of intransitive verbs.[3] As a noun, not a participle, שׂר balances with שׁפט in a stereotypical phrase.[4] And the fact that איש is found five times in four verses suggests a pattern that a single aberrancy as a relative would disconcert.[5]

Another proposal would change the conjunctive accent over לאיש to a disjunctive to eliminate a tautology.[6] Since איש can mean 'prince, king, leader or agent for another',[7] the phrase would then read 'a ruler, a prince and a judge'. Crown is unclear how this rendering is less rather than more a tautology than the usual 'prince and judge' translating the Hebrew pair that, in any case, many take for a hendiadys.[8]

In summary, no explanation yet improves the first one described. Among nonliteral translations, surely the cleverest is Durham's: 'Who set you as a prince among men and a judge over us?'[9]

Verse 15. וישׁב...וישׁב: 'settled...sat down'. This root has two fundamental meanings, 'Ortsgebundenheit' and 'Ruhestellung'.[10] Their apparent meeting in the same verse here disquiets some translators.[11]

1. Joüon, *Grammaire*, §131i n. 2.
2. Joüon, *Grammaire*, §82o; GKC §67z; Meyer, *Hebräische Grammatik*, §§79e, 80d.
3. GKC §67bb.
4. E.Z. Melamed, 'Break-up of Stereotype Phrases as an Artistic Device in Biblical Poetry', in *Studies in the Bible* (ed. C. Rabin; Scripta Hierosolymitana, 8; Jerusalem: Magnes Press, 1961), p. 131.
5. Verses 11e, 11f, 12c, 13c (in plural), 14a.
6. A.D. Crown, 'An Alternative Meaning for איש in the Old Testament', *VT* 24 (1974), p. 111. Also Lacocque, *Devenir*, p. 61.
7. 'Alternative Meaning', p. 110.
8. The first to call it so was Cassuto, *Commentary*, p. 23. Melamed ('Breakup', p. 131) and Houtman (*Exodus*, p. 288) agree.
9. *Exodus*, p. 18.
10. M. Görg, 'ישׁב *jāšab*', *ThWAT*, III, p. 1016, with reference to H. Schweizer.
11. *The Jerusalem Bible* is a good example of the consequent equivocation. Its 1966 edition (gen. ed. A. Jones; Garden City, NY: Doubleday) reads 'and made for

Houtman sums up two schools of interpretation.[1] Some, like Cassuto, deduce from the text that Moses settled in Midian, then one day went to a well.[2] Others, including Houtman himself, do not distinguish the two events in time: upon entering Midian, Moses went straight to a well which is naturally the first stop for a traveller. Moses was halting on his way through Midian but not settling there.[3]

The Septuagint has an additional clause between these two verbs: 'he came to the land of Midian'. Ehrlich and A. Aejmelaeus speculate that the Masoretic Text omitted it by homoioteleuton, the mischievous word being 'Midian'.[4] The original would have read, 'He settled in the land of Midian. He came to the land of Midian, and sat by a well.' This disarranged sequence, Ehrlich argues, is true to the Hebrew way of narrating. Other examples he cites are Exod. 19.1b-2 and Gen. 12.5. Greenberg comments to the same end and adds Gen. 37.21; 42.20.[5] However, König has reservations.[6] For him, v. 15e looks ahead, not back: Moses' rest by the well is more an introduction to the next story than a detail of his settlement in Midian.

To conclude, Ehrlich's textual criticism seems plausible, as do his and Greenberg's examples of such a disjointed narrative style. It is undiscoverable from the text whether we are to understand that Moses went immediately or subsequently to the well. And no reason exists in theory why a word cannot have two meanings in the same verse. The vocabulary analysis will try to understand the two וישב in the context of the entire pericope.

the land of Midian', with a note in the *Reader's Edition* (1971) that the 'exact meaning is uncertain'. *The New Jerusalem Bible* (London: Darton, Longman & Todd, 1985) revises the text to 'went into Midianite territory' and the note to '"He went" Gk Syr.; "he settled" Hebr.'.

1. *Exodus*, p. 290.

2. *Commentary*, p. 23. He sees a string of verbal repetitions for emphasis (pp. 23-24). Words other than ישב also change meaning: הרג means 'murder' in the mouth of Hebrew (v. 14b), but 'execute' in Pharaoh's order (v. 15b). In 2.21 ישב will mean 'to dwell'.

3. *Exodus*, p. 291.

4. Ehrlich, *Randglossen*, p. 265; A. Aejmelaeus, 'What Can We Know about the Hebrew *Vorlage* of the Septuagint?', *ZAW* 99 (1987), p. 80.

5. *Understanding Exodus*, p. 46.

6. *Syntax*, §369c.

Verse 15e. הבאר: 'a well'. The article can be used to designate something definite but still unknown.[1] Joüon[2] calls it 'a (certain) well', Houtman[3] 'the only well or the most important one to the area into which Moses came'.[4]

2. *Delimitation*

The break is plain between this pericope and the last. The story happens in the same place. But the princess, mother and sister have vanished in the lapse of Moses' infancy and childhood. New characters replace them in vv. 11 and 13. Moses is active now not passive, and this new episode in his life begins emphatically with a succession of four *e* sounds: ויצא אל־אחיו (v. 11c).[5]

Various techniques both link and distinguish the two episodes. The words משה and ויגדל come at the end of 2.1-10 and the beginning of 2.11-15,[6] but in the first the verb connotes 'to be weaned', and in the second, 'to arrive at manhood'.[7] The phonological likeness between המים and בימים makes them also transitional keywords.

The separation of 2.11-15 and 2.16-22 into two units is not so self-evident in the text or unanimous in the commentaries and translations.[8] But sufficient evidence does support it.

1. Joüon, *Grammaire*, §137n; GKC §126qr; König, *Syntax*, §289ac; H.L. Strack, *Die Genesis* (Kurzgefasster Kommentar zu den heiligen Schriften Alten und Neuen Testaments I.1; Munich: Beck, 2nd edn, 1905 [1896]), p. 108.

2. *Grammaire*, §137n.

3. *Exodus*, p. 291.

4. '[U]n (certain) puits'; 'de enige of de belangrijkste put van de streek, waar Mozes aankwam'.

5. Parunak, 'Transitional Techniques', p. 528: '*Phonological* similarity associates units of text marked by concentrations of similar sounds, such as clusters of plosives or of long *a* vowels'. This remark applies also to המים and בימים commented below.

6. The spelling in v. 10 is *wayigdal*.

7. Cassuto, *Commentary*, p. 21; Childs, *Exodus*, p. 29; Ackerman, 'Literary Context', p. 96.

8. A brief and random selection shows, for example, that the RSV begins a new paragraph at v. 15c; Fox (*Names*, p. 18) at v. 15e; the NJV and Boschi at v. 16; Ackerman, 'Literary Context', p. 102 and n. 38 at v. 15 beginning at the clause preserved in the Septuagint missing from the Masoretic Text. The NAB merges vv. 15 and 16 in one sentence. Schmidt (*Exodus*, pp. 80-83) sees vv. 15a-c as a transition and v. 15d as the beginning of a major new section.

Bar-Efrat says that the action of getting up and moving off and the separation of someone from a group as here in 2.15 can mark the end of a narrative segment.[1]

Grammatically, v. 16 stops the train of ו-conversive verbs with a nominal proposition and it introduces the third-person feminine plural. Narratively, it summons up new characters and opens the way for new turns in the plot. Stylistically and structurally, 2.11-15 has coherence, as the semantic and thematic inclusions to be discussed under 'Narrative Symmetry' will show; it is worth noting here simply that vv. 14f-15 mark the end of the one story with a series of repetitions: דבר, פרעה, הרג, משה, ישב. The next verse begins the other pericope with a new 'pastoral' semantic field.

The transition between 2.11-15 and 2.16-22 is marked lexically by the repetition of מדין and phonologically by the resemblance between וישב (v. 15d, e) and שבע (v. 16a).

3. *Narrative Structure*

Deep

The study of deep structure is especially useful when repetition is one of the dynamics of the plot.[2] In this pericope, we can better understand Moses' going out twice if we first reduce his activities to a skeletal structure.

At issue specifically is the relation between Moses' actions. Do his two excursions from the Egyptian court operate structurally in the same way? How are they related to each other and to the rest of the story? For Propp this sequentiality is always a key question.[3]

At first study, his two ventures and their consequences may seem to be two sets of twin functions in mirror image, 'wrong–wrong punished' and 'wrong–wrong unpunished'.[4] The doubling of the verb יצא (vv. 11c, 13a) in close succession in the plot (ביום השני) might encourage this impression. In fact, however, that verb is not the main

1. *Art*, pp. 142-43.
2. Propp, 'Structure', p. 83.
3. Propp, *Morphologie*, pp. 143-44; 'Structure', p. 73.
4. 'Wrong/wrong punished' is one of the three functions or 'action sequences' found in Gen. 2–3 by R.C. Culley ('Action Sequences in Genesis 2–3', *Semeia* 18 [1980], pp. 26-27). But this debt does not imply that we are trying to relate the functions of this pericope to any network common to all Hebrew Scripture.

action in either episode, and hence is not a clue to their structural functions.

The first part (vv. 11b-12d) is indeed reducible to the formula 'wrong–wrong punished'; that description omits no major plot element in those verses. However, the best structural analysis of the second day's events is not 'wrong–wrong unpunished'. We do not see the committing of the wrong, as we do on the first day. The narrator simply calls one of them רשע (v. 13c). Nor does Moses' question 'Why are you hitting your fellow?' (v. 13d) necessarily suggest a desire to punish, as we will see in the vocabulary section.

A more appropriate way to label the functions of the second day is 'accusation–counter-accusation'. Moses' question is juridical and provokes a response in kind. Leaving the study of the legal character till later, we should heed now the implications of the structural contrast and relation. As Propp quoted from Goethe, 'the study of forms is the study of transformations'.[1]

Scholars agree that form and content interact in narrative.[2] And so, if the second set of functions of the plot structure, the incident of the second day, is new, and not just a reworking of the first, then the idea of unlikeness may be a more useful key to the plot content here than oppositeness, which would be central if the structure were 'wrong–wrong punished' and 'wrong–wrong unpunished'. (Of course, a logical contrary is one aspect of the second set: Moses accuses, then is accused.) Other narrative elements will confirm that we can understand the pericope better if we concentrate on the differences rather than the similarities in Moses' two encounters.

While the first and the second sets of twin functions are thus joined by superficial similarities resting on structural differences, the second and the third stand to each other as mortise and tenon. Propp saw that one action can have two morphological meanings.[3] Here, the Hebrew's rejoinder to Moses (v. 14a-c) belongs alike to the twin function 'accusation–counter-accusation' and to the next, which is 'danger–

1. Years after the publication of his book, Propp ('Structure', p. 59) lamented that its English translator had betrayed it by omitting his quotations of Goethe.

2. *Morphologie*, p. 106. This was one of the insights of Russian Formalists according to Fokkema and Kunne-Ibsch, *Theories*, p. 26. Propp ('Structure', p. 77) rejects Levi-Strauss's criticism that he separated them. See also Milne, *Propp*, p. 103. Chatman (*Story*, pp. 23-26) expands on their relation.

3. *Morphologie*, pp. 84-85.

escape from danger'. It closes one structural sequence and opens the next, since it rebuts Moses' question by implying a threat. Again, the value of this observation must be judged with the fruit of reflection on other facets of the pericope.

Surface

With the surface pattern of tension, as with the underlying plot composition, the vocabulary of the pericope is deceptive. Just as the double יצא can mislead the study of functions, so the dramatic and thrice-used words נכה (*hiph.*) and הרג might seem a key to the rise of suspense. '[Moses] hit the Egyptian' (v. 12c) suggests itself as a peak of tension or indeed the climax. But a closer reading corrects this hasty conclusion.

The child Moses was pitied when he was seen (2.5, 6: ראה). Now he does the same. His empathy for the Hebrews over against the Egyptians is established early on when he 'sees their burdens at first hand' (v. 11c-f).[1] On the second day, as soon as he turns this way and that and sees no one, it is obvious that he will intervene, and not to lend a hand to the Egyptian oppressor. Moses' blow is just one more step of a steady build-up of suspense that does not become critical until v. 13c with והנה. Only here does the plot reach a turning point, a moment when its direction is all-important and undetermined.[2]

'[And] behold, two Hebrew men quarreling!' When we read or hear that he went out again 'and behold...', we naturally hope for information about the events of the day before. Has the body been discovered or moved? Instead the plot introduces new events that complicate but do not lessen the suspense. We are lured into what Sternberg calls 'a false certitude of knowledge',[3] or, here, of expectation. And so, instead of the dramatic relief that usually follows such a turning point as v. 13c, we and Moses experience surprise, which for us continues the tension while altering its cause.

1. The 'Notes on the Literal Translation' spoke of the subjective import of ראה ב.

2. Coats (*Moses*, p. 49) gives no support for his contention that the fundamental tension of the tale concerns Moses' reaction to the Egyptian's cruelty, other than to say that the Hebrew is called his brother twice. In 'Moses in Midian' (*JBL* 92 [1973], p. 5), he seems to contradict this conclusion of his: 'And in the second intervention, the crisis of the unit appears. Moses' deed is known.'

3. *Poetics*, p. 309.

For the first time in Exodus 1–2, this surprise affects us as readers and listeners as well. We knew already what was in the basket even though the princess did not, and we have our suspicions about the Pharaoh who did not know Joseph. The promises in Genesis made us hope that the more the Egyptians oppressed the Hebrews, the more they would increase (1.12a-c). But nothing has prepared us for the image of Hebrews fighting each other. In Chatman's terms,[1] surprise, complementary with suspense, operates here at both the 'story' and 'discourse levels', where story means the 'content or chain of events', and discourse, 'the expression, the means by which the content is communicated.[2]

The word הנה functions here similarly to its occurrence in Pharaoh's speech in 1.9 and at the discovery of the boy in the basket in 2.6. As the first word in Pharaoh's address, it was a direct appeal to his audience's attention and feelings. Used of the princess, it expressed both 'excited perception' and an important shortening of the focal distance.[3] Here too it registers internal, direct focalization especially through its combination with a participle. And the emotion it conveys is shock.

The practical effect of this surprise is to hold our attention on the Hebrews through any changes they may suffer in our judgment of them. We may not approve of the scuffle, especially when one of them is baldly named the 'wrongdoer' (v. 13d: רשע). But our interest in their lot does not lose its keenness, since new curiosity now supplies for any mitigation of our sympathy. As Sternberg concludes about the strategy of surprise, one of its central functions is the control of judgment.[4]

This pericope does not have the full arc of five narrative stages that we traced in the birth and adoption of Moses (2.1-10). Nor does it return to the double-peaked surface structure of the scene with the midwives (1.15-22).[5] Here nothing offers respite of tension until after

1. *Story*, p. 60.

2. Chatman, *Story*, p. 19.

3. The quoted expression is Kogut's ('הנה in Biblical Hebrew', p. 138). See further remarks and references in the section on 'Point of View and Narrative Gaps' in Chapter 4.

4. *Poetics*, p. 314.

5. That pericope had a turning point in 1.16g with Pharaoh's command, then relief when the midwives disobeyed it. Tension peaked again at v. 19e, Pharaoh's interrogation of the women. It slackened at God's intervention.

the second and last turning point, v. 15b: '[Pharaoh] sought to kill Moses'. But he escapes, fleeing to Midian.

4. *Point of View and Narrative Gaps*

As hitherto in Exodus and throughout Scripture,[1] the focalization here is mainly external, kept outside the characters. For example, the sight of the Egyptian hitting the Hebrew is taken in panoramically from the angle of no particular participant or observer. But, as earlier, the exceptions are instructive.

The external focalization sometimes looks within Moses and discloses his sympathies. He pities the Hebrews under their burdens (ראה ב: v. 11d). Narratively, he comes upon the Hebrews fighting in the same way as the princess discovers the boy in the basket: והנה accompanies inward-scanning focalization and introduces free indirect discourse that uses a nominal construction headed by the subject. The event is described emphatically and synchronically just as Moses himself experienced it.[2] Soon we learn too of his fears and further thoughts (v. 14).

In the birth story of Moses (2.1-10), the focalization was a play of perspectives that illustrated the ethical dilemmas in this conflict. The ambiguity continues here. Moses is rebuffed by one of the Hebrews, the people whom we have always supported and whom the narrator calls Moses' brothers. The wrongdoer distorts Moses' well-intentioned deed into one of self-incrimination. The focalization and the plot now together magnify the ambiguity by passing it through a prism of irony.[3]

1. Alter, *Narrative*, p. 114.

2. For more about הנה, free indirect discourse and the narrative effect of nominal constructions, refer to the remarks and notes in Chapter 4 under 'Point of View and Narrative Gaps'. The earlier cases of external focalization directed within have been: 1.8b (a new king 'did not know of Joseph'); 1.12c (the Egyptians 'shuddered in horror at the Hebrews'); 1.17a and 1.21a (the midwives 'feared God'); 2.2c-d (the mother 'saw him—that he was goodly') and, as mentioned, 2.6b-d (the princess saw the child, 'and, behold, a boy crying! She took pity on him.').

3. R. Scholes and R. Kellogg, *The Nature of Narrative* (London: Oxford University Press, 1966), p. 240: 'The problem of point of view is narrative art's own problem... In the relationship between the teller and the tale, and that other relationship between the teller and the audience, lies the essence of narrative art. The narrative situation is thus ineluctably ironical.'

Moses asks why the Hebrew is beating his fellow. He seeks intimate information about 'his brother', but neither he nor we get it. On the other hand, the Hebrew wants to penetrate Moses' thoughts about which we do know a little, at least that he looked on the Hebrews sympathetically and felt emotion at the sight of the quarrellers. That is, the focalization has led us into Moses' mind, and now the Hebrew sarcastically demands the same understanding: 'Do you think to kill me as you killed the Egyptian?' (v. 14c). In Chatman's language,[1] a character in the 'story' seeks a privilege already granted us through the 'discourse'. 'Content' impinges on 'expression'.

This contrast between plot and point of view underscores another. Until now we have sided with the Hebrews morally and optically; that is, we have agreed with them and often seen events through their eyes. That double solidarity now cracks. We still favour the Hebrews against the Egyptians, but not the Hebrew 'wrongdoer' against Moses. Our complaint against him is illuminated by the diffraction that separates his and our focalizations on Moses. In this narrative, as so often in life, a disagreement entangles principle and perspective.

This limited dissension, this specification of our support for Israel is an important step in its mature acceptance as a nation given to sin like others. It prepares us for later in the Book of Exodus when they will grumble even as God keeps his promise to their forefathers.[2]

Thus, external focalization aimed internally has shown us Moses' thoughts. We do not look within his Hebrew interlocutor in the same way, and we must accept the narrator's word that he is the wrongdoer in the quarrel. The elements seem in place for a 'character-elevating strategy' in favour of Moses. But a counter-strategy of 'informational gaps' blunts this effect.[3]

We are confused at first by the sight of the Hebrews fighting because we do not understand their relation to the dead Egyptian. Moses does not know more than we. We and Moses find out together when the Hebrew answers back to him, 'Do you think to kill me as you killed the Egyptian?'(v. 14c). Then we have to reconsider an earlier sentence, '[Moses] turned this way and that, and seeing that

1. *Story*, p. 19.

2. Ackerman, 'Literary Context', p. 99; e.g. Exod 16.8; 17.7.

3. The two terms are from Sternberg, *Poetics*, pp. 163, 186. See previous examples and comments in Chapters 2 and 4 under 'Point of View'.

there was no one, hit the Egyptian' (v. 12a-c).

Initially we had no reason to doubt that the middle phrase was true, that in fact no one else was around. We do not think to ask who is telling us כי אין איש, Moses or the narrator. But once we hear the Hebrew, we are unsure. The phrase may have been Moses' hasty misimpression. Perhaps he and the suffering Hebrew were not entirely alone with the Egyptian. We cannot tell how the wrongdoer knew of the killing. He may have secretly witnessed it himself or learned of it from the Hebrew who was beaten. We do not reject Moses as a source of information, but we cannot applaud him. In our judgment of him, the suspicions raised by the gapping balance out the intimacy of the focalization. Neither indicts him, but together they do not honour him. These narrative techniques have brought us to the thorny question of the quality of Moses' acts.[1]

The Jewish and classic Protestant position is that Moses was divinely inspired to kill the Egyptian. Augustine headed the school that believed he was wrongheaded.[2] Among recent exegetes, the division is perhaps sharpest between Coats, who sees Moses' identification with his brothers as heroic, and T.C. Butler, who finds an underlying anti-Mosaic tradition.[3]

It is important that this text itself 'neither praises nor condemns' Moses. The 'stress falls fully on the act not the decision itself'.[4] Nothing here even proves that Moses knew already that the Hebrews were his brothers;[5] Coat's point of departure is an unfounded assumption.

The studies of the vocabulary and rhetoric to follow will help understand whether Moses killed the Egyptian justifiably. By way of introduction now, we can say only that the data of the plot and narration are as neutral about Moses as the focalization and gapping are balanced.

1. G. Cordesse ('Narration et Focalisation', *Poétique* 76 [1988], pp. 487-98) discusses the inverse proportion of control exercised over the story by the narrator and any character in a sliding scale of focalization that he calls 'embrayage–débrayage' (p. 490).

2. B.S. Childs, *Biblical Theology in Crisis* (Philadelphia: Westminster Press, 1970), pp. 177-79.

3. Coats, *Moses*, p. 47. T.C. Butler, 'An Anti-Moses Tradition', *JSOT* 12 (1979), pp. 9-15.

4. Childs, *Exodus*, pp. 43, 44; also Houtman, *Exodus*, p. 286.

5. Ackerman, 'Literary Context', p. 98.

5. *Narrative Symmetry*

Unlike the last two pericopes, this one has no full chiasm. Instead, a range of three repetitions sets out its perimeters and centre. Two of them are on the level of semantic fields:

	Narrated Event	*Semantic Field*
A	[Moses] went out to his brothers (v. 11c).	motion
B	He saw their burdens at first hand. He saw an Egyptian man hitting a Hebrew man . . . (v. 11d-f).	perception, affliction
B′	When Pharaoh heard of this deed, he sought to kill Moses (v. 15a-b).	perception, affliction
A′	But Moses fled from Pharaoh (v. 15c).	motion

Another structure, encompassed by the first two, applies to the plot:

A	*the 'deed'*	He turned this way and that, and seeing that there was no one, hit the Egyptian and hid him in the sand (v. 12).
A′	*the 'deed' is known*	'Do you think to kill me as you killed the Egyptian?' Moses was afraid and thought, 'Surely the deed is known' (v. 14c-f).

Terminology is a problem here, however artificial. Some scholars would admit these patterns of ideas under the titles 'inclusion' or 'envelope figure'. More rigorous taxonomists insist that an inclusion be restricted to the verbal.[1]

1. Conroy (*Absalom*, p. 142 n. 102) speaks of 'material inclusions', 'the framing of a unit by two items similar in meaning though not in verbal form'. Cf. J.R. Lundbom, *Jeremiah: A Study in Ancient Hebrew Rhetoric* (SBLDS, 18; Missoula, MT: Scholars Press, 1975); M. Kessler, 'Inclusio in the Hebrew Bible', *Sem* 6 (1978), p. 48; and W.G.E. Watson, *Classical Hebrew Poetry: A Guide to its Techniques* (JSOTSup, 26; Sheffield: JSOT Press, 1984), pp. 282-86. Lundbom (pp. 16-17): 'The inclusion must therefore not be defined too narrowly. It is necessary only that the end show continuity with the beginning, and that this continuity be taken as a deliberate attempt by the author to effect closure.' Kessler lists cases of 'approximate inclusio' especially in biblical prose where 'synonymous or semantically related words occur' (p. 48). Watson on the other hand allows no such

J.-L. Ska holds that a true inclusion, as distinct from simple repetition, is a figure in which the first member announces the second. The second concludes the development and recalls the first.[1] These schemes conform to that rule. Moses' flight to Midian is the result and culmination of his first 'going out' or separation from the court. Pharaoh's attempt to kill him is because of his reaction to the Egyptian's violence against the Hebrew, and stands in continuity with that cruelty. The discovery of Moses' act worsens the risk he undertook in performing it and forces him to take on its full consequences. We can thus prudently call these patterns semantic and thematic inclusions respectively.

But a figure is always more important for its effect than its name. Taken together, these three inclusions help draw the borders of the pericope, as already noted under 'Delimitation'.[2] They stress the unity of the enclosed portion,[3] but also its diversity. According to J.-N. Aletti and J. Trublet, these devices set the periphery off from the centre, putting the emphasis not on one over the other, but on the contrast between them.[4] They brace and thus emphasize a new narrative technique for the pericope, dialogue, and new characters, the two quarrelling Hebrews. And since the centre thus disengaged (vv. 13a-14b) brings on stage the actions of the second day, the effect of the symmetry corroborates that of the narrative structure, to link yet distinguish the second day and the first.

'He hid him in the sand' (v. 12d). Certain material parallels run between 2.1-10 and 2.11-15 and contrast them. Both Moses and his mother hide something from Pharaoh. She is doubly successful because her child ends up taking refuge in the oppressor's own court. Moses fails to the same degree because it is another Hebrew who threatens him by abusing information that he saved a fellow-sufferer from assault.

liberality, at least in poetry. At most, the breakup of a wordpair 'provides an effect similar to an envelope figure' (p. 286).

1. The point was made in private correspondence.

2. For Lundbom (*Jeremiah*, p. 17), this is one of the most important functions of an inclusion.

3. S.F. Fogle, 'Envelope', *Princeton Encyclopedia of Poetry and Poetics* (ed. A. Preminger *et al.*; Princeton: Princeton University Press, 2nd edn, 1974 [1965]), p. 241.

4. J.-N. Aletti and J. Trublet, *Approche poétique et théologique des Psaumes* (Paris: Cerf, 1983), p. 109.

Moses is also a foil to the midwives. Their דבר (1.18) is an act of cooperation with God who recognizes and rewards them. Moses' דבר (2.14) is wasted initiative that becomes known to Pharaoh, who seeks to punish him. They fear God (ירא). He is afraid for his life (ירא) and will not fear in the sense that the midwives do until he stands before the awesomeness of God in his encounter at the Burning Bush (3.6).[1] While lexically the text keeps telling us that the Hebrews are Moses' 'brothers', its story line speaks more of their difference.

6. *Vocabulary and Rhetoric*

The narrative symmetry has already revealed several of the semantic fields. In all there are six:

Family: אח (2×)
Nationality: מצרי (3×), עברי (2×), רע (*rēa'*), פרעה (2×), ארץ מדין
Perception: ראה (3×), ידע, שמע, הנה, אמר (2×)[2]
Affliction: סבלת, נכה (*hiph.* 2×), נצה (*niph.*), הרג (3×), ירא, שים על,
שפט, שר[3]
Motion: יצא (2×), פנה כה וכה, ברח, ישב (2×)
Communication: אמר (2×), בקש (*pi.*)

The field 'Perception' is already familiar from the other pericopes where it has been a lexical reflection of the chapters' interest in the complexity and imperfection of human knowledge.[4] It keeps present the conclusion of previous development, that to know themselves the Israelites, including Moses, must know God.

'Affliction' includes death, and is the opposite of 'Fertile Life', the field that has figured in every pericope so far. The switch is of a piece

1. For previous reflections on the midwives' fear, see the 'Vocabulary' section of Chapter 3.

2. In v. 14b, e, אמר is best translated 'to think', a verb of perception; in vv. 13d, f, it is clearly 'to say', a form of communication so listed among the semantic fields.

3. שר and שפט are listed here as words of affliction because the aggressive tone of the Hebrew's question means them as such, not because they are necessarily offices always associated with oppression, as the vocabulary analysis will make plain.

4. See 'Vocabulary' in Chapter 2, and 'Point of View and Narrative Gapping' and 'Narrative Symmetry' in Chapter 4.

with the reversals in the plot: for the first time, an Egyptian is killed instead of a Hebrew, but the event brings greater misfortune instead of liberation. The only word relatable to the field of 'Family' is אח, but it is precisely Moses' 'brother' who turns on him.

The two largest fields are 'Affliction' and 'Nationality'. This shared preponderance is fitting, since the first field is due to the second: the Hebrews suffer because Pharaoh has stirred Egyptian national feeling against them, and Moses flees because he is rejected by both nationalities.

The key to the relation among the semantic fields and to the broader role of language in the passage lies in the nature of the exchange between Moses and the Hebrew (vv. 13-14) and in the juridical weight of certain words: ראה, למה, רשע, רע (*rēa'*), שים, שפט, הרג, שמע and דבר.

First, one must realize that the quarrel between the two Hebrews fits a pattern reported elsewhere in Scripture in narrative and legislation. It is a juridical ריב like that supposed in the Book of the Covenant (Exod. 21.18f: נכה (*hiph.*), רע [*rēa'*]).[1] The procedure to adjudicate in such a case is complex, but one of the motifs is a cross-examination that does not expect a reply.[2] Moses' question to the wrongdoer is not a strict interrogation, and it would be too much to interpret the scene as a full legal trial. Enough to remark that, digested together, the character dynamics and vocabulary smack of legal affairs.

Let us pass the words in review. רשע is often found in juridical scenes.[3] רע (*rēa'*) is a broad word best defined by its context,[4] but it does occur in legal texts, including both decalogues, where it refers to

1. B. Gemser, 'The *rib*- or Controversy-Pattern in Hebrew Mentality', in *Wisdom in Israel and in the Ancient Near East* (Festschrift H.H. Rowley; ed. M. Noth and D.W. Thomas; VTSup, 3; Leiden: Brill, 1955), p. 121, who cites Exod. 2.11-15.

2. K. Nielsen, *Yahweh as Prosecutor and Judge: An Investigation of the Prophetic Lawsuit (Rîb-Pattern)* (JSOTSup, 9; Sheffield: JSOT Press, 1978), pp. 15-16. See also J. Harvey ('Le "rîb-pattern", réquisitoire prophétique sur la rupture de l'alliance', *Bib* 43 [1962], p. 178), to whom Nielsen refers, but who presents the pattern somewhat differently.

3. Cf. van Leeuwen ('רשע *rš'* frevelhaft/schuldig sein', *THAT*, II, p. 816), who cites this passage as an example of a juridical context, although for him the word itself does not have a juridical meaning; Houtman, *Exodus*, p. 287. Childs (*Exodus*, p. 30, and 'Theology', p. 165) specifically calls it a legal term.

4. J. Kühlewein, 'רע *rēa'* Nächster', *THAT*, II, p. 788.

the individual to be dealt with according to the law.[1] ראה and שמע are used to mean taking cognizance of an offence.[2] שים is the verb indicating the official institution of judges and other authorities.[3] דבר can mean a dispute, lawsuit brought to a tribunal and decided there, sentence, judgment,[4] and might carry such connotations here. Even הרג can be used of the punishment for a crime.[5] (שפט will be dealt with later).

Next, we should recall that Pharaoh's question to the midwives applied a legal, or at least 'pre-judicial', formula. It is a 'Beschuldigungsformel': 'Why have you done this thing and let the male children live?' (1.18). Moses' question to the Hebrew is of the same kind: 'Why are you hitting your fellow?'[6] 'Why' and a mention of the offense are the common elements.

As a third step, one looks again at Moses' killing of the Egyptian. In the light of the juridical syntax and diction comprising the atmosphere of 'the second day', one sees the crucial fact about the first day's violence. The heart of the matter is not whether Moses was right to

1. J. Fichtner, 'Der Begriff des "Nächsten" im Alten Testament, mit einem Ausblick auf Spätjudentum und Neues Testament', in *idem*, *Gottes Weisheit* (Arbeiten zur Theologie, 2.5; Stuttgart: Calwer Verlag, 1965), pp. 99-100. Disputing with Childs, Durham (*Exodus*, p. 19) feels it is more general than legal here, but gives no reasons.

2. P. Bovati, *Ristabilire la Giustizia: Procedure, vocabulario, orientamenti* (AnBib, 110; Rome: Pontificium Institutum Biblicum, 1986), p. 59. One of the conclusions of his book is that the vocabulary and theme of justice are more frequent in the Hebrew Bible than commonly thought (p. 359).

3. Bovati, *Ristabilire*, p. 160 n. 21, citing this verse.

4. Bovati, *Ristabilire*, pp. 192-93.

5. H.F. Fuhs, 'הרג *hārag*, *ThWAT*, II, p. 492.

6. Boecker, pp. 30-31, 67 nn. 3, 4, who speaks of a 'vorgerichtliche Redeformen der Beschuldigerseite' (p. 66). Refer to 'Vocabulary' in Chapter 3.

Since 1.18 chooses מדוע and 2.13 למה, it is prudent to remark that J. Barr ('Why? in Biblical Hebrew', *JTS* NS 36 [1985], p. 28) finds that the two interrogatives are 'largely interchangeable. . . In many cases where the two come closely together, such as Exod. ii.8-20. . . common sense overwhelmingly argues that there is no semantic difference and it would be an absurd excess of pedantry to seek one.' He thus refutes A. Jepsen ('Warum? Eine lexikalische und theologische Studie', in *Das ferne und nahe Wort* [Festschrift L. Rost; ed. F. Maass; BZAW, 105; Berlin: de Gruyter, 1967], pp. 106-13), who makes a distinction between מדוע conveying pure information, amazement and sympathy, and למה for reproach or complaint.

intervene. It is that in choosing to kill the Egyptian he deliberately acted outside the law.

Moses 'looked this way and that' (v. 12a) beforehand; he did not strike in blind passion.[1] And he knew that his deed was illegal because he hid the evidence, the body.[2]

Any number of arguments can try to justify these actions. For example, a traditional plea is that he acted only when he saw that there was no one else to carry out the execution (*Exod. R.* 1.29). Or the incident may foreshadow the responsibility God will give him in Exodus 3–4.[3]

But once having taken matters into his own hands, properly or not, he cannot then attempt to act according to the standards from which he has previously dispensed himself. He cannot act extra-juridically one day and juridically the next, on his own authority then on that of the law. Childs is correct that 'the point of the. . . story emerges in the conflict between the motifs of active sympathy and required secrecy'. And he wonders if 'an act of justice can really be done in secret'.[4]

In other words, Moses lacks the physical and moral coherence of the midwives.[5] His self-contradiction injects tension into the contrast we noted in the structure between the functions 'wrong–wrong punished' and 'accusation–counter-accusation'. The Hebrew's barbed reply aims at this discrepancy. 'Who put you as ruler and judge over us?'(v. 14b).

Cassuto and Lacocque have us remark the anger expressed by consonance of the *r*, *š* and *ś* in the Hebrew's question (v. 14).[6] One also notes that assonance gives a certain ponderousness that might be interpreted as malicious: 14 times, the vowel is *a* in various lengths.

The word שפט is narrowly related to the idea of authority. It is a

1. Childs, *Exodus*, p. 30; Houtman, *Exodus*, p. 286. Bovati (*Ristabilire*, p. 251) cites Moses' deed as a 'reato senza testimoni'.

2. D. Kellermann ('טמן *ṭāman*', *ThWAT*, III, p. 367) says that the point is to hide the body, not to inter it

3. Coats, *Moses*, pp. 49-50.

4. Childs, 'Theology', pp. 166, 183. In *Old Testament Theology in a Canonical Context* ([Philadelphia: Westminster Press, 1985], pp. 76-77), Childs asks if Exod. 2.11-15 might be one of a series of stories through which the canon examines the problem of violence in a different light than the Decalogue.

5. See 'Vocabulary' in Chapter 3.

6. *Commentary*, p. 23; *Devenir*, p. 62.

charge of public interest. The substantive participle can mean generally 'authority, chief, leader'.[1] The verb apparently had two meanings originally, 'to rule', and 'to decide', with judgeship a function of kingly power.[2] משפט was known to prebiblical Semites, but as a private value. In the Bible it becomes the foundation of public law.[3]

The Hebrew wrongdoer is more accurate than he could have known in associating 'judge' with 'prince'. A שר is above all one who commands his men and exercises justice among them.[4]

> As commander, Moses would have been eo ipso a Judge. But because he is not a איש שר, he has no right to play the judge.[5]

The Hebrew's other remark bears heavy weight. 'Do you think to kill me as you killed the Egyptian?' (v. 14b). Niehr compares it to a similar rhetorical question about שפט as an intermediary in a dispute.[6] It is put by Absalom in 2 Sam. 15.4: מי ישימני שפט בארץ. More precisely, Exod. 2.15 is a '"rigged question" the terms [of which] require admission as part of *any* answer'.[7] The classic example is the well-worn joke, 'Have you stopped beating your dog?'. Similarly here, Moses cannot answer 'yes' or 'no' without admitting his offence. The question is a yawning rhetorical trap.

To sum up, Moses speaks to the Hebrew in a juridical 'Beschuldigungsformel', like Pharaoh's interrogation of the midwives. He is countered by a turn of rhetoric, like Pharaoh's speech to the

1. Bovati, *Ristabilire*, p. 155; also p. 159.

2. H.W. Hertzberg, 'Die Entwicklung des Begriffes משפט im AT', *ZAW* 40 (1922), pp. 256-58. H. Niehr (*Herrschen und Richten: Die Wurzel špṭ im alten Orient und im Alten Testament* [Forschung zur Bibel, 54; Würzburg: Echter Verlag, 1986], pp. 136, 170) cites Crüsemann and sees the taunting choice of the word here as a protest against the Israelite monarchy.

3. H. Cazelles, 'Aspirations à la justice dans le monde prébiblique: La réponse divine selon la révélation biblique', in *idem*, *Autour de l'Exode (Etudes)* (SB; Paris: Gabalda, 1987 [1978]), p. 380. It was not exclusively a public function, however, especially after the fall of the monarchy. M. Weinfeld (*Justice and Righteousness in Israel and the Nations* [Jerusalem: Magnes Press, 1985], p. 125 [Hebrew]) speaks of the 'democratization' of the term.

4. Van der Ploeg, 'Les chefs', p. 60; also p. 40.

5. Hertzberg, 'Entwicklung', p. 258.

6. *Herrschen und Richten*, p. 135.

7. Lanham, *Handlist*, p. 51.

Egyptians.[1] Moses has 'gone out' of the court, but has brought with him its patterns of speech. He first acts against Pharaoh, then unwittingly tries to play him. Mimicking Pharaoh, he is silenced by someone who can do so better. And by associating with Pharaoh's enemies, the Hebrews, he loses the means to express his favour for them. The irony saps Moses' language of all its vigour and deprives him of every remedy to his dilemma. He can only leave and return with another, omnipotent authority, that of God: 'Say this to the people of Israel, "YHWH, the God of your fathers...has sent me to you"...And they will listen to your voice...' (Exod. 3.15, 18).[2]

It was mentioned earlier that Moses may not have known that the Hebrews were his brothers. Regardless of who he thinks he is, his failed attempts to help the oppressed extend the question of his identity into his adulthood and show that it cannot be resolved or even clarified by his own action or words, by proofs of personal sympathy or appeals to external norms.

Alter has reflected on the 'bias of stylization in the Bible's narration-through-dialogue'.[3] In vv. 13-14 direct speech deprives us of the reliable narrator, and the very existence of dialogue invests the scene with added ambiguity, as 'we are led to ponder the different possible connections between [the characters'] spoken words and [their] actual feelings or intentions' (p. 67).

We saw earlier that the beginnings of the Israelites' nationhood rest on their oppression, that is, the events of history. However, exactly for that reason and as represented by the ambiguity of Moses' birth to Hebrews and adoption by Egyptians, the Israelites' identity remains

1. See the section on 'Rhetorical Analysis' in Chapter 2.

2. Fischer (*Jahwe unser Gott*, p. 188) is perhaps unaware of this rhetorical impasse facing Moses when he writes that Moses does speak well despite his protests in Exod. 3–4 that he cannot.

Without touching on language, Childs ('Theology', p. 166) also remarks that Moses has no commission here. He intervenes by natural right only. On the contrary, Ackerman ('Literary Context', p. 99) believes that the legal vocabulary shows that Moses does have the authority to act, as though he could confer it on himself. As a point of reference, the broad legal question of the capacity to judge in Israel is reviewed by L. Köhler (*Deuterojesaja [Jesaja 40–55] stilkritisch untersucht* [BZAW, 37; Giessen: Töpelmann, 1923], p. 110). He maintains that only resident freeman ('Bürger') who are apt for the cult, for war and for marriage can enter into the role of judges, they alone are צדיק'.

3. *Narrative*, p. 69.

unstable unless constantly rooted in a knowledge of God who alone is suprahistorical.

Similarly, Moses can never create his own mission or his own self-understanding, any more than the sons of Israel can make themselves into a people. His initiative fails for want of God, whose intervention will be more successful than Moses' exactly because it will teach true perception and service. Liberation is here an exercise of knowledge as well as power.[1]

The double יצא is thus a kind of 'non-Exodus', and Moses' escape an 'anti-liberation'.[2] It is a flight from the past rather than an advance towards its fruition, a necessity brought on by powerlessness and carried out in the ambivalence of irony.

Having failed to find identification with the 'brothers', Moses must seek his sense of himself in the events of the future. His identity will become clear with his authority, in his commission at the Bush when God, who is the first to call him by his name since the princess, reveals himself in terms of Moses' past: 'Moses, Moses! . . . I am the God of your father, the God of Abraham, the God of Isaac, and the God of Jacob' (Exod. 3.4, 6). Moses will again be afraid (ירא), but this time, like the midwives (1.21), it will be before the awesomeness of God.[3]

It is not by Moses' acting alone, but through him as emissary of God, that the Israelites will satisfy the need first seen at his birth and adoption—the need to build their inchoate sense of nationhood into an

1. See 'Narrative Symmetry' in Chapter 4.

2. יצא is a standard word for the Exodus, according to H.D. Preuss, 'יצא *jāṣā*'', *ThWAT*, III, p. 804. Note its emphasis on the event as a datum in the history of salvation: E. Jenni, 'יצא *jṣ*' hinausgehen', *THAT*, I, p. 761. Ironically here, given the slavery of the Hebrews, it is also the technical term for the release of a slave or prisoner: J. Wijngaards, 'הוציא and העלה: A Twofold Approach to the Exodus', *VT* 15 (1965), pp. 92-93.

3. D.M. Gunn ('The "Hardening of Pharaoh's Heart": Plot, Character and Theology in Exodus 1–14', in *Art and Meaning: Rhetoric in Biblical Literature* [ed. D.J.A. Clines *et al.*; JSOTSup, 19; Sheffield: JSOT Press, 1982], p. 87) looks beyond Exod. 1–2 and concludes that although Moses is 'puppet-like' (as Pharaoh is) for most of the Exodus, he will re-emerge as a man of initiative at the Sea. He finally becomes a true servant with all the tensions that exist between freedom and service.

enduring and collective faith in God by learning who they are in the light of their past.[1]

In this passage and through Moses, God's empowering self-revelation becomes a condition for the Israelites' further self-discovery. His impending declaration, 'I AM WHO I AM' (3.14), implies a corollary ratified by events here: 'And therefore you are who you are or will soon become'.

God's absence and activity totally condition the Israelites' understanding, because, as we noted, the motif of knowledge in Exodus 1–2 sets the ground for the Exodus as the making of a covenant after the damage of the Fall. The creation of a need for God out of Moses' failure and flight shows that here Moses is eminently the postlapsarian man. He is subject to the vagaries of human language that are the consequence of that first plunge into error and our disastrous misappropriation of authority.

A few short notes will complete the study of the vocabulary. The specification of time by the phrase 'in those days' (v. 11c) gives a certain realism.[2] But, perhaps more important here, it reinforces the connection between this passage and the oppression that has come before: expressions like בימים ההם are the easiest way to show synchronity in Scripture.[3] And indeed, as we have seen, the pericope describes how the oppression lasts and even spreads as the Hebrews turn on each other.

מכה (v. 11f) as a noun is, of course, also the word for the plagues. Its position at the end of a string of *wayyiqtol* verbs gives it stress.

1. Again the relevant section is in 'Narrative Symmetry' in Chapter 4, and the point is the evocations in Exod. 1–2 of the promises to the patriarchs.

2. N. Tucker, 'Several Perspectives concerning the Organization of Time', *Beth Mikra* 93 (2) (January–March) (1983), p. 168 (Hebrew); cf. also Duvshani ('Time in Biblical Narrative', p. 224), who discusses the realistic quality of expressions of time in terms of a theory of a specifically biblical concept of time—a notion rejected by J. Barr, *Biblical Words for Time* (SBT, 1st Series, 33; London: SCM Press, 2nd edn, 1969 [1962]), especially p. 109.

3. Talmon, 'Synchroneity and Simultaneity', p. 11. However, Cassuto (*Commentary*, p. 21) says the expression describes only the events immediately to be related, not the entire period of oppression. Schmidt (*Exodus*, p. 90) and Dillmann (*Exodus und Leviticus*, p. 23) say the opposite.

For Houtman, the recurrence of the root in vv. 12d and 13e implies that violence breeds violence.[1]

The pericope uses extensive repetition in the diction: נכה (*hiph.* 3×), אח, איש (4×; *pl.* 1×), כה, יצא, הרג (3×), מצרי (3×), פרעה, משה (3×), יום-ימים, דבר, ראה (3×), אמר (4×), ישב. (We have already noted that ויגדל is repeated from the last pericope.) Some of these cases might be practical, like משה. But the total effect gives verbal weight to the dual structure of the two days while perhaps emphasizing again the continuation of the situation. This would hold especially for the two וירא (v. 11d-e) found in the same position, the beginning of the phrase. The device is called anaphora.[2] Coats notes astutely that on the second day, when Moses is betrayed, the Hebrews are not called his 'brothers' again.[3]

The reappearance of עברי with its connotation of foreignness is seen as appropriate by Lemche,[4] because Moses 'acts as a high-ranking Egyptian and not as an Israelite'.[5]

שר is not a derogatory term in itself,[6] but here, in the Hebrew's retort (v. 14a), its proximity recalls the שרי מסים imposed by the Egyptians (1.11).[7]

Moses' misjudgment is stressed by אכן, which points to a 'contrast, ...expressing the reality in opp. to what had been wrongly imagined'.[8]

The passage's interest in the thematic over the dramatic may be reflected in the choice of ברח over נוס. With ברח the emphasis is the avoidance of danger, not on its acuity.[9] When it applies to an individual, it is almost always a slave or a dependent who leaves one allegiance for another, as Moses does here when he abandons the court and stays with Reuel.[10]

1. *Exodus*, p. 279.
2. Lausberg, *Handbuch*, I, §§629-30.
3. *Moses*, p. 50.
4. 'Hebrew', p. 14.
5. See the beginning of 'Vocabulary' in Chapter 3.
6. Van der Ploeg, 'Les chefs', p. 40.
7. We noted in 'Vocabulary' in Chapter 2, that the שרי מסים may in turn recall the Israelites' position in Egypt as שרי מקנה before their oppression.
8. BDB, p. 38; also Muraoka (*Emphatic Words*, pp. 132-33), with reference to Ehrlich; König, *Syntax*, §351b.
9. J. Gamberoni, 'ברח', *ThWAT*, I, p. 779.
10. E. Jenni, '"Fliehen" im akkadischen und im hebräischen Sprachgebrauch',

7. *Conclusions*

Exod. 2.11-14 reifies the moral complexity alluded to in Exod. 2.1-10 by embroiling the narrative in the ambivalence inherent in violence and language—that is, the twin poles of human experience: acts and words. This passage describes two false answers to the question of the last pericope, 'Who are the Israelites in the light of the past?'. Moses' self-contradiction matches that of the Hebrew who rejects him, his brother's rescuer. Moses' self contradiction in action shows the futility of his initiative without divine authority; the incongruous reaction of the Hebrew points up the narrow limits of Israelite nationhood without the Lord of history. The two cases situate the action to come, including the Exodus, deep within the difficult and confused terrain of the fallen world. The Israelites' cry for help in 2.24 will be a call for the restoration of truth as much as for the end of oppression. In that sense, only God, not Moses, can be the saviour of Israel.[1]

Or 47 (1978), p. 357, citing this verse; also S. Schwertner, 'נוס *nūs* fliehen', *THAT*, II, p. 48, who stresses that ברח means leaving one's habitual milieu to become a refugee or emigrant elsewhere.

1. For a historical-critical attempt to answer the question, 'Who Saved Israel, God or Moses?', see W.H. Schmidt, 'Jahwe in Ägypten: Unabgeschlossene historische Spekulationen über Moses Bedeutung für Israels Glauben', *Kairos* ns 18 (1976), pp. 43, 53. He suggests that Moses' original function in the story is not that of a charismatic leader in the style of a saviour, but rather as the link between YHWH the Sinai mountain god and the god of the patriarchs.

Chapter 6

EXODUS 2.16-22

1. *Literal Translation*

16a Now belonging to the priest of Midian there were seven daughters,
16b and they came
16c to draw [water]
16d and to fill the troughs
16e in order to water the flock of their father.
17a But shepherds came
17b and drove them away.
17c Moses rose up
17d and delivered them
17e and watered their flock.
18a They came to Reuel their father,
18b and he said,
18c 'Why did you hurry
18d in coming today?'
19a They said,
19b 'An Egyptian man rescued us from the hand of the shepherds
19c and also drew, yes, drew [water] for us,
19d and watered the flock'.
20a He said to his daughters,
20b 'And where is he?
20c Why is this that you have left the man?
20d Call him,
20e that he may eat bread!'
21a Moses was willing
21b to settle down with the man,
21c and he gave Zipporah his daughter to Moses.
22a She bore a son,
22b and he called his name Gershom,
22c for he said,
22d 'A sojourner have I been in a foreign land'.

Notes on the Literal Translation

Verse 17b, e. ויגרשום: 'and drove them away'; צאנם: 'their flocks'. The masculine object suffixes obviously refer to the daughters. Lacocque speculates that צאנם was written instead of צאנן either by analogy with ויגרשום or to prevent haplography between the two *nuns*.[1] He also suggests with Cassuto that ם was written instead of ן in ויגרשום to distinguish it from the נ paragogicum.[2] As in 1.21, the common phenomenon of anomalous grammatical concord is being overexplained.[3]

Verse 19c. דלה דלה (*dāloh dālāh*): 'drew, yes, drew [water]'. This rendering of the infinitive absolute proposed by Fox is satisfyingly literal for our purposes.[4] However, it does risk the misimpression that the emphasis is necessarily on the verb. Rather, the infinitive absolute much more often underscores a 'modality' than a 'verbal idea'.[5] Here the point could be an 'opposition or antithesis', perhaps that of a citified Egyptian's labouring at this menial work.[6]

Verse 20b. ואיו: 'And where is he?' Joüon cites this sentence as an instance of 'le waw de sentiment' expressing more a nuance than a logical link.[7] Lacocque calls it a 'waw d' "excitation"'.[8] GKC §154b isolates here a kind of ו 'at the beginning of speech in loose connexion with an act or speech of another person'. Cassuto says much the same.[9] Ehrlich[10] and Schmidt[11] read the ו as a light reproach.

1. *Devenir*, p. 65.
2. *Commentary*, p. 24.
3. Brockelmann, *Hebräische Syntax*, §124b; GKC, §135o, both citing this verse.
4. *Names*, p. 20.
5. Muraoka, *Emphatic Words*, pp. 86-87, citing Joüon, *Grammaire*, §123d. 'Opposition or antithesis' is one of the eight modalities he suggests, other instances of which are Josh. 24.10; Num. 23.11; 1 Sam. 12.25 and Ps. 118.13. Joüon (*Grammaire*, §123e-k) lists these phenomena differently.
6. So Childs, *Exodus*, p. 31. For Durham (*Exodus*, p. 21), on the other hand, the emphasis is on the verb, and he translates the infinitive absolute as 'all the water', or 'vigorously drew'.
7. *Grammaire*, §177m.
8. *Devenir*, p. 66.
9. *Commentary*, p. 25.
10. *Randglossen*, p. 266.
11. *Exodus*, p. 94.

2. *Delimitation*

The last chapter has already discussed the transition between this pericope and the preceding.

The break at the end of this episode, at v. 22, is easily spotted. The action comes to a pause. A set pattern in vv. 21-22 describes a marriage, birth and naming.[1] At v. 23 the locality and characters will change. And time will leap ahead: 'In the course of those many days...' The letter פ in the Masoretic Text before v. 23 signals that the Masoretes recognized it as the beginning of a separate unit, a פתוחא or open paragraph.

3. *Narrative Structure*

Deep

This pericope presents topics that have become familiar to us since the beginning of the Book; for example, rescue, the punishment of wrong and the danger Moses faced. But here no particular weight is given to these in themselves.

When the plot is refined to its base elements, a new deep structure stands out: 'exploit–exploit rewarded'. This pattern is the only one that runs beneath the whole episode from the clash with the shepherds to the birth of Moses' son. Its stress on the bravery of Moses' deed helps account structurally for the relatively ample description of the rescue that is given by the daughters to their father. (Their report will be given attention under 'Repetition'.)

Surface

Again we find certain features of the story so far, but now in different combinations. The episodes of the midwives (1.15-22) and Moses' interventions in Egypt (2.11-15) both had two crescendos of tension. In 1.15-22, the second worked up from a certain relaxation and was greater than the first; the order to all Egyptians to kill every son was more dangerous than the instruction to the midwives. In 2.11-15 the two turning points have built directly on top of one another: no respite follows 'When [Moses] went out the next day, and behold...'

1. For details about this pattern, refer to 'Vocabulary' in Chapter 4, the birth of Moses.

(2.13a-b) until after Pharaoh has 'sought to kill Moses' (2.15b) and Moses has made good his escape.

Here the suspense peaks twice with dramatic relief in between, as in the scene with the midwives, where God breaks through in the middle. But it eventually ends with a complete restoration of equilibrium, like the calm in 2.15e after Moses' flight, when he sits by the well to rest.

The first turning point here is 2.17c: 'Moses rose up'. What happens next is immediate and determinative: he delivers the young women and waters their flock. Tension slackens as the daughters tell their adventure to their father. The second decisive point in the story is v. 20e, when he has them invite Moses to a meal. It results that Moses settles and marries.

The alleviation of the suspense at the middle and the end prepares for a contrast with vv. 23-25. That scene will shift abruptly from the pastoral to the intolerable—to the Hebrews back in Egypt crying out in despair.

4. *Point of View*

So far in Exodus 1–2, the point of view has often penetrated a discrete but clear window into the function and relations of the characters. A frequent technique has been external focalization directed within the characters to inform us of their state of mind. This pericope is different. Its focalization shows us nothing of their inner life.

In the first part of the episode, the daughters' routine, their harassment and rescue are observed panoramically, from no particular angle. Once the women return home, some of the characters break into speech, but their thoughts and feelings stay veiled, glimpsed only through little devices like the 'waw de sentiment' in v. 20b.

We learn only that Moses 'was willing to settle down with the man' (v. 21a-b), but we will see in the vocabulary study that ויואל is from a root whose exact meaning must be fixed by context.

The role of this dimmed focalization is more readily accounted for after presenting another important quality of this story—its high degree of repetition, both of material from other pericopes, and of its own parts.

5. *Repetition*

This section of Exodus 1–2 is one of the most commented on because it is seen by many as a 'type-scene', an instance of a convention repeated variously in Genesis 24, Genesis 29 and John 4.

The theory owes much to the pioneering work of A. Lord on oral narrative poetry. He wrote that a type-scene 'contains a given set of repeated elements or details, not all of which are always present, nor always in the same order, but enough of which are present to make the scene a recognizable one'.[1]

With small discrepancies, three scholars have listed the repeated elements of the encounters at the well in the Hebrew Bible.[2] The protagonist or his emissary travels to a foreign land far away and stops at a well. He meets one or several maidens who come to draw water at the well. He does something for the woman, who runs home to report. The stranger is invited into her father's household, and he or his master marries her.

Many differences of varying importance obtain among the three stories. For example, special property laws apply to the well that is closed up with a stone in Genesis 29.[3] More interestingly, the girls in Exodus 2 are not reported to be beauties or relatives of the male protagonist, like Rebekah (Gen. 24.15-16) and Rachel (Gen. 29.10, 17). Nor is Midian Moses' old homeland.

All three authors maintain that the parallels in the plot lines were not drawn by chance. Culley studied 'repeated elements of narrative in

1. *The Singer of Tales* (Cambridge, MA: Harvard University Press, 1960), quoted in R.C. Culley, *Studies in the Structure*, p. 23. Alter (*Narrative*, p. 50) says he himself adopted the term from the classicist W. Arend, although it appears in Culley's monograph which Alter cites.

2. Alter, *Narrative*, p. 52; Culley, *Studies in the Structure*, p. 42; J.G. Williams, 'The Beautiful and the Barren: Conventions in Biblical Type-scenes', *JSOT* 17 (1980), p. 109. Only Alter mentions that the girl at the well is always called a נערה or someone's daughter. Williams sees a superhuman quality in the man's action. Culley discerns a phase called 'proposed sign' in Gen. 24 and 'discussion with shepherds (learned with relatives)' in Gen. 29. The common ground for this stage, missing in Exodus, is unexplained.

3. H. Gilead, 'Encounters at the Well', *Beth Mikra* 70 (1977), p. 221 (Hebrew), whose whole article is given over to such social, geographical and legal differences.

the light of the discussion of oral prose', although he does not insist that biblical stories must have an oral origin.[1] Unfairly, Alter accuses Culley of hypothesizing a single oral '*ur*-story' behind all type-scenes.[2] He himself ascribes the similarities to a 'grid' of 'analogous conventions through which the biblical narrators variously worked out their tacit contract with their contemporary audiences', just as modern moviemakers draw from a stock of formula plots in every Hollywood western (pp. 47, 49).

By all evidence, the stories do contain some products of convention, but more than that is hard to say. Alter admits:

> [C]ertain narrative conventions that are observable on the 'microscopic' level of the text, like the formulas for beginning and ending narrative units, can be identified with considerable confidence because one can locate fifteen, twenty, or even more instances in the Hebrew Bible. Other conventions, however, which determine larger patterns of recurrence in the 'macroscopic' aspects of the stories and which are not strictly tied to stylistic formulas. . . are bound to be more conjectural because, given the limited corpus with which we have to work, we may be able to locate confidently no more than five or six signal occurrences.[3]

1. *Studies in the Structure*, pp. 64-66, 25, 31.

2. *Narrative*, p. 50; Cf. J.G. Williams, 'The Beautiful', p. 117 n. 6, in which D.M. Gunn defends Culley against Alter's charge and cites Culley, *Studies in the Structure*, p. 40.

3. Some would say that Alter's corpus is unnecessarily limited, since his attention is too closely to the foreground rather than the background of the biblical text, and he does not deal with its cultural milieu. Cf. R. Cohn, 'On the Art of Biblical Narrative', *BR* 31 (1986), p. 13. Also D. Edelman, 'An Appraisal of Robert Alter's Approach', *BR* 31 (1986), p. 24: '[Especially in his work on type scenes, h]is lack of willingness to accept the relevance and usefulness of related methods has prevented him from reaping the benefits of existing biblical scholarship'. On the other hand, in an article subsequent to his book, Alter ('Convention', p. 118) says that 'the extant body of antecedent and circumambient [*sic*] Near Eastern literature may also be used, with caution, to give us guidelines to how these biblical works differ from literature composed later and elsewhere'. At least in this case, however, little is to be learned from other Near Eastern texts. Houtman (*Exodus*, p. 302) turns to the story of Si-nuhe (*ANET*, pp. 18-22) and a letter about the pursuit of runaway slaves (*ANET*, p. 259), but can conclude only that those menaced in Egypt often sought refuge abroad. Si-nuhe's story is otherwise inapplicable, since it deals with voluntary exile and an Egyptian's love of his homeland.

Considered practically, the cardinal question for analysing this text does not seem to be addressed by any of the speculations raised by the articles cited; it lies neither in the written or oral origin of the conventions, nor in the existence of a primary version, nor in similarities with other literatures.

Rather, the key question lies in the perhaps insoluble problem of gauging the true breadth of the convention at hand, of fixing its place on the scale from the 'microscopic' to the 'macroscopic'. Given the differences between them, are the encounters at the well one extensive but flexible convention played out three times, or are they three clusters of smaller independent conventional gestures and remarks? What methodology is to be used for this decision?

Culley concedes that his criterion was experimental, a 'rule of thumb' that judged 'non-essential parts' of a story as 'what could be left out and still leave a story'.[1] Perhaps a more direct approach to this pericope is to begin from whatever theoretical model explains the most.

Exod. 2.16-22 may well belong to one 'type-scene' or family of Hebrew narratives, other members of which are Genesis 24 and Genesis 29. But it responds better to analysis if called by the simpler name of 'repetition'.

Culley, Alter and Williams have listed the actions common to Genesis 24, Genesis 29 and Exodus 2. Some of the diction too is shared: שקה (*hiph.*), ישב, צאן, נערה. The key, however, is not these elements for their own sake, but the characters whose story they construct. When Moses rescues the women at the well, eats with the family, then marries into it and has a child, his action is significant because it re-enacts the histories of Jacob and the servant of Abraham.

For Cassuto the parallels in Genesis are to inculcate the Torah's 'familiar lesson that the experiences of the fathers prefigure those of their descendants'.[2] But here the context recommends the inverse: it is more his destiny to emulate them than theirs to prefigure him.

It was mentioned in the last chapter that Moses may be ignorant of his origins. But he is now, knowingly or not, acting like his forefathers.[3] 'The Midianite wilderness transforms [him] into shepherd,

1. *Studies in the Structure*, p. 111.
2. *Commentary*, p. 27.
3. *Exod. R.* 1.32; also Buber, *Moïse*, p. 53.

foreigner, father and seer—in short, into a son of the Patriarchs. . . '[1]

Moses' journey to Midian is '. . . within himself, to find his true identity and calling. . . '[2] That quest will not culminate until Horeb, 'the mountain of God': 'Who am I that I should go to Pharaoh and bring the sons of Israel out of Egypt?' (Exod. 3.11). But by imitating the Patriarchs now, he associates himself with their own theophanies in Genesis, and by establishing a commonality with them, he prepares for his bond with the Lord who will speak of himself as 'the God of [Moses'] father, the God of Abraham, the God of Isaac, and the God of Jacob' (Exod. 3.6, 15, 16; 4.5).

God's promise of descendants and land to Abram is especially relevant: 'Know, yes, know that your descendants will be sojourners (היה גר) in a land that is not theirs, and will be slaves there, and they will be oppressed for four hundred years' (Gen. 15.13). Moses, the 'brother' of the slaves in Egypt (Exod. 2.11), calls his son 'Gershom', for he said, 'A sojourner have I been (גר היה) in a foreign land' (2.22).

We have seen that Exodus 1–2 treats the purpose and nature of the past within God's plan of history. The self-contradiction that Moses showed in the Egyptian workfields raised the question about him that we had already asked of the Israelites: 'Who is he in the light of this divine project?'[3] Now the element of repetition within this episode begins to answer the question by alluding to him as the successor of the Patriarchs.

He who as a foundling lost his history now submits to it by copying his forefathers. Hotheaded in Egypt, he was a failed parody of Pharaoh.[4] Now he imitates his ancestors and is successful. The incoherence of his two actions in Egypt[5] is corrected by his insertion into the trajectory of his people's history traced by God's promises to the Patriarchs. As in the specially ordered genealogy at the beginning of the Book (1.2-4), the past is understood in function of God's mercy.[6]

1. Fox, *Names*, pp. 19-20.
2. Fox, *Names*, p. 7.
3. See Chapter 5, 'Conclusions'.
4. Both used the 'Beschuldigungsformel', 'Why did you do such and such?'. See 'Vocabulary and Rhetoric' in Chapter 5.
5. One was outside, and the other inside, juridical restraints. See 'Vocabulary and Rhetoric' in Chapter 5.
6. See 'Vocabulary' in Chapter 1.

The prelude, Exod. 1.1-7, showed us by repeating motifs from Genesis that the Hebrews' past will shape their present.[1] Exod. 2.16-22 now forms a thematic inclusion by applying this method and conclusion to Moses as well.[2]

We will see later how this passage fails to bring to completion either our understanding of Moses or his of himself.[3] He remains a powerful but opaque force reaching out toward Horeb and the future. But here he does gain a foothold in the past. He achieves a certain historical congruence that prepares him for his encounter with 'the God of Abraham, the God of Isaac, and the God of Jacob' (Exod. 3.6).

That is to say, Moses will soon find God by following his fathers' footsteps. We concluded that to know themselves, the Israelites must know God.[4] That is true for the adult Moses as well. But in order for Moses to know God, he must as a first step learn his ancestors' ways.

Evocation of Genesis 24 and Genesis 29 is only one kind of repetition in Exod. 2.16-22. Another is internal, the report that the girls

1. See 'Repetition', Chapter 1.

2. By identifying Moses' resemblance to the Patriarchs as the main point, I am disagreeing with many scholars. Schmidt (*Exodus*, p. 85) writes that the reason for the story is to bring about his marriage to a Midianite. Quoting K. Koch, he says it will be important that the Hebrews have relations with these Beduins when they flee into the wilderness (p. 87). Coats ('Moses in Midian', pp. 9-10) stresses the Midianite father-in-law, such that 'the closest point of contact for Exod. 2.11-22 [is] not in 3.1–4.18 but in 18.1-27', where the Midianite sacrifices to God and gives Moses advice. For Lacocque (*Devenir*, p. 65), Moses is acting on the Law in advance. A.H.J. Gunneweg ('Mose in Midian', *ZTK* 61 [1964], p. 9) believes that the purpose is 'überlieferungsgeschichtlich', to unify once-independent themes under a 'gesamtisraelitisch' and yahwistic umbrella. G.A.F. Knight (*Theology as Narration*: *A Commentary on the Book of Exodus* [Grand Rapids, MI: Eerdmans], p. 13) stresses that he finds peace, love and creative work in a kindly home, Houtman (*Exodus*, p. 282) that he is safe and not assimilated, in accord with the Genesis promises of providence.

3. For more about this laconic description of Moses, see 'Point of View and Narrative Gaps' in Chapter 4, about the inconclusiveness of Moses' future at his birth and adoption. In Chapter 5, 'Point of View and Narrative Gaps' explains that both these narrative techniques give a disinterested picture of him. The vocabulary and rhetoric reflect the ambiguity of his actions in the light of juridical standards.

4. See 'Narrative Symmetry' in Chapter 4, where we noted that Moses and Israel are associated such that the obscuring of his identity through his adoption means that only God, who is beyond the hazards of human life, can guarantee a lasting sense of nationhood for the Israelites.

give their father in v. 19. Alter has written much about the eloquence of such repetition as a register whose changes from the narrator's description can index a passage's characterization and purpose.[1] But the remarkable thing about the daughters' words is how little they add to narrator's. The only news for us is that they mistook him for 'an Egyptian man' (v. 19b), and that he drew more water for the flock. Repetition here is almost the opposite of gapping: it is superfluity rather than suppression of information.

For Sternberg, repetition in narrative immediately raises questions about the purpose of its existence.[2] The brevity of this pericope prompts one especially to ask why an entire verse of it is near-duplication. So also does the close proximity of the event and the report.[3] The aim here cannot be as often elsewhere to draw attention to the reporter,[4] since the daughters speak in the plural as a collectivity, and they otherwise have no importance in the story.[5] Moses is the principal figure. As a technique of his characterization, the girls' words function more as control than development. Like a disembodying stage effect, the repetition shines a spot light on Moses' deeds, but keeps the actor himself in the wings. We admire him more, but know him only a little better.

The women's talk is set against his taciturnity. He says only one thing, at the end: 'A sojourner have I been in a foreign land'. In the last pericope Moses became trapped between the juridical language in which he parroted Pharaoh and the rhetorical question by which the Hebrew tricked him.[6] In the moral sense, he lost the power of speech. Moses' one statement is odd in ways we will study under 'Vocabulary and Characterization'. For now it is simply noted that it is neither

1. *Narrative*, pp. 88-113.

2. Sternberg, 'Repetition', p. 110.

3. G.W. Savran, *Telling and Retelling: Quotation in Biblical Narrative* (Indiana Studies in Biblical Literature; Bloomington, IN: Indiana University Press, 1988), pp. 5, 41.

4. Savran, *Telling*, pp. 41, 80.

5. Although Moses' wife has a name, it is bland derivation from צִיפּוֹר, 'bird', according to Stamm (*Frauennamen*, p. 126) and Noth (*Exodus*, p. 37).

6. See 'Vocabulary and Rhetoric' in Chapter 5 for more details about the juridical 'Beschuldigungsformel', 'Why are you hitting your fellow?', and the trick question, 'Do you think to kill me as you killed the Egyptian?'.

long enough nor clear enough for him to share the authority of the narrator.[1]

His authority, when it comes, will be directly from God. Moses' self-contradiction in Egypt, his flight, then his victory in Midian show that, like John Milton's Adam, he is 'sufficient to stand though free to fall'. But even his exploit does not fill in the emptiness, the subtraction of personality that draws him to the Burning Bush as in a vacuum. His imitation of the Patriarchs gives him a past, but does not flesh in his present. And the internal repetition, like the fixed focalization, heightens the celebration of his bravery without diminishing the freedom of his unmeritable election by God.

6. *Narrative Symmetry*

Since most scholars see this pericope as a bridge between Exodus 2 and 3, they have tried to place it symmetrically within its surroundings rather than look within it for a self-standing narrative construct. C. Wiéner makes out a chiasm:[2]

A	In Egypt (2.1-15a).
B	In Midian (2.15b-22).
C	At Horeb (3.1–4.17).
B[1]	Return to Midian and New Departure (4.18-26).
A[1]	In Egypt (4.27–6.13).

The outline demonstrates the centrality of the experience at Horeb. But the number of verses assigned to each term is very uneven. Further, one naturally asks what real reward the scheme brings beyond the gratification of slight taxonomic pleasures.

Weimar also isolates a chiasm:[3]

1. By contrast, cf. G. Savran, 'The Character as Narrator in Biblical Narrative', *Prooftexts* 5 (1985), p. 11: 'A Storyteller such as Abraham's servant [in the well scene in Gen. 24] is cast precisely in the mold of *his* maker, that equally anonymous, half-hidden, omniscient narrator who brings him to life in the story'. Incidentally, the girls themselves do not have the full authority of the narrator either, since they make a mistake and call him an Egyptian.

2. C. Wiéner, *Le livre de l'Exode* (Cahiers Evangile, 54; Paris: Casterman, 1985), p. 15.

3. *Berufung*, p. 223.

A Pharaoh's order and the saving from death by the midwives
B Exposure of the baby; its rescue and adoption
B^1 Rescue of the shepherdesses; Moses' marriage and son
A^1 Theophany in the Bush; the institution of Moses

The thematic resemblance is clear between B and B^1, but less so between A and A^1. Weimar says they are related because the royal order is frustrated by Moses' institution as God's authoritative and powerful emissary.[1] Perhaps they bond better as opposites, like the pattern within 1.15-22 that contrasted the reactions made by Pharaoh and God to the midwives' defiance.[2]

Inside 2.12-22a, Weimar sees a triptych with each of its three parts subdivided in two:[3]

(A) 2.16-17:
(1) '. . . and they came. . . '
the activity of the daughters
'. . . in order to water the flock of their father'
the intention of the daughters

(2) 'But shepherds came. . . Moses. . . delivered [the daughters]'
the activity of the shepherds and Moses
'. . . and watered their flock'.
Moses' success

(B) 2.18-19:
(1) 'Why did you hurry in coming today?'
the father's question
(2) 'An Egyptian man rescued us. . . '
the girls' answer

(C) 2.20-22a:
(1) 'Call him that he may eat bread!'
the father's initiative
'Moses was willing to settle down with the man'.
Moses' reaction
(2) '. . . and he gave Zipporah his daughter to Moses'
the father's initiative
'She bore a son and he called his name Gershom'
Moses' reaction

1. *Berufung*, p. 224.
2. See details in 'Narrative Symmetry', Chapter 3.
3. *Berufung*, pp. 219-20.

In 'A', both subunits include the 'Stichwort' בוא and close with שקה (*hiph.*). The name גרשם given to the son in 'C' reflects Moses' deed in 'A': ויגרשום. The women's report in the middle panel 'B' is a 'Rettungsformel' and is the thematic centre, anticipated by 'A' and resulting in 'C'.

Weimar's analysis of 2.20-22a (his part C above) accurately describes a certain passivity in Moses, consonant with the restraint we have noticed in the focalization and repetition. But the total scheme has some flaws.

If בוא indicates a new subunit, what of תבאנה and בא (*bo'*), both in the first section of Part B? Also, Weimar's break between parts B and C seems somewhat contrived, since it splits up the conversation between the girls and their father.

More seriously, Weimar seems unsure where to lay proportionate weight in the passage. He says that the saving act of Moses in part A indicates the theological perspective of the story, but that the centre and emphasis of the unit is in Part B. He might have been clearer if he had handled the report as a case of repetition.

Another scheme altogether might help:

(Introduction) 2.16
    the daughter's activity
(A) 2.17
    Moses' exploit
(B) 2.18-20
    the dialogue
        'They came to Reuel their father'
            introduction
        (a) 'Why did you hurry. . . ?'
            question
        (b) 'An Egyptian man rescued us. . . '
            report as answer
        (a′) 'And where is he? Why is this. . . ?'
            questions
        'Call him. . . '
            conclusion
(A′) 2.21-22a
    Moses' reward
(Conclusion) 2.22b-d
    the son's name

The first phrase of the introduction (2.16) and the last phrase of the conclusion (2.22b-d) both begin with nouns (ולכהן and גר). Both mention countries ('Midian' and 'a foreign land'), and fathers and their children (Reuel's daughters and Moses' son).

Between these semantic and lexical inclusions fit two chiasms. The first, Moses' exploit–Moses' reward, is thematic and brings to the surface these terms of the deep structure. It in turn surrounds an inner grammatical pattern, alternation between the interrogative and the affirmative in the dialogue. This second pattern's introduction ('They came to Reuel their father') and conclusion ('Call him that he may eat bread!') both imply movement toward Reuel.

The centre of the passage is not Moses' deed, but the daughters' report of it. The structure thus becomes here another mode of indirection like the focalization, the internal repetition, and Moses' silence. Working together in a narrative strategy, they feature Moses but put him off-centre, making him pivotal but keeping him from full view.

Like the repetition that helps create it, the symmetry of this passage is both internal and external. Its parts stands to each other in the ways we have seen. But, as a whole, its plot also bears on the last episode as its inverse: success not failure; foreigners not his people; a welcome not a rejection; entrance into a new relation of marriage not flight from the old one, adoption. In the first, the Egyptian is the enemy who oppresses; in the second, Moses is called an Egyptian as he offers help against the oppressor. Moses flees his home; he finds a home.[1]

Two other points recall the beginning of his life. In 2.1-10 his parents married and his mother bore him. Now he marries and his wife gives him a son. He was named in a significant way just as he himself names his son here and finds a meaning in his choice.[2]

These referential and repetitive qualities of the symmetry give a cyclical movement to Moses' early life.[3] This will change at his encounter on Mount Horeb, after which God will effect a wholly new kind of salvation: 'Do not fear, stand firm, and see the salvation of

1. Fox, *Names*, p. 21; Childs, *Exodus*, p. 32, for the last two points.

2. Houtman, *Exodus*, p. 281; Cassuto, *Commentary*, p. 27.

3. N. Tucker ('Some Principles of Composition of Biblical Stories', *Beth Mikra* 68 [1] [September–November] [1976], pp. 52-53 [Hebrew]) divides biblical stories into two broad types. Another cyclical story is Jacob's; the other kind is linear like Abraham's and Joseph's.

YHWH, which he will do for you today; for you see the Egyptians today, you will not ever see them again' (Exod. 14.13).

7. *Vocabulary and Characterization*

The six semantic fields are:

Fertile Life and Family: בת־בנות (3×), אב (2×), בן, נתן ל (i.e. as wife), קרא שם, ילד
Nationality: נכרי, גר, מצרי, מדין
Motion: בוא (4×), מהר (*pi.*), קום
Affliction: גרש (*pi.*)
Pastoral: דלה (2× + infin. absol.), רהטים, מלא (*pi.*), רעים (*ro'îm*) (2×), שקה (*hiph.*; 3x), צאן (3×)
Rescue: ישע (*hiph.*), נצל מיד (*hiph.*)
Hospitality: עזב, קרא, לחם, ישב אכל

One notes the absence of the field of 'Perception', frequent in the parts about Moses in Egypt (2.1-10; 2.11-15). Also missing are the more violent examples of the vocabulary of 'Affliction' already seen through most of the units from 1.8 to 2.15. Only גרש (*pi.*) is to be found (v. 17b), and it is comparatively mild. Two words alone describe the rescue. Again, emphasis is away from the witnessing of the harassment and Moses' reaction to it.

'Motion' has been a frequent category. It has occurred in the prologue, 1.1-7, and in the earlier pericopes about Moses (2.1-10; 2.11-15), and reminds us that, at least until the Burning Bush, the characters prefer activity to reflection. This is one reason why the narrative devices carry so much of the burden of significance in these chapters.

Two entirely new fields reflect the change in setting and tone: 'Pastoral' and 'Hospitality'. 'Pastoral' and 'Motion' are the fields that dominate at the well and in the daughters' report, until v. 20c when 'Hospitality' comes to the fore.[1] With the expression נתן ל (v. 21c), that category in turn overlaps with and yields to a concentration of words about 'Fertile Life and Family': Reuel gives his daughter in marriage to the visitor. Like the chiasms in the structure, this smooth and tidy succession in the vocabulary lays stress on the continuity of the story, in which the rescue leads quickly to the invitation and marriage. It also points up the whole incident's programmatic

1. עזב is included under 'Hospitality' as its opposite.

nature as a repetition of similar incidents in Genesis.

The words for 'Nationality' are at the beginning (v. 16a: מדין), middle (v. 19b: מצרי) and end (v. 22d: גר, נכרי). The effect is to help the pericope represent for Moses a transformation by stages from an adopted Egyptian prince to an adopted Midianite son-in-law.

The individual words and phrases of the pericope suggest at least four interesting studies. The first is קום. The second is the pair ישע (*hiph.*) and נצל (*hiph.*). The third is Moses' exclamation: גר הייתי בארץ נכריה. The fourth is the verb יאל (*hiph.*).

'Moses rose up and delivered' the women (v. 17c). If the verb ישב at the end of the last episode (v. 15e) is literally 'he sat down [by a well]', then קום can mean 'rose up'. Otherwise it is often linked to verbs of action as an imprecise auxiliary indicating the beginning of the movement.[1] Consonant with the repetitive pattern noted above, the verb has occurred earlier: 'Now a new king arose over Egypt who did not know Joseph' (1.8). That verse announced the tribulations of the Israelites and the theme that oppression begins in ignorance. Now Moses arises to stop the oppression of the women. We just recalled under 'Repetition' that in his clash with the quarrelsome Hebrew in Egypt, Moses used the legal style of Pharaoh's question to the midwives: 'Why are you doing such and such?' Now he performs the same action as Pharaoh, but to opposite ends and with better results.

At the end of their relation, קום will again apply to both leaders:

> And Pharaoh rose up (ויקם) in the night, he and all his servants and all Egypt and there was a great cry in Egypt, for there was not a house where one was not dead. And he summoned Moses and Aaron by night, and said, 'Rise up (קומו), go forth from among my people, both you and the people of Israel; and go, serve YHWH, as you have said. Take your flocks and your herds, as you have said, and be gone. . .' (Exod. 12.30-32).

The link between the passages is underscored by the number of other words in Exod. 12.30-32 that are also found in Exodus 1–2: פרעה (cf. 1.11, 19, 22; 2.5, 7, 8, 9, 10, 15 [2×], כל (cf. 1.5, 6 [2×], 14 [2×], 22 [3×]), מצרים (cf. 1.1, 5, 8, 13, 15, 17-18; 2.23), בית (cf. 1.1, 22; 2.1), מות (cf. 1.6; 2.23), קרא (cf. 1.18; 2.7, 8, 10, 20, 22), יצא (cf. 1.5; 2.11, 13), עם (cf. 1.9, 20, 22), בני ישראל (cf. 1.1, 7, 9, 12, 13; 2.23, 25), עבד (cf. 1.13, 14 [5×]; 2.23), צאן (cf. 2.16, 17, 19), לקח (cf.

1. S. Amsler, 'קום *qūm* aufstehen', *THAT*, II, p. 638; J. Gamberoni, 'קום *qûm*', *ThWAT*, VI, p. 1257.

2.1, 3, 5, 9), הלך (cf. 2.1, 5, 7, 8, 9).[1] Applied to both Pharaoh and Moses, קום is a token of their complex association as rival leaders standing under the judgment of God.

Alter writes that 'when there is no divergence between a statement as it occurs in narration and as it recurs in dialogue [as here], the repetition generally has the effect of giving a weight of emphasis to the specific terms which the speaker chooses for his speech'.[2] Of Moses' exploit, the narrator says ישע (*hiph.*), the women נצל (*hiph.*).

J.F.A. Sawyer has done exacting work on the Hebrew words for salvation. He concludes that in the narrative portions of the historical books and the Pentateuch ישע (*hiph.*) has two distinct meanings, a 'heilsgeschichtlicher' and a 'profaner Gebrauch'.[3]

Only God can be the subject in the soteriological meaning. When a person is the subject, as here, the context is juridical or political. In plain fact, the use of ישע (*hiph.*) here is probably due to מושיע in Deut. 22.25-29, where the issue is legal protection from rape in the open countryside.[4] Even more prosaically, some references define the word as 'help at work'.[5]

In this juridical context, the emphasis is not on the delivery, but on the intervention and conflict on behalf of what is right.[6] Nevertheless, at his greatest, the person in question is a representative of God who rights wrong with divine justice.[7]

ישע (*hiph.*) is thus of a piece with two classes of vocabulary we have already seen in Exodus 1–2. First, like חמל, יצב (*hithp.*) and צפן from the birth story (2.1-10), it reconfirms the future appointment of

1. See also the discussion about Exod. 12.31-32 in 'Vocabulary', Chapter 4, in relation to the princess's imperative: לכי.

2. *Narrative*, p. 77.

3. J.F.A. Sawyer, 'ישע *jš*'', *ThWAT*, III, pp. 1045-46.

4. Sawyer, *ThWAT*, III, p. 1048. Also *idem*, 'What was a mošia'?', *VT* 15 (1965), p. 482 n. 2.

5. F. Stolz, 'ישע *jš*' hi. helfen', *THAT*, I, p. 786; *HALAT*, II, p. 428.

6. So Sawyer ('mošia'', p. 482 n. 2), who quotes the example of Exod. 2.

7. Sawyer, *ThWAT*, III, p. 1407; *idem*, *Semantics in Biblical Research: New Methods of Defining Hebrew Words for Salvation* (SBT, 2.24; Naperville, IL; A.R. Allenson, 1972), p. 103: 'There is some evidence that HOŠIA' is one of a small group of "disinfected" words (cf. BARA' "to create"), properly used only in contexts where YHWH or his appointed leader is subject, its application in other contexts being conspicuously avoided and even explicitly condemned'.

Moses as a leader chosen by God. Second, its juridical import demonstrates the gravity of the shepherds' offence despite the lack of detail.[1] It sets the story within the chapters' continuing theme that oppression is a matter of injustice and that true liberation therefore requires adherence to a clearer moral vision of the world and entails a revaluing of creation.[2] In this it is like the other juridical words. In the first episode of the oppression in 1.8-14, these were ענה (*pi.*), בפרך and הבה; in the birth story (2.1-10) נער and the adoption formula היה ל ל. In the account of Moses' efforts at justice in Egypt (2.11-15), we noted ראה, למה, רשע, רע (*rēa'*), שים, שפט, הרג, שמע and דבר. In 1.18 Pharaoh asked the midwives a legal-style 'Beschuldigungsfrage'.

The women choose the word נצל (*hiph.*) to recount Moses' deed. It too recurs later in the book, as a 'Leitwort' in the account of the Exodus.[3] But it is not necessarily laden with theological content.[4] And it is weaker even in its profane sense. It implies simply a distancing from a threat, while ישע (*hiph.*) suggests the elimination of the threatener.[5] In other words, the women do not see him as a representative of divine justice. Indeed, in the same v. 19b they mistake him for 'an Egyptian man', ironically the same expression used of the attacker in 2.11.[6]

Thus they unwittingly attenuate the force of ישע (*hiph.*) and so draw the curtain back over whatever it implies about Moses' future. In this sense the contrast between the two words functions like the focalization,

1. Greenberg (*Understanding Exodus*, p. 56) speaks of a 'scale of disinterestedness' that rises with each incident. First Moses defended an Israelite against an outsider, then one Israelite against another, now Gentiles against other Gentiles. For Houtman (*Exodus*, p. 280), this incident is a chance for Moses to become a great man ('een man van formaat').

2. About injustice as a distortion of creation, see the 'Conclusions' in Chapter 2.

3. Cf. F.L. Hossfeld and B. Kalthoff ('נצל *nṣl*', *ThWAT*, V, p. 574), who cite Exod. 3.8; 5.23; 18.10. It occurs five times in Exod. 18, for example (vv. 4, 8, 9, 10 [2×]).

4. Hossfeld and Kalthoff, 'נצל', p. 574; U. Bergman ('נצל *nṣl* hi. retten', *THAT*, II, p. 98) is more categorical, saying that it has no such content at all.

5. Hossfeld and Kalthoff, 'נצל', pp. 573-74; Sawyer (*Semantics in Biblical Research*, p. 103) adds that the historical evidence from other Semitic languages confirms this view. Houtman (*Exodus*, p. 296) wonders if נצל (*hiph.*) is not sometimes stronger, but without explanation cites as evidence only Gen. 37.21.

6. Houtman, *Exodus*, p. 296.

repetition and structure that mark Moses' importance, but between discrete parentheses.

This bright but unfocused image of Moses is exhibited in miniature in the conclusion of the pericope and Moses' only statement: גר הייתי בארץ נכריה. His remark presents certain exegetical problems because it is out of context.

The major philological sources agree: a גר is distinct from a זר or a נכרי, in that he is a foreigner who establishes himself for a certain time in a country and to whom is attributed a particular juridical configuration.[1] He leaves his village and clan to flee because of war, natural disaster or 'Blutschuld'.[2] His status and privileges depend on the hospitality of those, not his relatives, who take him in.[3] The Israelites in Egypt were גרים.[4] So were the patriarchs.[5]

Moses names his son Gershom. For, he says, he 'a sojourner (גר) has [he] been (הייתי) in a foreign land'. The statement is baffling.

An Israelite by race, he originally shared his people's status as foreigners in Egypt. But he became the princess's son, and we do not know enough about adoption in the ancient world to decide how it would affect his condition.[6] One must also distinguish between Egyptian and Israelite law, the latter of which in any case would have to be retrojected onto this early moment of their history.

Some believe Moses' choice of the name Gershom is a play on the words גר and שם ('there').[7] If one accepts this idea, 'there' would imply Egypt, not Midian where he was speaking. Furthermore, the

1. R. Martin-Achard, 'גור *gūr* als Fremdling weilen', *THAT*, I, p. 410. By contrast, a נכרי is a 'foreigner who has not given up his original home', according to M. Guttman ('The Term "Foreigner" [נכרי] Historically Considered', *HUCA* 3 [1926], p. 1).

2. *HALAT*, I, p. 193.

3. D. Kellermann, 'גור', *ThWAT*, I, p. 983.

4. Martin-Achard, 'גור', p. 410: Exod. 22.20 (= Exod. 23.9 = Lev. 19.34 = Deut. 10.19); Lev. 25.23.

5. Kellermann, 'גור', p. 986: Abraham in Gen. 17.8; 23.4; Jacob in Gen. 28.4; Isaac in Gen. 35.27; 37.1; Esau and Jacob in Gen. 36.7.

6. See C.F.D. Moule ('Adoption', *IDB*, I, p. 48) about the Hebrew Bible; M. Kurlowicz ('Adoption on the Evidence of the Papyri', *The Journal of Juristic Papyrology* 19 [1983], pp. 61, 66, 75) stresses the lack of data about Egyptian adoption even in later periods.

7. Schmidt, *Exodus*, p. 95; Fox, *Names*, p. 20.

qatal of היה almost certainly refers to the past, not the present.[1] The nub of the problem is that he is more evidently a גר as a refugee in Midian and the guest of Reuel than he was as a prince in Egypt.

If he is referring to Egypt we do not know how or when he discovered his origins. If he means his status in Midian, why does he use the *qatal*, perhaps making a pun? The commentators are as unagreed, since the text is ambiguous.[2]

This verse is one that might be explained more smoothly in a diachronic rather than a synchronic analysis. It could be an editorial comment put in the mouth of Moses to lend his weight to later social legislation defending the weak—including foreigners—on the grounds that the Israelites themselves had been גרים in Egypt.[3] But whatever its origin, every text has an effect on the act of reading in context. This verse functions as a three-ply reinforcement. It strengthens Moses' tie to the patriarchs already noted under 'Repetition', since God told Abraham that his descendants would be 'sojourners in a land that is not theirs' (Gen. 15.13). It increases the unity of Exodus 1–2 because

1. Meyer, *Hebräische Grammatik*, §101 2c; Joüon, *Grammaire*, §111i: '*est* (rare)'. Citing this verse as an example of *qal* perfect in the temporal sense, G.S. Ogden ('Time, and the Verb היה in OT Prose', *VT* 21 [1971], pp. 451-52) writes, 'A survey of all the examples of the Perfect היה leads to the conclusion that in whatever aspect it may occur either as a copula, existential, or transitional, a statement about the past is being made'.

2. Noth (*Exodus*, p. 37), Greenberg (*Understanding Exodus*, p. 49) and Houtman, (*Exodus*, p. 300) believe that he is a גר in Midian, but do not say why Moses should use the past tense. Schmidt (*Exodus*, p. 77) and Houtman (*Exodus*, p. 300) translate the word as 'guest' ('Gast'; 'gast'), applicable to his status in Midian but scarcely to that in Egypt where he has been condemned to death. On the other hand, Lacocque (*Devenir*, pp. 67-68) thinks Moses was foreign in Egypt. He sees other word play between גרש (*pi.*) and גר: Moses is expelled after having been a foreigner there. Cassuto (*Commentary*, p. 26), Ackerman ('Literary Context', p. 105) and Greenberg (*Understanding Exodus*, p. 49) make the same lexical connection as Lacocque, but call it the true etymology of the name. And they draw the opposite conclusion from Lacocque about where Moses was a sojourner. Cazeaux ('Naître', p. 411) detects the inconsistency that, he says, adds to the tension of the next pericope. Fokkelman ('Exodus', p. 60) thinks the name anticipates Exod. 11.1: 'when [Pharaoh] lets you go, he will drive you utterly away (גרש יגרש)'.

3. For example, Exod. 22.20-21; 23.9; Lev. 19.33-34 cited by J.D. Amusin ('Die Gerim in der sozialen Legislatur des *Alten Testaments*', *Klio* 63 [1981], p. 19), who notes that the imperative in such cases is often negative. Note Deut. 23.8, but also Deut. 10.19.

the themes in Genesis 15 of proliferation, knowledge, slavery and judgment have already been evoked in Exodus 1.[1] It also intensifies the ambivalence about Moses already created by the narrative techniques just studied.

To amplify the last point, when Moses put himself in conflict with the Egyptian and the Hebrew in the previous pericope, we learned that he could not create his own self-understanding.[2] Here the confusion of his one remark about himself repeats that conclusion. It is implied that people and events can bestow social status on him, as an adopted son or as a גר. But they cannot give him the clarity and fullness of personality that come only after his encounter at the Bush, from the knowledge and service of God.[3]

One more word calls for notice here. 'Moses was willing (יאל [*hiph.*]) to settle down with the man' (v. 21a-b). Another verb here could have been an insight into Moses' state of mind, and a valuable one. However, this one remains just beyond the range of practical analysis. It is difficult to translate because its value changes with its setting. Its usual meaning is in reference to a beginning made difficult by shyness, politeness or other obstacles. But it can also mean simply 'to decide', so that the verse could be rendered 'Moses decided to remain with the man'.[4] Again the passage is

1. See especially 'Vocabulary', Chapter 2 about 1.8-14, although the semantic field of proliferation is found in all the pericopes until 2.11-15.

2. See 'Vocabulary and Rhetoric' in Chapter 4, where the point is made that both the Israelites' and Moses' identity must be rooted in a knowledge of God because he alone is above the flux of history. See also the comments on ידע and עבד in 'Vocabulary' in Chapter 2.

3. The later development and exposition of Moses' character lie well beyond the field of this study, but as here they seem to hinge on his relation with God. It would be profitable to trace the changes in Moses as these are reflected in his dealings with God. Beginning in fear and hesitation in Exod. 3, he grows in confidence, even daring to remind God of his promises to the patriarchs (32.13). God speaks to him as a friend (33.11), and Moses in turn is sharp with him (Num. 11.11-15) and even rhetorically conniving (Num. 14.13-19). Moses' mysterious punishment could be examined (Num. 20.12; Deut. 32.51). The narrator's accounts of the Exodus (Exod. 14.15-31) and the Golden Calf (Exod. 32.1-24) could be compared with Moses' report of them (Deut. 9.7-21; 29.1-13).

4. A.S. Kapelrud, 'יאל *j'l*', *ThWAT*, III, p. 384. Under this entry, BDB (pp. 383-84) reads 'shew willingness to do anything, accept an invitation, acquiesce', and for this verse adds 'and Moses was willing to dwell with the man (and did

sketching Moses with oblique shadow strokes.

One sees now how utterly the presentation of Moses differs from modern, Western principles of characterization. J. Ewen has drawn up models to categorize figures in Western literature.[1] He works with three ideas that he admits are ill-defined and overlapping: development, compositeness and mimesis–symbolism.[2] Each is conceived as a scale. That of development runs from the fully static, like an entirely allegorical character, to the dynamic, as in a novel about the changes of adolescence. 'Compositeness' (מורכבות) is his word for psychological complexity, the upper register of which is occupied by nineteenth-century Russian and French novels of social relations. The mimetic–symbolic scale is the least precise, but it defines a range from the particular to the typical, from the character who is irreducibly individual to those like Don Quixote who embody certain values.

Moses strains against this order. In fact, aspects of his character could be placed on any of the categories' extremes. He is the most particular of all biblical personalities, but his birth is symbolic.[3] He is psychologically rich enough to have been analysed by Freud himself, but we have been noting how the text hitherto resists such study.[4] The change is great from nobleman to semi-nomad, but for this son of the Patriarchs it is more an act of conformity than of individuation.

The characterization of Moses is difficult because it is so fixed in the very unfolding of the story. Moses knows and reveals himself only insofar as God reveals himself. His birth story has already shown how he and Israel can be two faces of the same reality.[5] Now we can

so) = Ju 17,11'. P. Joüon ('Notes de lexicographie hébraïque—II הואיל', *MUSJ* 6 [1913], p. 162) translates it here as 'began'.

1. J. Ewen, *Character in Narrative* (Tel Aviv: Sifriat Poalim, 1986), pp. 33-44 (Hebrew).

2. *Character*, p. 33.

3. See that heading in Chapter 4.

4. For an evaluation of Freud's conclusion about Exod. 1–2 that Moses was an Egyptian nobleman by birth, see Zeligs, *Moses*, especially pp. 26-27. Zeligs's own theory, borrowing from O. Rank and H. Sachs, is that the chapters are a blend of the myth of the birth of a hero and the 'family romance myth', a typical boyhood fantasy that reflects the loss of idealization of the parents and manifests itself in the conviction that the parents are not really his (pp. 28-29).

5. 'Narrative Symmetry' in Chapter 4 disagrees with D.W. Wicke, and holds that Israel gains its identity just as Moses' is confused. Play on the word בן signifies the relation.

recognize as well the union between his character and the scripture traditionally attributed to him.[1] The traditional identification is true in the narrative as in the maxim: Moses is the Torah and the Torah is Moses.

8. *Conclusions*

Looking beyond Egypt and the Israelites, the pericope continues to investigate the twinned themes of oppression and self-understanding, the former of which has already been linked to disturbed human relations, and the latter to the knowledge of God. Moses' rescue of the women advances the first theme by further defining the Israelites' liberation as an act that consolidates society from an historical foundation, since it places Moses both in the stream of his own people's past and within an ordered community as husband and son-in-law. But any fuller development of Moses' narrative presence is commensurate with his mission. A postlapsarian man of God in a morally ambiguous world, Moses projects a human complexity that grows apace with his godliness in the process of restoring truth through the experience of the Exodus. He is evaluated in relation to God like the midwives and Pharaoh,[2] and stands to him as the most radically contingent. In this way he is 'very meek, more than all men that were on the face of the earth' (Num. 12.3).

1. R. Martin-Achard, 'Moïse, figure du médiateur selon l'Ancien Testament', in *La figure de Moïse: Ecriture et relectures* (ed. R. Martin-Achard *et al.*; Geneva: Publications de la Faculté de théologie de l'Université de Genève, 1978), p. 9. He says that a close relation exists between the three fundamental elements of biblical revelation: the Pentateuch, Israel and Moses. They have a common origin and destiny according to the Old Testament. He also cites the maxim to follow.

2. See the 'Conclusions' of Chapter 3. The midwives cooperate with God in fearlessness and reverence, and so prefigure the new covenant. Pharaoh usurps God's dominion over life and death, and so loses control over events.

Chapter 7

EXODUS 2.23-25

1. *Literal Translation*

23a	In [the course of] these many days,
23b	the king of Egypt died.
23c	The Israelites groaned from the work
23d	and cried out,
23e	and their call went up to God from the work.
24a	God heard their moaning,
24b	and God remembered his covenant with Abraham, with Isaac and with Jacob.
25a	God saw the Israelites
25b	and God knew.

Notes on the Literal Translation

Verse 23c, e. מן העבדה: 'from the work'. The literal translation makes for awkward English in the first case especially, but at least plainly brings across the repetition. In 'groaned from the work', the preposition designates the logical cause,[1] and could be more elegantly rendered with something like 'because'. In 'their call went up to God from the work', מן together with אל is directional.[2]

The translation offered for the words of lamentation will be explained along with their connotations in the 'Vocabulary' section.

Verse 25b. וידע אלהים: 'and God knew'. This half-verse is one of the most discussed in the two chapters and a challenge to translators. The Septuagint reads καὶ ἐγνώσθη αὐτοῖς, 'he made himself known to them', which would give ויוודע (*niph.*). Most accept the Masoretic

1. *HALAT*, II, p. 566; Williams, *Hebrew Syntax*, §319.
2. *HALAT*, II, p. 565: '[Es] bezeichnet d[ie] Richtung e[iner] Bewegung'.

Text, but choose circumlocutions: 'cared for kept in mind',[1] 'sorgte sich (um sie)',[2] 'tat sich kund',[3] 'trok zich hun lot aan'.[4] I have kept the basic translation to give relief to the repetition of ידע, used already in 1.8.

In Chapter 2 I adduced Huffmon, who argues that the verb ידע has parallels in Hittite treaty passages and so could mean 'recognize by covenant'. If one accepts this hypothesis, וידע could be linked closer to זכר את ברית.

2. *Delimitation*

This pericope begins with an expression of time (ויהי בימים הרבים ההם) much like the opening clause of an earlier pericope (2.11: ויהי בימים ההם). As mentioned in the last chapter, the narration time[5] and the setting shift, the first to a long range, and the second back to Egypt. The characters are those we last encountered in 2.11-15, the Pharaoh and the Hebrews. In the next pericope, announced by a ס as a סתומא, the action will suddenly return to Midian.

3. *Narrative Structure*

Deep

The basic functions of the plot are obvious: 'cry–response'. This deep structure is new for the simple reason that the actions are unprecedented.

Surface

Like the prelude 1.1-7, this passage is not a fully developed narrative.[6] The prelude had no tension. This unit borrows it from the story told so far. But both 1.1-7 and 2.23-25 do advance the plot. After

1. D.W. Thomas, 'A Note on וידע אלהים in Exod. II.25', *JTS* 49 (1948), p. 143.
2. Weimar, *Berufung*, p. 374.
3. Schmidt, *Exodus*, p. 77.
4. Houtman, *Exodus*, p. 304.
5. About the meaning of this idea, refer to the section on the 'Complication' in 'Narrative Structure, Surface', Chapter 4.
6. Fokkelman ('Exodus', p. 58) says that the primary function of both units is 'articulative' to frame the short stories of Exod. 1–2.

Joseph's death at the beginning of the Book, the divine promises from Genesis nourished the Israelites and they proliferated; now Pharaoh dies and the Israelites begin to cry out in despair.

The plot development around the issues of life and death constitutes a thematic inclusion that braces the entire two chapters and adds to the delimiting signs noted in the Introduction.

At the end of the unit, God notices the Israelites' plight and so brings the inherited tension to a turning point. By returning just then to Midian and Moses' shepherding, the narrative tarries over the suspense and makes the surface structure a bridge between Exodus 1–2 and Exodus 3.

4. *Point of View*

As in the last pericope in Midian, the point of view is external. This outside focalization never penetrates the Israelites: we are aware that they are in misery because of their cries, but we have no interior view of their state of mind. Instead we have special access to God. We know that 'God remembered...and God knew' (vv. 24b; 25b).

With the midwives in 1.20, God intervened silently; we learned nothing of his thoughts: 'God dealt well with the midwives; the people increased and became very strong'. Now we see briefly within his mind, and his salvation is all the more to be hoped for.

5. *Narrative Symmetry*

The most notable symmetry in these three verses is the disposition of the diction according to the deep structure described above. Four words or expressions communicate the 'cry' and four the 'response': אנח (*niph.*), זעק, עלה שועה אל and נאקה; and שמע, זכר את ברית, ראה and ידע. The words for crying all precede those for responding except for נאקה and שמע: וישמע אלהים את־נאקתם (v. 24a). The reverse order there forms a small chiasm that ties the two fields together, giving some structure to the newly intensified relation between God and his people.

The balance in the verbs is replicated in the nouns, and to the same effect: אלהים or האלהים appears five times, and five is also the sum of the two occurrences of בני ישׂראל and the three Patriarchs, Abraham, Isaac and Jacob.[1]

Greenberg also points out that the four clauses concerning God (vv. 24-25) are in parallelism: a verb of sensation is followed by one of mental activity: 'heard–saw'; 'remembered–knew'. He does not attempt to explain the effect of this pattern. It might be to demonstrate the quality of God's actions here, which, as we will see, are at once cognitive and real.

6. *Vocabulary*

Familiar and new semantic fields are represented:

Family: אברהם, יצחק, יעקב
Nationality: מלך מצרים, בני ישׂראל
Affliction: מות, עבודה (2×), אנח (*niph.*), זעק, שׁועה, נאקה
Motion: עלה . . . אל . . . מן
Perception: שׁמע, זכר, ראה, ידע
Divinity: אלהים, ברית

The large number of words in the field of 'Affliction' here recalls their frequency at the beginning of the oppression: 'The Egyptians made the Israelites work with rigour. They made their life bitter with hard work, with mortar and with bricks and with every work in the field, all their work which they had done by them with rigour' (1.13-14). At that time the words preceded a new measure against the Israelites, the order to the midwives. Now they are answered by God's response.

Broadcast by words with specific resonances, the cries of the Israelites will guide us deeper into the pericope. The first thing to notice is that the text does not say the Israelites are praying. (Hence there is no semantic field of 'Communication'.) Their petitions reach God, but they are not overtly directed to him. In fact, unlike other words such as בקשׁ (*pi.*), שׁאל or דרשׁ, the terms here imply no relation between the one crying and the one cried to.[2]

The first three words for crying in v. 23 mount a scale of intensity.

1. Greenberg (*Understanding Exodus*, p. 55) calls the effect of the short clauses about God 'iterative', like 'a tolling bell'.

2. R.N. Boyce, *The Cry to God in the Old Testament* (SBLDS, 103; Atlanta: Scholars Press, 1988), p. 14.

The first, אנח (*niph.*), is an 'inarticulate exclamation' lacking explicit content, beyond a mere reaction to pain.[1] It is not an attempt to reach someone who can perhaps help. זעק is more an appeal; it is both a cry of pain and a cry for help, and one aspect or the other dominates, depending on the situation.[2] שועה is most specific, unambiguously meaning a cry for help.[3] Combined here with אל...מן, it is also the most closely aimed at a rescuer. נאקה is less precise, but it is the word that 'hooks' the others to God's response by means of the chiasm noted in 'Narrative Symmetry' above.[4]

זעק joins the list of many words in Exodus 1–2 that can have juridical overtones.[5] It is at times associated with the salvation expressed by ישע (*hiph.*),[6] and so looks forward to that root in Exod. 14.13, 30 when God saves Israel. In the meantime, it harmonizes with God's hearing and seeing; for שמע and ראה can mean taking cognizance of a misdeed.[7]

שמע is in turn matched by זכר, which, by its very meaning 'to remember', brings this legal accent into the present.[8] The next part of the vocabulary study will show how the words of this episode fix it as a bridge between what is past and what is to come. It is a moment of

1. Boyce, *Cry*, p. 19. Cf. also R. Albertz, 'צעק *ṣ'q* schreien', *THAT*, II, p. 569. Incidentally זעק differs from צעק in an orthographic or dialectical way only: Boyce, *Cry*, p. 8; Albertz, 'צעק', p. 568; G.F. Hasel, 'זעק *zā'aq* צעק *ṣā'aq*', *ThWAT*, II, pp. 629-30.

2. Albertz, 'צעק', p. 570; Boyce, *Cry*, pp. 22, 67.

3. Boyce, *Cry*, p. 18.

4. It is also the verb used in the second account of Moses' call in 6.5.

5. Daube, *Exodus Pattern*, p. 27. Hasel, 'זעק', p. 633: It can be a cry for the 'Rechtshilfe' of the king, as in 1 Kgs 20.39 (cf. 2 Sam. 14.4); 2 Kgs 6.26; 8.3, 5. Or it can be addressed to the community: 2 Sam 13.19; Isa. 5.7; Jer. 20.8; Job 19.7; 31.38-40; Prov. 21.13. The juridical-sociological sphere of meaning can overlap with the religious-theological.

6. Boecker, *Redeformen*, pp. 62-66. Note also the comments on ישע (*hiph.*) in 'Vocabulary and Characterization' in Chapter 6, where we noted that it would be wrong to associate Moses' activity too closely with God's later intervention.

7. Bovati, *Ristabilire*, p. 58 n. 16, citing this verse.

8. Boecker, *Redeformen*, p. 109: The word does not imply a 'romantischen Sich-Zurückversetzen in die Vergangenheit'. Rather, '[d]er Bezug auf Vergangenes, der mit זכר fraglos in irgendeiner Weise intendiert ist, hat im Zusammenhang mit dem Rechtsverfahren den Sinn, Fakten und Ereignisse der Vergangenheit als Rechtsgrundlage für die Rechtsentscheidung in der Gegenwart heranzuziehen'.

short but brilliant intensity both for the Israelites and for God. It enlivens the past and gives a foretaste of the future.

First note the sheer number of times that the verbs שמע, זכר and ראה occur also in Genesis to indicate the paternal relationship of God to his suffering people.[1] Thus God remembered Noah (8.1; also 9.15, 16), Abraham with regard to Lot (19.29), Rachel who was barren (30.22), Leah who was afflicted (29.31), and the suffering Jacob (31.12, 42). He heard the oppression of Hagar (16.11), the voices of Ishmael (21.17), Leah (29.33) and Rachel (30.6), and the prayer of these women (30.17, 22). He saw the affliction of Leah (29.31, 32), of Jacob (31.42), of Sarah (16.13 [disputed text]) and of Abraham (22.14 [disputed text]).

In his rescue at the well, Moses repeated the actions of the Patriarchs and gained some consistency with history in preparation for the authority that is to be given him. By contrast, God who sees, hears and remembers here is repeating himself, demonstrating his self-consistency and hence his authority over time itself.

Except in Amos 1.9, ברית is the object of זכר only when God is the subject.[2] It is not an abstract notion, but a commitment to do or give something definite.[3] When God remembers his covenant made long ago, he is not just performing a mental act—he is in action.[4] And he is working now, approaching his people with salvation.

But the expression also extends the past into the present.[5] With this phrase, God reveals himself not in an absolutely new way, but rather in continuity with the past. זכר את ברית here refers to the covenant as God's current self-engagement within history on behalf of his people as represented by the three patriarchs. And so we are reminded of what Exodus has already said: through the ordered genealogy of the

1. As Cassuto did (*Commentary*, p. 29), although his list is incomplete. When God remembers, he does so only in matters related or important to humankind (H. Eising, 'זכר *zākar*', *ThWAT*, II, p. 578).

2. W. Schottroff, '*Gedenken' im Alten Orient und im Alten Testament*: *Die Wurzel zākar im semitischen Sprachkreis* (WMANT, 15; Neukirchen–Vluyn: Neukirchener Verlag, 1964), p. 202.

3. E. Kutsch, 'Sehen und Bestimmen: Die Etymologie von ברית', in *Archäologie und Altes Testament* (Festschrift K. Galling; ed. A. Kusche and E. Kutsch; Tübingen: Mohr, 1970), p. 170.

4. Schottroff, *Gedenken*, p. 339, 209.

5. H. Gross, 'Zur Wurzel zkr', *BZ* ns 4 (1960), p. 229.

ancestors (1.1-7) and Moses' imitation of the patriarchs (2.16-22) we have learned that history in Exodus 1–2 is the proof of God's mercy and the ground of responsible freedom.[1]

ברית is a complex biblical phenomenon.[2] The object of much debate, it can be a broadly legal matter in the profane sphere;[3] in all domains it indicates a commitment[4] largely defined by context.[5] The context here is the promises made to the patriarchs, sealed forever.[6] When the patriarchs are mentioned in relation to the memory of the covenant, it does not mean that God will act because of those who are dead, but rather that their names will be witnesses to his free and present faithfulness to his own word.[7]

In Genesis 17, the covenant made with Abraham was threefold. It held out fertility, land and God's promise to be their God. Exodus 1, of course, has fulfilled the first clause, and Chapter 1 above saw the similarity of vocabulary. Here the covenant refers to another of the three elements. The entrance into the land lies in the future, but God's presence is real now, incipient in his very act of turning to the covenant.

The verb ראה builds onto these points. It is juridical, as mentioned. In the sense of 'to look upon sympathetically, to care for', it is also

1. See 'Repetition and Narrative Gaps' in Chapter 1, and 'Repetition' and 'Conclusions' in Chapter 6.

2. D.J. McCarthy, 'Covenant-relationships', *Questions disputées d'Ancien Testament: Méthode et théologie* (ed. C. Brekelmans; BETL, 33; Louven: Presses Universitaires, 1974), p. 103: 'As an amalgam of negotiations, of relationships specified, of signs relating to all parties, covenant cannot be reduced to any one element in the whole nor to any aspect of its total meaning, however important that aspect may be in a given case'. Also J. Barr, 'Some Semantic Notes on the Covenant', in *Beiträge zur Alttestamentlichen Theologie* (Festschrift W. Zimmerli; ed. H. Donner *et al.*; Göttingen: Vandenhoeck & Ruprecht, 1977), p. 31. D.J. McCarthy (*Treaty and Covenant: A Study in Form in the Ancient Oriental Documents and in the Old Testament* [AnBib, 21A; Rome: Pontificium Institutum Biblicum, 2nd edn, 1978], pp. 1-24) gives a survey of the issue.

3. McCarthy, 'Covenant-relationships', p. 91 n. 2: 'Because it was stylized, publically known, and enforceable, covenant may be properly called a legal matter'.

4. McCarthy, 'Covenant-relationships', p. 17.

5. Barr, 'Covenant', p. 37, citing Kutsch.

6. M. Weinfeld, 'ברית', *ThWAT*, I, p. 799.

7. Schottroff, *Gedenken*, p. 211.

parallel to זכר and ידע according to P.A.H. de Boer and H. Yalon.[1] And so it recalls its previous uses to express the pity of the mother and the princess for the infant Moses (2.2, 6) and of Moses for the Hebrews who toiled under burdens and beatings (2.11 [2×]).

It also looks ahead. The angel of the Lord will soon 'appear' to Moses (3.2), who 'looks' and says to himself that he will 'see this great sight' (המראה), then is afraid to 'look at God' (3.6) who has 'seen the Israelites' oppression' (3.9).[2] As זכר את ברית links the past and the present to God's imminent action, ראה bridges the past and the future.

The mention of the patriarchs' names is also a narrative technique to locate the unit historically. It looks back to the stories of the men themselves in Genesis, including the promises made to them, and it looks ahead to their frequent mention in the rest of the Exodus story (Exod. 3.6, 15, 16; 4.5; 6.3, 8).

Seen in the context of all these words, וידע can be more easily accepted as it stands in the Masoretic Text at 2.25b. For Lacocque, the very absence of an object obliges us to consider the full force of the verb.[3] It does not mean a theoretical act of thought, but rather a practical relation with the object known.[4] This tallies well with the participation of God implied in זכר את ברית. And so וידע forms a contrasting inclusio with 1.8: the new king did not know of Joseph and brutalized the relations between the Egyptians and the Israelites.

To close this vocabulary study, one should turn to Exod. 3.7-12, in which many of the words in 2.23-25 and others from earlier in Exodus 1–2 are taken up in God's direct speech:

> I have seen (ראה ראיתי) the affliction of my people (עמי) who are in Egypt (מצרים), and their cry have I heard (ואת צעקתם שמעתי) because of their taskmasters; I know (ידעתי) their sufferings. I will descend to save them from the hand (להצילו מיד) of Egypt and to bring them up from that land (ולהעלות מן־הארץ ההוא)...And now, behold, the cry of the Israelites has

1. Cf. P.A.H. de Boer (*Gedenken und Gedächtnis in der Welt des Alten Testaments* [Stuttgart: Kohlhammer, 1962], p. 32), who cites the prayer of Hannah in 1 Sam. 1.11, which also contains all three verbs; H. Yalon, 'The Meaning of ידע, למד', *Tarbiz* 36 (1966–67), p. 396 (Hebrew); G.J. Botterweck ('ידע *jāda*'', *ThWAT*, III, p. 491) notes the coincidence of that verb and ראה in Gen. 18.21; Deut. 4.35; 1 Sam. 6.9; 18.23; Isa. 5.19; Ps. 31.8.

2. See 'Vocabulary' in Chapter 4.

3. *Devenir*, p. 69.

4. Schottroff ('ידע', *THAT*, I, p. 690), already cited in Chapter 2.

> come (הנה צעקת בני־ישׂראל באה) to me, and I have seen (וגם ראיתי) the oppression with which Egypt oppresses them. Now go (לכה), I will send you to Pharaoh (ואשׁלחך אל פרעה) that you may bring out (והוציא) my people, the Israelites (עמי בני־ישׂראל) from Egypt... You will serve (תעבדון) God on this mountain.

And later one finds at 6.5: 'Moreover I have heard the moaning of the Israelites (וגם אני שׁמעתי את־נאקת בני ישׂראל) whom Egypt makes work (מצרים מעבדים), and I have remembered my covenant (ואזכר את־בריתי)'.

7. *Conclusions*

This final unit of Exodus 1–2 summarizes many of the previous themes and announces others to come. In preparation for Moses' call, it fixes the positions of those between whom he will mediate, as in a dramatic tableau. The Israelites are poised in attitudes of petition; God is nearby, solicitous but no less supreme.

God's actions are unambiguous, and hence different from the unfocused picture of Moses in the last pericope and the inarticulate cry of the people. His actions draw on the past, excite the present and presage the future. Anticipated and represented by his successful intervention with the midwives, they will also be efficacious.

CONCLUSION

1. *Overview of Narrative Elements*

After reading the pericopes in order, it is good to look back over Exodus 1–2 as a whole. The aspects of the narrative that we have already examined singly combine in overarching patterns of textual design. These reinforce the ideological thrust of the units.

Narrative Structure

Deep. The deep structures of the pericopes all divide most rewardingly into double or triple functions. These have been:

> the second halves of
> (danger)–escape from danger,
> (promise)–fulfilment (*the prelude*: 1.1-7),
>
> problem–attempted solution–result (Pharaoh's speech and the beginning of the oppression: 1.8-14),
>
> (problem from 1.8-14)–attempted solution–result (*the story of the midwives*: 1.15-22),
>
> danger–escape from danger (*the birth of Moses*: 2.1-10),
>
> wrong–wrong punished,
> accusation–counter accusation and
> danger–escape from danger (*all three about Moses in the workfields and his escape*: 2.11-15),
>
> exploit–exploit rewarded (*Moses at the well*: 2.16-22)
>
> cry–response (*the conclusion*: 2.23-25)

The two sets of functions, 'problem–attempted solution–result' and 'danger–escape from danger', both occur twice. 'Danger–escape from danger' is also the deep structural link between Genesis 50 and Exod. 1.1-7. But in all, the deep structures are more varied than consistent, and the unity of the chapters rests on other elements.

Surface. Nor is the surface structure of tension integral. No single turning point and climax overshadows the others, perhaps because no one character monopolizes the action.

The pericopes vary along the scale of structural complexity. The first has no suspense. The second has suspense, relaxation, then more suspense. The third has the same pattern, except that the second suspense is greater than the first. The fourth has five full stages of dramatic presentation.

The next three units progressively allow greater scope for relief of tension. The fifth has none until after the second climax, when the story regains equilibrium. The sixth also has two climaxes, but there is relief between them and a final equilibrium. The seventh has no new tension, but ends at the turning point.

Point of View

The focalization remains external throughout the chapters, although on five occasions it takes the liberty of scanning within characters.[1] The focalization is often an instrument to marshal the audience's perception and judgment of the characters. In the first pericope, it becomes fixed in time. Then it can moderate our empathy for the Hebrews in the second unit and stimulate our sympathy in the third. It signifies the ethical ambiguity of the fourth and fifth pericopes. The strict reserve in the sixth adds to the complexity of Moses' characterization. Its access to the mind of God heightens the suspense of the final unit.

Narrative Symmetry

Ackerman presents and explains a graphic representation of the symmetry of the two chapters:[2]

1. See especially 'Point of View' in Chapter 2, and 'Point of View and Narrative Gaps' in Chapter 4.
2. 'Literary Context', pp. 109-12.

For Ackerman, the first two units belong together as an introduction because in both a Genesis story is alluded to, Israel is passive, God is behind the scenes, and the fivefold repeated root עבד in 1.13-14 matches the five verbs for proliferation in 1.7. Our analysis has shown, however, that all of Genesis is a sounding board for Exodus 1, not just the story of Creation and the Tower of Babel. God remains hidden in other pericopes, in fact until the end of the two chapters, with the brief exception of his intervention for the midwives. And while עבד may contrast with the verbs of proliferation, it also recurs inconveniently outside Ackerman's pattern in 2.23-25, as do the verbs of fertility in 1.15-22.

Ackerman sets the pericope of the midwives with that of Moses and the two Hebrews (1.15-21; 2.11-15). He and they act against injustice. For Ackerman, the craven remark of the Hebrew wrongdoer clashes with the midwives' bravery, establishing two opposing types within the Hebrew community. Pharaoh's attempt to kill Moses parallels his earlier command against all Hebrew newborn males. However, by comparing Moses to the midwives, Ackerman lessens Moses' failure in the workfields. And he ignores the more revealing parallel between the language of Moses and Pharaoh.

Neither do the birth and the Midian scenes (2.1-10, 16-22) line up as closely as Ackerman hopes. They do involve one family, water and the misuse of power. Both end in a name-giving. But he ignores the important repetition by Moses of his ancestors' deeds in 2.16-22. The semantic fields are very different. (We noted the absence in 2.16-22 of the important field of 'Perception'.) And we have seen in Chapter 6 on 2.16-22 that its points of contrast with 2.11-15 are thematically richer than those in common with the birth story in 2.1-10.

Ackerman has tried too hard to find an all-encompassing symmetry. For the sake of tidiness, he has simplified a complex network of thematic and linguistic correlations that runs from Genesis through Exodus 1–2 and into the rest of the Exodus story.

A great part of this study has scrutinized the internal workings of the pericopes and their particular place in the train of events. As Buber remarked, the continuity of the events is more important to the original narrator of Exodus than the individual units.[1] Looking back

1. *Moïse*, pp. 21-22.

now from the height of the conclusion, one sees a vaster range of congruencies.

A loose similarity pairs off many of the incidents in Exodus 1–2 and weaves a strong but unobtrusive web among the seven pericopes. The Israelites and the Egyptians are both a 'people'. The Egyptians shudder in horror (קוץ) at the Israelites, the princess has compassion (חמל) on the Israelite baby. There are two scenes by the water, one when Moses is saved, the other when he saves the maidens. He rescues them, they report on his action. He fails in Egypt, he succeeds in Midian. The new Pharaoh arose, Moses arose at the well. The new Pharaoh did not know Joseph, God did know. Joseph and Pharaoh died. Joseph and Moses, two egyptianized Israelites, are responsible for the arrival and departure of Israel in Egypt.[1] Moses is rejected by his own people in Egypt, then welcomed by foreigners in Midian. He flees his adoption in Pharaoh's household and enters a marriage in that of the Midianite priest. His parents had married; he does too.

In addition, Fox notices that almost every key event in Moses' early life foreshadows Israel's experience later in Exodus: the rescue from death by royal decree, the escape by water, the flight into the desert, and the encounter with God on the sacred mountain.[2]

This doublet pattern makes for the unity of the chapters. It also gives a design to events, a context of coherence that announces and prepares for the element of meaningfulness in all this suffering, the providence of God.

Vocabulary

In his book on Exodus 3–4, Fischer found that the semantic fields of those chapters fell together such that one field dominated in each of four sections.[3] Exodus 1–2 has a less tidy disposition of vocabulary. Some fields are repeated throughout the chapters; others are peculiar to a single pericope. The largest and most widely diffused semantic fields are 'Fertile Life and Family', 'Nationality', 'Affliction' and 'Perception'. The first often uses vocabulary from Genesis, and

1. Buber, *Moïse*, p. 26.

2. *Names*, p. 5.

3. Fischer, *Jahwe unser Gott*, pp. 67-83, with a summary scheme on p. 82. The fields and the sections where each is dominant are: 'Sehen' (3.1-9); 'Sendung' (3.10-22); 'Glaubwürdigkeit' (4.1-9); 'Sprechen' (4.10-17).

'Perception' is a common field later in Exodus.[1] Through these words here, life and death are confronted, and questions are raised about discerning providence and penetrating the consciousness of Moses and the Israelites.

Key words give specificity to these issues. Near the beginning (1.8-14) and at the end (2.23-25), עבד directs attention to the purpose of the Israelites' and Moses' struggle for existence. ידע is an important word, more for its wealth of connotation than its frequency.[2] ראה is more common[3] and perhaps is punned with ירא.[4] The forceful presence of these words presses the question of God's mysteriousness and invisibility here, and hints at his awesome intervention soon to be described in the same language. קרא is another much-used word in various pericopes, perhaps as preparation for the call of Moses (3.4) and the giving of the Name.[5]

As for the many juridical words, they underline the notion that oppression is a matter of injustice and that it can be remedied only by a renewed moral vision of the world.[6] Frye comments that the narrative sequence of the Hebrew Bible, in which the giving of the law at Sinai follows the Exodus so closely, is 'logically and psychologically' correct.[7] 'A shared crisis gives a community a sense of involvement with its own laws, customs, and institutions, a sense of being a people set apart.' A people that has known revolution takes on a deductive way of thinking which is often encoded in constitutional law. Frye proposes the Americans' reverence for their constitution as a parallel to the Bible's sense of Israel as a people created by its law.

1. See 'Vocabulary' in Chapters 1 and 4.
2. It is found in 1.8; 2.4, 25.
3. 1.16; 2.2, 5, 6, 11 (2×); 12.25.
4. 1.17, 21; 2.14.
5. 1.18; 2.7, 8, 10, 20, 22, to which, for completeness, one adds a probable occurrence of קרא II = קרה in 1.10.
6. In 1.8-14 these were ענה (*pi.*), בפרך and הבה; in the birth story (2.1-10) נער and the adoption formula היה ל ל. In the account of Moses' efforts at justice in Egypt (2.11-15) we noted ראה, למה, רשע, רע (*rēa'*), שים, שופט, הרג, שמע and דבר. In 1.18 Pharaoh asked the midwives a legal-style 'Beschuldigungsformel'. In 2.16-22 ישע (*hiph.*) can be a legal word.
7. *The Great Code*, p. 118.

2. *Thematic Synthesis*

The introduction to the study stated that its interpretative interest was to consider Exodus 1–2 rhetorically as a text that persuades its audience through its language and narrative techniques. The chapters' purpose is not just to transmit information, but also to win adherence to the ideology that informs the storytelling. This study has had regard for both the ways and ends of the text, or better, the harmonization of its argument and content. After scrutinizing the pericopes successively and laying bare the narrative strategies that have been summarized immediately above, we can now consider this ideology synthetically. The one condition is that we do not imagine ideology as something practically separable from the narrativity that shaped and bore it.

Fischer laid stress on the essential coherence and unity of Exodus 3–4 in the conclusion to his book.[1] No part may be subtracted without destroying the logic of the narrative. Exodus 1–2 has changes of scene and character that Exodus 3–4 does not. Its thematic unity is appropriately looser. Under the general principle that providence can derive good from evil (Gen. 50.20), three ideas are confederated in Exodus 1–2. This study does not try to prove that they hold throughout the Bible. But they are themes that later portions of Exodus will develop. And without adverting to them, any reading of these chapters would be incomplete.

History

In Exodus 1–2, the entire past is constitutive of the present under the lordship of the God of history. In Genesis, God worked mainly through intrafamily conflicts.[2] Now, in the process of revelation from Creation to the Exodus, he is preparing to intervene more directly. But he always builds the present on the past, even when his project is revolutionary, 'the salvation of YHWH, which he will do for you today' (Exod. 14.13). The Israelites act as foreseen in Genesis, and Moses is set within the context of his ancestors' ways. Hence the Exodus revolution has a quality of both liberation and rootedness. The

1. *Jahwe unser Gott*, pp. 201-202.
2. Fox, *Names*, p. 3.

Israelites are freed from oppression to live a life fully consonant with what is providential in their past.

Israel and Moses

It is unwise to psychologize the Bible, and it can be anachronistic to speak too freely about the 'identity' of Moses and the Israelites. But in a real sense, Exodus 1–2 is about the birthpains of Israel's self-awareness as a people. That is to say, their purpose, their place in the world, springs from God who will free them from servitude in Egypt to know and serve him.

Suffering and promise are the stimulants to consciousness here. The two chapters stress God's promise more than his love,[1] and this emphasis is worth recalling in relation to the ever-urgent mysteries of the presence of pain and the apparent absence of God from the world.

The full contingency upon God inherent in Moses' and Israel's identity is expressed more insistently in Moses' case, he whom the narrative presents obliquely as though present and foreshadowed at the same moment in the story. The difference between the energy of his interventions and the reticence of his characterization reflects the difference between God's will and our freedom.[2] This blurred picture of Moses develops through a series of separations from his parents, the Court and his 'brothers'. The same process will mark both the coming Plague Narrative, with its important distinctions between Israel and Egypt, and the entire Israelite legal and ritual system, which values holiness and separation.[3]

Justice

Through legal vocabulary that perhaps anticipates the importance of law later in Exodus, stress falls on the oppression of the Hebrews as a matter of injustice. Therefore liberation will not be just an escape from cruelty, but an initiation into a sharper moral vision of things that focuses on the acknowledgment of God's supremacy in history

1. Gunn, 'Hardening of Pharaoh's Heart', p. 82.

2. According to Walzer (*Exodus and Revolution*, p. 82), the Book of Exodus invented what political scientists now call 'positive freedom', true but not unrestrained.

3. So Fox (*Names*, p. 17), who nonetheless speaks more of 'personality changes' in Moses than of techniques in his characterization. See also p. xxxiv.

and of his people's service of him. In the meantime, the confusion of Moses' upbringing and of his actions in the workfields shows the ambiguity inherent in any situation of injustice, where right and wrong will always overlap.

3. *Conclusion*

These truths are not astonishing. Some, like God's role in history, are biblical commonplaces. What the present essay brings to the study of Scripture is the demonstration that such truths lie embedded in the deceptively simple narrative of Exodus 1–2. This work has also contributed to refining the methodology of synchronic criticism by making fully eclectic use of various tools like rhetorical analysis and structural formalism. It has shown that one can use common sense to apply elements of literary criticism to the Bible and still treat it as a unique and theological book. No one methodology answers all the questions asked by a text, and no experience of reading can fully satisfy. Each reading is a pledge to engage the text again.

APPENDIX

Combinations in Genesis of Key-Words in Exodus 1.1-7

Genesis	שרץ	פרה	רבה	מלא	ארץ	עצם	במאוד מאוד
1.20	×				×		
1.22		×	× (2×)	×	×		
1.28		×	×	×	× (2×)		
6.11				×	× (2×)		
6.13				×	× (2×)		
7.17			×		× (2×)		
7.18			×		×		
7.21	× (2×)				× (2×)		
8.17	×	×	×		× (3×)		
9.1		×	×	×	×		
9.7		×	× (2×)		×		
17.2			×				×
17.6		×					×
17.20		×	×				×
18.18					×	×	
26.4			×		× (2×)		
26.22		×			×		
28.3		×	×		×		
35.11		×	×				
41.52		×			×		
47.27		×	×		× (2×)		
48.4		×	×		×		

Notes

This is a chart of the words' occurrences together, not alone. The verse of the MT has been chosen arbitrarily as the unit of analysis.

The expression במאוד מאוד is used in Genesis only in combination with one or two of the other key words: רבה (17.2), פרה (17.6) and both together (17.20).

In Genesis, the verb עצם is used only with ארץ (18.18) and מאוד (26.16).

The phrase 'to fill the earth' is common in the Old Testament. Before Exod. 1.1-7 it is found twice as an imperative (1.28; 9.1; of water: 1.22) and twice as an affirmation that the earth was filled with violence (6.11 is a *niphal wayyiqtol*, as in Exod. 1.7. Gen. 6.13 is a *qal qatal*).

The combination of פרה, רבה and מלא is used three times before Exod. 1.1-7: Gen. 1.22 (of every creaturely life); 1.28 (of mankind); 9.1 (of Noah).

BIBLIOGRAPHY

Abrams, M.H., *A Glossary of Literary Terms* (New York: Holt, Rinehart & Winston, 3rd edn, 1971 [1941]).

Ackerman, J.S., 'The Literary Context of the Moses Birth Story (Exodus 1–2)', in *Literary Interpretations of Biblical Narratives* (ed. K.R.R. Gros Louis *et al.*; Nashville: Abingdon Press, 1974), I, pp. 74-119.

Aejmelaeus, A., 'What Can we Know about the Hebrew *Vorlage* of the Septuagint?', *ZAW* 99 (1987), pp. 58-89.

—'Function and Interpretation of כי in Biblical Hebrew', *JBL* 105 (1986), pp. 193-209.

Ahuviah, A., '"I Will Bring you up from Egyptian Affliction"', *Beth Mikra* 74 (3) (April–June) (1978), pp. 301-303 (Hebrew).

Albertz, R., 'צעק *ṣ'q* schreien', *THAT*, II, pp. 568-75.

Albright, W.F., 'The Refrain "And God saw ki tob" in Genesis', *Mélanges bibliques* (Festschrift A. Robert; Travaux de l'Institut catholique de Paris, 4; Paris: Blond & Gay, 1957), pp. 22-26.

Aletti, J.-N., and J. Trublet, *Approche poétique et théologique des Psaumes: Analyses et méthodes* (Paris: Editions du Cerf, 1983).

Alonso-Schökel, L., 'Nota estilistica sobre la partícula הנה', *Bib* 37 (1956), pp. 74-80.

Alter, R., *The Art of Biblical Narrative* (New York: Basic Books 1981).

—'How Convention Helps us Read: The Case of the Bible's Annunciation Type-Scene', *Prooftexts* 3 (1983), pp. 115-30.

Amsler, S., 'קום *qūm* aufstehen', *THAT*, II, pp. 635-41.

Amusin, J.D., 'Die Gerim in der sozialen Legislatur des Alten Testaments', *Klio* 63 (1981), pp. 15-23.

Andersen, F.I., *The Sentence in Biblical Hebrew* (Janua Linguarum, Series Practica, 231; The Hague: Mouton, 1974).

Auzou, G., *De la servitude au service: Etude du livre de l'exode* (Connaissance de la bible, 3; Paris: L'Orante, 1961).

Avishur, Y., *Stylistic Studies of Word-Pairs in Biblical and Ancient Semitic Literatures* (AOAT, 210; Neukirchen–Vluyn: Neukirchener Verlag, 1984).

Balentine, S., 'A Description of the Semantic Field of Hebrew Words for "Hide"', *VT* 30 (1980), pp. 137-53.

Bar-Efrat, S., 'Some Observations on the Analysis of Structure in Biblical Narrative', *VT* 30 (1980), pp. 154-73.

—*The Art of Narration in the Bible* (Tel Aviv: Sifriat Poalim, 2nd edn, 1984 [1979]) (Hebrew).

Barr, J., *Biblical Words for Time* (SBT, First Series, 33; London: SCM Press, 2nd edn, 1969 [1962]).

—'The Symbolism of Names in the Old Testament', *BJRL* 52 (1969–70), pp. 11-29.

—'Some Semantic Notes on the Covenant', in *Beiträge zur Alttestamentlichen Theologie* (Festschrift W. Zimmerli; ed. H. Donner *et al.*; Göttingen: Vandenhoeck & Ruprecht, 1977), pp. 23-38.

—'Why? in Biblical Hebrew', *JTS* ns 36 (1985), pp. 1-33.

Baumgartner, W. *et al.* (eds.), *Hebräisches und Aramäisches Lexikon zum Alten Testament* (Leiden: Brill, 3rd edn, 1983 [1953]).

Becker, J., *Gottesfurcht im Alten Testament* (AnBib, 25; Rome: Pontificium Institutum Biblicum, 1965).

Ben-Reuven, S., 'בן in Contrast to ילד and ניר in the Bible', *Beth Mikra* 93 (2) (January–March) (1983), pp. 147-49 (Hebrew).

Berlin, A., 'On the Meaning of *rb* ', *JBL* 100 (1981), pp. 90-93.

—'Point of View in Biblical Narrative', in *A Sense of Text: The Art of Language in the Study of Biblical Literature* (*JQR* Supplement; Winona Lake, IN: Eisenbrauns, 1982), pp. 71-113.

—'On the Bible as Literature', *Prooftexts* 2 (1982), pp. 323-32.

Blank, S.H., 'Wisdom', *IDB*, IV, pp. 852-61.

Blau, J., 'Zum angeblichen Gebrauch von *'t* vor dem Nominativ', *VT* 4 (1954), pp. 7-19.

Bleich, D., 'Epistemological Assumptions in the Study of Response', in *Reader-Response Criticism: From Formalism to Post-Structuralism* (ed. J.P. Tompkins; Baltimore: Johns Hopkins University Press, 1980), pp. 134-63.

Boecker, H.J., *Redeformen des Rechtslebens im Alten Testament* (WMANT, 14; Neukirchen–Vluyn: Neukirchener Verlag, 1964).

Boer, P.A.H. de, *Gedenken und Gedächtnis in der Welt des Alten Testaments* (Stuttgart: Kohlhammer, 1962).

Bollnow, O.F., 'Die Welt der Symbole', in *Leben und Tod in den Religionen: Symbol und Wirklichkeit* (ed. G. Stephenson; Darmstadt: Wissenshaftliche Buchgesellschaft, 1985), pp. 1-14.

Boschi, B., *Esodo* (Nuovissima Versione della Bibbia dai Testi Originali, 2; Rome: Edizioni Paoline, 1978).

Botterweck, G.J., 'ידע *jāda'* ', *ThWAT*, III, pp. 486-512.

Bovati, P., *Ristabilire la Giustizia: Procedure, vocabolario, orientamenti* (AnBib, 110; Rome: Pontificium Institutum Biblicum, 1986).

Boyce, R.N., *The Cry to God in the Old Testament* (SBLDS, 103; Atlanta: Scholars Press, 1988).

Bratsiotis, N.P., 'איש', *ThWAT*, I, pp. 238-52.

Breck, J., 'Biblical Chiasmus: Exploring Structure for Meaning', *BTB* 17 (1987), pp. 70-74.

Bremond, C., 'La logique des possibles narratifs', *Communications* 8 (1966), pp. 60-76.

Brockelmann, C., *Hebräische Syntax* (Neukirchen: Moers, 1956).

Brongers, H.A., and A.S. van der Woude, 'Wat is de betekenis van *' ābnāyîm* in Exodus 1.16', *NedTTs* 20 (1965–66), pp. 241-54.

Brown, F., S.R. Driver and C.A. Briggs, *A Hebrew and English Lexicon of the Old Testament: With an Appendix Containing the Biblical Aramaic: Based on the Lexicon of William Gesenius as Translated by Edward Robinson* (Oxford: Clarendon Press, 1906).

Brueggemann, W., 'The Kerygma of the Priestly Writers', *ZAW* 84 (1972), pp. 397-414.

Buber, M., *Moïse* (trans. A. Kohn; Heidelberg: L. Schneider, 1952 [Paris: Presses Universitaires, 2nd edn, 1957]).

Bullinger, E.W., *Figures of Speech Used in the Bible: Explained and Illustrated* (Grand Rapids, MI: Baker, 1968 [London, 1898]).

Butler, T.C. 'An Anti-Moses Tradition', *JSOT* 12 (1979), pp. 9-15.

Carson, D.A., *Exegetical Fallacies* (Grand Rapids: Baker, 1984).

Casanowicz, I.M., *Paranamasia in the Old Testament* (dissertation, Boston, n.p., 1894).

Cassuto, U., *A Commentary on the Book of Exodus* (trans. I. Abrahams; Jerusalem: Magnes Press, 1967).

Cazeaux, J., 'Naître en Egypte: Exode 1–7,7—Etude littéraire', *RHPR* 60 (1980), pp. 401-27.

Cazelles, H., 'Aspirations à la justice dans le monde prébiblique: La réponse divine selon la révélation biblique', in *Autour de L'Exode (Etudes)* (SB; Paris: Gabalda, 1987 [1978]), pp. 371-87.

Ceresko, A.R., 'The Chiastic Word Pattern in Hebrew', *CBQ* 38 (1976), pp. 303-11.

Chatman, S., *Story and Discourse: Narrative Structure in Fiction and Film* (Ithaca, NY: Cornell University Press, 1978).

Chiesa, B., 'Sull'utilizzazione dell'*Aggadah* per la restituzione del testo ebraico in *Esodo* 1, 22', *Henoch* 1 (1979), pp. 342-52.

Childs, B.S., 'The Birth of Moses', *JBL* 84 (1965), pp. 109-22.

—*Biblical Theology in Crisis* (Philadelphia: Westminster Press, 1970).

—*The Book of Exodus: A Critical, Theological Commentary* (Philadelphia: Westminster Press, 1974).

—*Old Testament Theology in a Canonical Context* (Philadelphia: Fortress Press, 1985).

Chouraqui, A., *Noms* (La Bible, 2; Bruges: Desclée de Brouwer, 1974).

Clements, R.E., *Exodus* (Cambridge Bible Commentary; Cambridge: Cambridge University Press, 1972).

Clements, R.E., and H.-F. Fabry, 'מים *majim*', *ThWAT*, IV, pp. 843-66.

Clines, D.J.A., *The Theme of the Pentateuch* (JSOTSup, 10; Sheffield: JSOT Press, 1978).

Coats, G.W., 'A Structural Transition in Exodus', *VT* 22 (1972), pp. 129-42.

—'Moses in Midian', *JBL* 92 (1973), pp. 3-10.

—'The Moses Narrative as Heroic Saga', in *Saga, Legend, Tale, Novella, Fable: Narrative Forms in Old Testament Literature* (ed. G.W. Coats; JSOTSup, 35; Sheffield: JSOT Press, 1985), pp. 33-44.

—'Tale', in *Saga, Legend, Tale, Novella, Fable: Narrative Forms in Old Testament Literature* (ed. G.W. Coats; JSOTSup, 35; Sheffield: JSOT Press, 1985), pp. 63-70.

—*Moses: Heroic Man, Man of God* (JSOTSup, 57; Sheffield: JSOT Press, 1988).

Cogan, M., 'A Technical Term for Exposure', *JNES* 27 (1968), pp. 133-35.

Cohn, R.L., 'On the Art of Biblical Narrative', *BR* 31 (1986), pp. 13-18.

Cole, D., 'Obstetrics for the Women of Ancient Egypt', *Discussions in Egyptology* 5 (1986), pp. 27-33.

Conroy, C., *Absalom Absalom!: Narrative and Language in 2 Sam 13–20* (AnBib, 81; Rome: Pontificium Institutum Biblicum, 1978).

Cook, J., 'Text and Tradition: A Methodological Problem', *JNSL* 9 (1981), pp. 3-11.

Cordesse, G., 'Narration et Focalisation', *Poétique* 76 (1988), pp. 487-98.

Costacurta, B., *La vita minacciata: Il tema della paura nella Bibbia Ebraica* (AnBib, 119; Rome: Pontificium Institutum Biblicum, 1988).

Couroyer, B., 'A propos d'Exode, II, 14', *RB* 89 (1982), pp. 48-51.

Crown, A.D., 'An Alternative Meaning for איש in the Old Testament', *VT* 24 (1974), pp. 110-12.

Culley, R.C., *Studies in the Structure of Hebrew Narrative* (SBL Semeia Supplements, 3; Philadelphia: Fortress Press; Missoula, MT: Scholars Press, 1976).

—'Action Sequences in Genesis 2–3', *Semeia* 18 (1980), pp. 25-33.

Dahood, M., 'Ugaritic-Hebrew Syntax and Style', in *Ugarit-Forschungen*, I (ed. K. Bergerhof *et al.*; Neukirchen–Vluyn: Neukirchener Verlag, 1969).

—'Hebrew-Ugaritic Lexicography ix', *Bib* 52 (1971), pp. 348-49.

—'Vocative *Lamedh* in Exodus 2, 14 und [*sic*] Merismus in 34, 21', *Bib* 62 (1981), pp. 413-15.

Daube, D., *The Exodus Pattern in the Bible* (All Souls Studies, 2; London: Faber & Faber, 1963).

Dillmann, A., *Exodus und Leviticus* (Kurzgefasstes exegetisches Handbuch zum Alten Testament, 12; Leipzig: Hirzel, 3rd edn, 1897).

Döller, A., '"Obnajim" Ex. 1, 16', *BZ* 7 (1909), pp. 255-59.

Driver, G.R., 'Hebrew Mothers (Exodus i 19)', *ZAW* 67 (1955), pp. 246-49.

Durham, J.I., *Exodus* (WBC, 3; Waco, TX: Word Books, 1987).

Duvshani, M., 'Time in Biblical Narrative', *Beth Mikra* 73 (2) (January–March) (1978), pp. 224-36 (Hebrew).

Edelman, D., 'An Appraisal of Robert Alter's Approach', *BR* 31 (1986), pp. 19-25.

Ehrlich, A.B., *Randglossen zur Hebräischen Bibel: Textkritisches, Sprachliches, und Sachliches*. I. *Genesis und Exodus* (Leipzig: Hinrichs, 1908).

Eichrodt, W., *Theologie des Alten Testament*. II.3. *Gott und Mensch* (Stuttgart: Ehrenfried Klotz, 4th edn, 1961).

Eising, H., 'זכר *zākar* ', *ThWAT*, II, pp. 571-93.

Eliade, M., *Traité de l'histoire des religions* (Paris: Payot, 1949).

Ewen, J., *Character in Narrative* (Tel Aviv: Sifriat Poalim, 1980) (Hebrew).

Exum, J.C., '"You Shall Let Every Daughter Live": A Study of Exodus 1.8–2.10', *Semeia* 28 (1983), pp. 63-82.

Fichtner, J., 'Der Begriff des "Nächsten" im Alten Testament mit einem Ausblick auf Spätjudentum und Neues Testament', in *idem*, *Gottes Weisheit: Gesammelte Studien zum Alten Testament* (Arbeiten zur Theologie, 2.3; Stuttgart: Calwer, 1965), pp. 88-114.

Fischer, G., *Jahwe unser Gott: Sprache, Aufbau und Erzähltechnik in der Berufung des Mose (Ex. 3–4)* (OBO, 91; Freiburg: Universitätsverlag, 1989).

Fish, S.E., 'Literature in the Reader: Affective Stylistics', in *Reader-Response Criticism: From Formalism to Post-Structuralism* (ed. J.P. Tompkins; Baltimore: Johns Hopkins University Press, 1980), pp. 70-100.

Fishbane, M., *Text and Texture: Close Readings of Selected Biblical Texts* (New York: Schocken Books, 1979).

Fisher, L.R. (ed.), *Ras Shamra Parallels: The Texts from Ugarit and the Hebrew Bible*, I (AnOr, 49; Rome: Pontificium Institutum Biblicum, 1972); II (AnOr, 50; Rome: Pontificium Institutum Biblicum, 1975).

Fogle, S.F., 'Envelope', *Princeton Encyclopedia of Poetry and Poetics* (ed. A. Preminger *et al.*; Princeton: Princeton University Press, 2nd edn, 1974 [1965]), pp. 241-42.

Fokkelman, J.P., *Narrative Art in Genesis: Specimens of Stylistic and Structural Analysis* (Studia Semitica Neerlandica, 17; Assen: Van Gorcum, 1975).

—'Exodus', in *The Literary Guide to the Bible* (ed. R. Alter and F. Kermode; Cambridge, MA: Harvard University Press, 1987), pp. 56-65.

Fokkema, D.W., and E. Kunne-Ibsch, *Theories of Literature in the Twentieth Century:*

Structuralism, Marxism, Aesthetics of Reception, Semiotics (London: C. Hurst, 2nd edn, 1979 [1978]).

Fontinoy, C., 'La naissance de l'enfant chez les Israélites de l'Ancien Testament', in *L'enfant dans les civilisations orientales* (ed. A. Théodoridès *et al.*; Acta Orientalia Belgica, 2; Leuven: Peeters, 1980), pp. 103-18.

Fowl, S., 'The Ethics of Interpretation, or What's Left Over after the Elimination of Meaning' (SBLSP, 27; Atlanta: Scholars Press, 1988), pp. 69-81.

Fox, E., *Now These are the Names: A New English Rendition of the Book of Exodus* (New York: Schocken Books, 1986).

Freund, E., *The Return of the Reader: Reader-Response Criticism* (London: Methuen, 1987).

Frie, N., 'Symbol', *Princeton Encyclopedia of Poetry and Poetics* (ed. A. Preminger *et al.*; Princeton: Princeton University Press, 2nd edn, 1974 [1965]), pp. 833-36.

Frye, N., *The Great Code: The Bible and Literature* (New York: Harcourt, Brace & Jovanovich, 1981).

Fuchs, E., 'Who is Hiding the Truth? Deceptive Women and Biblical Androcentrism', in *Feminist Perspectives on Biblical Scholarship* (ed. A.Y. Collins; SBL Biblical Scholarship in North America, 10; Chico, CA: Scholars Press, 1985), pp. 137-44.

Fuhs, H.J., 'הרג *hārag*', *ThWAT*, II, pp. 483-94.

—'ירא *jāre'* ', *ThWAT*, III, pp. 870-93.

—'נער *na'ar*', *ThWAT*, V, pp. 507-18.

Gaboriau, F., *Le thème biblique de la connaissance: Etude d'une racine* (Paris: Desclée, 1969).

Gamberoni, J., 'ברח', *ThWAT*, I, pp. 778-81.

—'קוּם *qûm* ', *ThWAT*, VI, pp. 1252-74.

Gelio, R., 'È possible un *'îš* relativo/dimostrativo in ebraico biblico?', *RivB* 31 (1983), pp. 411-34.

Gemser, B., 'The *rîb*—or Controversy-Pattern in Hebrew Mentality', in *Wisdom in Israel and the Ancient Near East* (Festschrift H.H. Rowley; ed. M. Noth and D.W. Thomas; VTSup, 3; Leiden: Brill, 1955), pp. 120-37.

Genette, G., *Figures, III* (Paris: Editions du Seuil, 1972).

—*Nouveau discours du récit* (Paris: Editions du Seuil, 1983).

Gerstenberger, E.S., 'ענה II *'ānāh*', *ThWAT*, VI, pp. 247-70.

Gilead, H., 'Encounters at the Well', *Beth Mikra* 70 (1977), pp. 220-23 (Hebrew).

Görg, M., 'ישב *jāšab*', *ThWAT*, III, pp. 1012-32.

Goldberg, M., 'Exodus 1.13-14', *Int* 37 (1983), pp. 389-91.

Good, E.M., *Irony in the Old Testament* (Bible and Literature Series, 3; Sheffield: Almond Press, 2nd edn, 1981 [1965]).

Gottlieb, W., 'The Term "Nepes" in the Bible: A Re-appraisal', *Transactions of the Glasgow University Oriental Society* 25 (1973–74), pp. 71-84.

Greenberg, M., *Understanding Exodus* (Heritage of Biblical Israel, 2.5; New York: Behrman House, 1969).

Greenstein, E.L., 'Deconstruction and Biblical Narrative', *Prooftexts* 9 (1989), pp. 43-71.

Gross, H., 'Zur Wurzel *zkr*', *BZ* ns 4 (1960), pp. 227-37.

Gunn, D.M., 'The "Hardening of Pharaoh's Heart": Plot, Character and Theology in Exodus 1–14', in *Art and Meaning: Rhetoric in Biblical Literature* (ed. D.J.A. Clines *et al.*; JSOTSup, 19; Sheffield: JSOT Press, 1982), pp. 72-96.

Gunneweg, A.H.J., 'Mose in Midian', *ZTK* 61 (1964), pp. 1-9.

Guttmann, M., 'The Term "Foreigner" (נכרי) Historically Considered', *HUCA* 3 (1926), pp. 1-20.

Hackett, J.A., 'Women's Studies and the Hebrew Bible', in *The Future of Biblical Studies: The Hebrew Scriptures* (ed. R.E. Friedman and H.G.M. Williamson; SBL Semeia Studies, 16; Atlanta: Scholars Press, 1987), pp. 141-64.

Harvey, J., 'Le "Rîb-Pattern", réquisitoire prophétique sur la rupture de l'alliance', *Bib* 43 (1962), pp. 172-96.

Hasel, G.F., 'זעק *z ā'aq* צעק *ṣā'aq*', *ThWAT*, II, pp. 628-39.

Hertzberg, H.W., 'Die Entwicklung des Begriffes משפט im AT', *ZAW* 40 (1922), pp. 256-87.

Hoftijzer, J., 'Remarks concerning the Use of the Particle *'t* in Classical Hebrew', *OTS* 14 (1965), pp. 1-99.

Hogg, J.E., 'Exod. 1.21: "He made them houses"', *AJSL* 41 (1924–25), pp. 267-70.

—'A New Version of Exod. 1.19', *AJSL* 43 (1926–27), pp. 297-99.

Holladay, W.L., '*'Ereṣ*—"Underworld": Two More Suggestions', *VT* 19 (1969), pp. 123-24.

Hossfeld, F.L., and B. Kalthoff, 'נצל *nṣl*', *ThWAT*, V, pp. 570-77.

Houtman, C., *Exodus: Vertaald en Verklaard*, I (Commentaar op het Oude Testament; Kampen: J.H. Kok, 1986).

Huffmon, H.B., 'The Treaty Background of Hebrew YĀDA'', *BASOR* 181 (1966), pp. 31-37.

Huffmon, H.B., and S.B. Parker, 'A Further Note on the Treaty Background of Hebrew YĀDA'', *BASOR* 184 (1966), pp. 36-38.

Isbell, C., 'Exodus 1–2 in the Context of Exodus 1–14: Story Lines and Key Words', in *Art and Meaning: Rhetoric in Biblical Literature* (ed. D.J.A. Clines *et al.*; JSOTSup, 19; Sheffield: JSOT Press, 1982), pp. 37-61.

Iser, W., 'The Reading Process: A Phenomenological Approach', in *Reader-Response Criticism: From Formalism to Post-Structuralism* (ed. J.P. Tompkins; Baltimore: Johns Hopkins University Press, 1980), pp. 50-69.

Janzen, J.G., 'Kugel's Adverbial *kî ṭôb*: An Assessment', *JBL* 102 (1983), pp. 99-106.

Jenni, E., 'יצא *jṣ'* hinausgehen', *THAT*, I, pp. 755-61.

—' "Fliehen" im akkadischen und im hebräischen Sprachgebrauch', *Or* 47 (1978), pp. 351-59.

Jepsen, A., 'Warum? Eine lexikalische und theologische Studie', in *Das ferne und nahe Wort* (Festschrift L. Rost; ed. F. Maass; BZAW, 105; Berlin: de Gruyter, 1967), pp. 106-13.

The Jerusalem Bible (Garden City, NY: Doubleday, 1966).

The Jerusalem Bible: Reader's Edition (Garden City, NY: Doubleday, 1971).

Johnson, A.R., *The Vitality of the Individual in the Thought of Ancient Israel* (Cardiff: University of Wales Press, 2nd edn, 1964 [1949]).

Joüon, P., 'Notes de critique textuelle (AT): Exode 2, 9', *MUSJ* 5 (1911–12), p. 453.

—'Notes de lexicographie hébraïque—II הואיל', *MUSJ* 6 (1913), pp. 162-64.

—*Grammaire de l'hébreu biblique* (Rome: Pontificium Institutum Biblicum, 1982 [1923]).

Kapelrud, A.S., 'יאל *j'l*', *ThWAT*, III, pp. 383-84.

Katsumura, H., 'Zur Funktion von *hinneh* [*sic*] und *w^ehinnēh* in der biblischen Erzählung', *Annual of the Japanese Biblical Institute* 13 (1987), pp. 3-21.

Kautsch, E. (ed.), *Gesenius' Hebrew Grammar* (trans. A.E. Cowley; Oxford: Clarendon Press, 1910).

Kedar, B., *Biblische Semantik: Eine Einführung* (Stuttgart: Kohlhammer, 1981).

Kellermann, D., 'גור', *ThWAT*, I, pp. 979-91.

—'טמן *ṭāman*', *ThWAT*, III, pp. 366-69.

—'סבל *sābal*', *ThWAT*, V, pp. 744-48.

Kennedy, G.A., *New Testament Interpretation through Rhetorical Criticism* (Chapel Hill, NC: University of North Carolina Press, 1984).

Kessler, M., 'Inclusio in the Hebrew Bible', *Semitics* 6 (1978), pp. 44-49.

Kikawada, I.M., 'Literary Convention of the Primaeval History', *Annual of the Japanese Biblical Institute* 1 (1975), pp. 3-21.

—'Some Proposals for the Definition of Rhetorical Criticism', *Semitics* 5 (1977), pp. 67-91.

Knight, G.A.F., *Theology as Narration: A Commentary on the Book of Exodus* (Grand Rapids: Eerdmans, 1976).

Köhler, L., *Deuterojesaja (Jesaja 40–55) stilkritisch untersucht* (BZAW, 37; Giessen: Töpelmann, 1923).

König, F.E., *Historisch-kritisches Lehrgebaüde der Hebräischen Sprache* (Leipzig: Hinrichs, 1881).

—*Historisch-comparative Syntax der Hebräischen Sprache* (Leipzig: Hinrichs, 1897).

Kogut, S., 'On Chiasm and its Role in Exegesis', *Šnaton* 2 (1977), pp. 196-204 (Hebrew).

—'On the Meaning and Syntactical Status of הנה in Biblical Hebrew', in *Studies in Bible 1986* (ed. S. Japhet; Scripta Hierosolymitana, 31; Jerusalem: Magnes Press, 1986), pp. 133-54.

Kovacs, B.W., 'Structure and Narrative Rhetoric in Genesis 2–3: Reflections on the Problem of Non-convergent Structuralist Exegetical Methodologies', *Semeia* 18 (1980), pp. 139-47.

Kühlewein, J., 'איש *'îš* Mann', *THAT*, I, pp. 130-38.

—'רע *rēaʿ* Nächster', *THAT*, II, pp. 786-91.

Kugel, J.L., 'The Adverbial Use of *kî ṭôḇ*', *JBL* 99 (1980), pp. 433-35.

—'On the Bible and Literary Criticism', *Prooftexts* 1 (1981), pp. 217-36.

—'James Kugel Responds', *Prooftexts* 2 (1982), pp. 328-32.

Kurylowicz, M., 'Adoption on the Evidence of the Papyri', *The Journal of Juristic Papyrology* 19 (1983), pp. 61-75.

Kutsch, E., 'Sehen und Bestimmen: Die Etymologie von ברית', in *Archäologie und Altes Testament* (Festschrift K. Galling; ed. A. Kuschke and E. Kutsch; Tübingen: Mohr, 1970), pp. 165-78.

Kutscher, Y., 'For a Biblical Dictionary: Exod. 1.19', *Leš* 21 (1956–57), pp. 251-52 (Hebrew).

Labuschagne, C.J., 'The Particles הן and הנה', *OTS* 18 (1973), pp. 1-14.

Lack, R., *Letture Strutturaliste dell'Antico Testamento* (Rome: Borla, 1978).

Lacocque, A., 'L'idée directrice de l'Exode I à IV', *VT* 15 (1965), pp. 345-53.

—*Le Devenir de Dieu* (Paris: Editions Universitaires, 1967).

Lämmert, E., *Bauformen des Erzählens* (Stuttgart: Metzler, 1955).

Lambert, M., 'Notes Exégétiques III: Exode, I, 10 et Osée, II, 2', *REJ* 39 (1899), p. 300.

Langlamet, F., 'Poétique du récit biblique', *RB* 99 (1987), pp. 464-68.

Lanham, R.A., *A Handlist of Rhetorical Terms: A Guide for Students of English Literature* (Berkeley: University of California Press, 1968).

Lausberg, H., *Handbuch der Literarischen Rhetorik: Eine Grundlegung der Literaturwissenschaft* (2 vols.; Munich: Max Huebner, 2nd edn, 1973 [1960]).

Lawton, R.B., 'Irony in Early Exodus', *ZAW* 97 (1985), p. 414.

Leeuwen, C. van, 'רשע *rš'* frevelhaft/schuldig sein', *THAT*, II, pp. 813-18.

Lemche, N.P., '"Hebrew" as a National Name for Israel', *ST* 33 (1979), pp. 1-23.

Licht, J., *Storytelling in the Bible* (Jerusalem: Magnes Press, 1978).

Lundbom, J.R., *Jeremiah: A Study in Ancient Hebrew Rhetoric* (SBLDS, 18; Missoula, MT: Scholars Press, 1975).

Lurker, M., 'Wasser', in *Wörterbuch biblischer Bilder und Symbole* (Munich: Kusel, 1973), pp. 338-41.

Luyster, R., 'Wind and Water: Cosmogonic Symbolism in the Old Testament', *ZAW* 93 (1981), pp. 1-10.

McCarthy, D.J., 'Covenant-relationships', in *Questions disputées d'Ancien Testament: Méthode et théologie* (ed. C. Brekelmans; BETL, 33; Leuven: Presses Universitaires, 1974), pp. 91-103.

—*Treaty and Covenant: A Study in Form in the Ancient Oriental Documents and in the Old Testament* (AnBib, 21A; Rome: Pontificium Institutum Biblicum, 2nd edn, 1978).

—'The Uses of *w^ehinnēh* in Biblical Hebrew', *Bib* 61 (1980), pp. 330-42.

MacDonald, J., 'The Particle את in Classical Hebrew: Some New Data on its Use with the Nominative', *VT* 14 (1964), pp. 264-75.

—'The Status and Role of the *Na'ar* in Israelite Society', *JNES* 35 (1976), pp. 147-70.

McKnight, E.V., *Post-Modern Use of the Bible: The Emergence of Reader-Oriented Criticism* (Nashville: Abingdon Press, 1988).

Margalit, O., 'Studies in Several Biblical Expressions for Time', *Beth Mikra* 89-90 (2-3) [sic?] (January–June) (1982), pp. 183-213.

Martin-Achard, R., 'גור *gūr* als Fremdling weilen', *THAT*, I, pp. 409-12.

—'Moïse, figure du médiateur selon l'Ancien Testament', in *La figure de Moïse: Ecriture et relectures* (ed. R. Martin-Achard *et al.*; Geneva: Publications de la Faculté de Théologie de l'Université de Genève, 1978), pp. 9-30.

Melamed, E.Z., 'Break-up of Stereotype Phrases as an Artistic Device in Biblical Poetry', in *Studies in the Bible* (ed. C. Rabin; Scripta Hierosolymitana, 8; Jerusalem, 1961), pp. 115-53.

Meyer, R., *Hebräische Grammatik* (Sammlung Göschen, 763, 764, 5765, 4765; Berlin: de Gruyter, 3rd edn, 1972 [1915]).

Michaeli, F., *Le Livre de l'Exode* (CAT, 2, Neuchâtel: Delachaux & Niestlé, 1974).

Milne, P.J., *Vladimir Propp and the Study of Structure in Hebrew Biblical Narrative* (Bible and Literature Series, 13; Sheffield: Almond Press, 1988).

Moule, C.F.D., 'Adoption', *IDB*, I, pp. 48-49.

Muilenburg, J., 'Form Criticism and Beyond', *JBL* 88 (1969), pp. 1-18.

Muraoka, T., *Emphatic Words and Structures in Biblical Hebrew* (Jerusalem: Magnes Press, 1985).

Murtonen, A., *The Living Soul: A Study of the Meaning of the Word næfæš in the Old Testament Hebrew Language* (StudOr, 23.1; Helsinki: Societas Orientalis Fennica, 1958).

Neusner, J., 'Beyond Historicism, after Structuralism: Story as History in Ancient Judaism', *Henoch* 3 (1981), pp. 171-99.

The New Jerusalem Bible (ed. H. Wansbrough; London: Darton, Longman & Todd, 1985).

The New Oxford Annotated Bible with the Apocrypha: Expanded Edition: Revised Standard Version (ed. A.G. May and B.M. Metzger; New York: Oxford University Press, 1977 [1962]).

Niccacci, A., 'Sullo sfondo egiziano di Esodo 1–15', *Liber Annuus* 36 (1986), pp. 7-43.
—*Syntax of the Verb in Classical Hebrew Prose* (trans. W.G.E. Watson; JSOTSup, 86; Sheffield: JSOT Press, 1990 [originally published in Italian as *Sintassi del verbo ebraico nella prosa biblica classica* (Studium Biblicum Fransiscanum Analecta, 23; Jerusalem: Franciscan Printing Press, 1986)]).
Niehr, H., *Herrschen und Richten: Die Wurzel špṭ in alten Orient und im Alten Testament* (Forschung zur Bibel, 54; Würzburg: Echter Verlag, 1986).
Nielsen, K., *Yahweh as Prosecutor and Judge: An Investigation of the Prophetic Lawsuit (Rîb-Pattern)* (JSOTSup, 9; Sheffield: JSOT Press, 1978).
Nohrnberg, J., 'Moses', in *Images of Man and God: Old Testament Short Stories in Literary Focus* (ed. B.O. Long; Bible and Literature Series, 1; Sheffield: Almond Press, 1981), pp. 35-57.
North, R., 'מס *mas* סבל *se bæl*', *ThWAT*, IV, pp. 1006-1009.
Noth, M., *Exodus: A Commentary* (trans. J.S. Bowden; Philadelphia: Westminster Press, 1962).
Odelain, O., and R. Séguineau (eds.), *Dictionnaire des noms propres de la Bible* (Paris: Editions du Cerf, 1978).
Ogden, G.S., 'Time, and the Verb היה in OT Prose', *VT* 21 (1971), pp. 451-69.
Olley, J.W., '"The Many": How is Isa. 53, 12a to be Understood?', *Bib* 68 (1984), pp. 330-56.
Olson, D.T., *The Death of the Old and the Birth of the New: The Framework of the Book of Numbers and the Pentateuch* (BJS, 71; Chico, CA: Scholars Press, 1985).
Orlinsky, H.M. (ed.), *Notes on the New Translation of The Torah: A Systematic Account of the Labors and Reasoning of the Committee that Translated The Torah* (Philadelphia: Jewish Publication Society of America, 1969).
Parunak, H.V.D., 'Oral Typesetting: Some Uses of Biblical Structure', *Bib* 62 (1981), pp. 153-68.
—'Transitional Techniques in the Bible', *JBL* 102 (1983), pp. 525-48.
Perelman, C., and L. Olbrechts-Tyteca, *Traité de l'argumentation: La nouvelle rhétorique* (Brussels: Editions de l'Université de Bruxelles, 1988 [1958]).
Perelman, C., *The Realm of Rhetoric* (trans. W. Kluback; Notre Dame, IN: University of Notre Dame Press, 1982).
Perrot, C., '*Petuhot* et *Setumot*: Etude sur les alinéas du Pentateuque', *RB* 76 (1969), pp. 50-91.
Plath, S., *Furcht Gottes: Der Begriff* ירא *im Alten Testament* (Arbeiten zur Theologie, 2.2; Stuttgart: Calwer Verlag, 1963).
Ploeg, J. van der, 'Les chefs du peuple d'Israël et leurs titres', *RB* 57 (1950), pp. 40-61.
Plum, K.F., 'Genealogy as Theology', *SJOT* 1 (1989), pp. 66-92.
Pons, J., *L'oppression dans l'Ancien Testament* (Paris: Letouzey et Ané, 1981).
Pope, M.H., 'Seven, Seventh, Seventy', *IDB*, IV, pp. 294-95.
Preuss, H.D., 'יצא *jāṣā* ', *ThWAT*, III, pp. 795-822.
Prince, G., *Narratology: The Form and Functioning of Narrative* (Janua Linguarum, Series Maior, 108; Berlin: Mouton, 1982).
Pritchard, J.B., *Ancient Near Eastern Texts Relating to the Old Testament* (Princeton, NJ: Princeton University Press, 3rd edn with supplement, 1969).
Propp, V., *Morphologie du conte* (trans. M. Derrida *et al.* from the Russian 2nd edn, 1969; Collection Points, 12; Paris: Editions du Seuil, 1970).

—'Structure and History in the Study of the Fairy Tale' (trans. H.T. McElwain from Italian) *Semeia* 10 (1978), pp. 57-83.

Ramsey, G.W., 'Is Name-Giving an Act of Domination in Genesis 2.23 and Elsewhere?', *CBQ* 50 (1988), pp. 24-35.

Redford, D.B., 'The Literary Motif of the Exposed Child (cf. Ex. ii 1-10)', *Numen* 14 (1967), pp. 209-28.

Reigbeder, O., *La Symbolique* (Que Sais-je?, 749; Paris: Editions du Seuil, 5th edn, 1981 [1957]).

Reymond, P., *L'eau, sa vie, et sa signification dans l'Ancien Testament* (VTSup, 6; Leiden: Brill, 1958).

Riesener, I., *Der Stamm* עבד *im Alten Testament: Eine Wortuntersuchung unter Berücksichtigung neuer sprachwissenschaftlicher Methoden* (BZAW, 149; Berlin: de Gruyter, 1979).

Rimmon-Kenan, S., *Narrative Fiction: Contemporary Poetics* (London: Methuen, 1983).

Ringgren, H., 'חיה *ḥājāh*', *ThWAT*, II, pp. 874-98.

—'חמר *ḥmr*', *ThWAT*, III, pp. 1-4.

Ron, M., 'Free Indirect Discourse, Mimetic Language Games and the Subject of Fiction', *Poetics Today* 2.2 (1981), pp. 17-39.

Rummel, S. (ed.), *Ras Shamra Parallels: The Texts from Ugarit and the Hebrew Bible*, III (AnOr, 51; Rome: Pontificium Institutum Biblicum, 1981).

Rupprecht, K., 'עלה מן הארץ (Ex 110 Hos 22): "sich des Landes bemächtigen"?', *ZAW* 82 (1970), pp. 442-47

Sarna, N.M., *Exploring Exodus* (New York: Schocken Books, 1986).

Savran, G.W., 'The Character as Narrator in Biblical Narrative', *Prooftexts* 5 (1985), pp. 1-17.

—*Telling and Retelling: Quotation in Biblical Narrative* (Indiana Studies in Biblical Literature; Bloomington, IN: Indiana University Press, 1988).

Sawyer, J.F.A., 'What was a mošia'?', *VT* 15 (1965), pp. 475-86.

—*Semantics in Biblical Research: New Methods of Defining Hebrew Words for Salvation* (SBT, 2.24; Naperville, IL: A.R. Allenson, 1972).

—'ישע *jš'* ', *ThWAT*, II, pp. 1035-59.

Saydon, P.P., 'Meanings and Uses of the Particle את', *VT* 14 (1964), pp. 192-210.

Schmid, H., *Die Gestalt des Mose: Probleme alttestamentlicher Forschung unter Berücksichtigung der Pentateuchkrise* (Erträge der Forschung, 237; Darmstadt: Wissenschaftliche Buchgesellschaft, 1986).

Schmidt, W.H., *Die Schöpfungsgeschichte der Priesterschrift* (WMANT, 17; Neukirchen–Vluyn: Neukirchener Verlag, 1964).

—'Jahwe in Ägypten: Unabgeschlossene historische Spekulationen über Moses Bedeutung für Israels Glauben', *Kairos* ns 18 (1976), pp. 43-54.

—*Exodus, Sinai und Mose* (Erträge der Forschung, 191; Darmstadt: Wissenschaftliche Buchgesellschaft, 1983).

—*Exodus*. I. *Exodus 1–6* (Neukirchen–Vluyn: Neukirchener Verlag, 1988).

Scholes, R., *Structuralism in Literature: An Introduction* (New Haven: Yale University Press, 1974).

Scholes, R., and R. Kellogg, *The Nature of Narrative* (London: Oxford University Press, 1966).

Schoors, A., 'The Particle כי', *OTS* 21 (1981), pp. 240-76.

Schottroff, W., 'ידע *jd'* erkennen', *THAT*, I, pp. 682-701.

—*'Gedenken' im alten Orient und im Alten Testament: Die Wurzel zākar im semitischen Sprachkreis* (WMANT, 15; Neukirchen–Vluyn: Neukirchener Verlag, 1964).
Schweizer, H., 'Wovon reden die Exegeten? Zum Verständnis der Exegese als verstehender und deskriptiver Wissenschaft', *TQ* 164 (1984), pp. 161-85.
Schwertner, S., 'נוס *nûs* fliehen', *THAT*, II, pp. 47-50.
Ska, J.-L., *Le passage de la mer: Etude de la construction, du style et de la symbolique d'Ex 14, 1-31* (AnBib, 109; Rome: Pontificium Institutum Biblicum, 1986).
Spiegelberg, W., *Aegyptologische Randglossen zum Alten Testament* (Leipzig: Hinrichs, 1904).
Spreafico, A., *Esodo: Memoria e promessa: Interpretazioni profetiche* (Supplementi *RivB*, 14; Bologna: Associazione biblica italiana, 1985).
Stähli, H.P., *Knabe–Jüngling–Knecht: Untersuchungen zum Begriff* נער *im Alten Testament* (Beiträge zur biblischen Exegese und Theologie, 7; Frankfurt am Main: Peter Lang, 1978).
Stamm, J.J., 'Hebräische Frauennamen', in *Hebräische Wortforschung* (Festschrift W. Baumgartner; ed. B. Hartmann *et al.*; VTSup, 16; Leiden: Brill, 1967), pp. 301-39.
Steinberg, N., 'The Genealogical Framework of the Family Stories in Genesis', *Semeia* 46 (1989), pp. 41-50.
Steiner, G., 'Real Presences', in *idem*, *Le Sens du Sens* (Paris: J. Vrin, 1988), pp. 69-91.
Sternberg, M., 'Repetition Structure in Biblical Narrative: Strategies of Informational Redundancy', *HaSifrut* 25 (1977), pp. 109-50 (Hebrew).
—*Expositional Modes and Temporal Ordering in Fiction* (Baltimore: Johns Hopkins University Press, 1978).
—*The Poetics of Biblical Narrative: Ideological Literature and the Drama of Reading* (Indiana Literary Biblical Series, 1; Bloomington: Indiana University Press, 1985).
Stoebe, H.J., 'רחם *rḥm* pi. sich erbarmen', *THAT*, II, pp. 761-68.
Stolz, F., 'ישע *jšʿ* hi. helfen', *THAT*, I, pp. 785-90.
—'שלך *šlk* hi. werfen', *THAT*, II, pp. 916-19.
Strack, H.L., *Die Genesis: Übersetzt und ausgelegt* (Kurzgefasster Kommentar zu den heiligen Schriften Alten und Neuen Testaments, 1.1; Munich: Beck, 2nd edn, 1905 [1896]).
Strickland, G., *Structuralism or Criticism? Thoughts on How we Read* (Cambridge: Cambridge University Press, 1981).
Taber, C.R., 'Semantics', *IDBSup*, pp. 800-807.
Talmon, S., 'The Presentation of Synchroneity and Simultaneity in Biblical Narrative', in *Studies in Hebrew Narrative Art through the Ages* (ed. J. Heinemann and S. Werses; Scripta Hierosolymitana, 27; Jerusalem: Magnes Press, 1978), pp. 9-26.
Terrien, S., 'Fear', *IDB*, II, pp. 256-60.
Thomas, D.W., 'A Note on וידע אלהים in Exod. II.25', *JTS* 49 (1948), pp. 143-44.
Thompson, T.L., and D. Irvin, 'The Joseph and Moses Narratives', in *Israelite and Judaean History* (ed. J.H. Hayes and J.M. Miller; London: SCM Press, 1977), pp. 149-212.
The Torah: The Five Books of Moses: A New Translation of the Holy Scriptures according to the Masoretic Text (Philadelphia: Jewish Publication Society, 2nd edn, 1967 [1962]).
Tompkins, J.P., 'An Introduction to Reader-Response Criticism', in *Reader-Response Criticism: From Formalism to Post-Structuralism* (ed. J.P. Tompkins; Baltimore: Johns Hopkins University Press, 1980), pp. ix-xxvi.
Traduction Œcuménique de la Bible (Paris: Sociétés bibliques, 1975).

Tsevat, M., 'חמל *ḥāmal*', *ThWAT*, II, pp. 1042-45.

Tucker, N., 'Some Principles of Composition of Biblical Stories', *Beth Mikra* 68 (1) (September–November) (1976), pp. 46-63 (Hebrew).

—'Several Perspectives concerning the Organization of Time', *Beth Mikra* 93 (2) (January–March) (1983), pp. 168-76 (Hebrew).

Vaux, R. de, *Les institutions de l'Ancien Testament* (Paris: Editions du Cerf, 2nd edn, 1961 [1957]).

Vries, S.J. de, 'The Fall', *IDB*, II, pp. 235-37.

Vriezen, T.C., 'Exodusstudien Exodus 1', *VT* 17 (1967), pp. 334-53.

Wagner, S., 'צפן *ṣpn*', *ThWAT*, VI, pp. 1107-12.

Wainwright, J.A., 'Zoser's Pyramid and Solomon's Temple', *ExpTim* 91 (1979–80), pp. 137-40.

Walzer, M., *Exodus and Revolution* (New York: Basic Books, 1986).

Watson, N., 'Reception Theory and Biblical Exegesis', *AusBR* 36 (1988), pp. 45-56.

Watson, W.G.E., *Classical Hebrew Poetry: A Guide to its Techniques* (JSOTSup, 26; Sheffield: JSOT Press, 1984).

Watters, W.R., *Formula Criticism and the Poetry of the Old Testament* (BZAW, 138; Berlin: de Gruyter, 1976).

Wehmeier, G., 'עלה *ʿlh* hinaufgehen', *THAT*, II, pp. 272-90.

Weimar, P., 'Aufbau und Struktur der priesterschriftlichen Jakobsgeschichte', *ZAW* 86 (1974), pp. 174-203.

—*Untersuchungen zur Redaktionsgeschichte des Pentateuch* (BZAW, 146; Berlin: de Gruyter, 1977).

—*Die Berufung des Mose: Literaturwissenschaftliche Analyse von Exodus 2,23–5,5* (OBO, 32; Freiburg: Universitätsverlag; Göttingen: Vandenhoeck & Ruprecht, 1980).

Weinfeld, M., 'ברית', *ThWAT*, I, pp. 781-808.

—*Justice and Righteousness in Israel and the Nations: Equality and Freedom in Ancient Israel in the Light of Social Justice in the Ancient Near East* (Jerusalem: Magnes Press, 1985) (Hebrew).

Welch, J.W. (ed.), *Chiasmus in Antiquity: Structures, Analyses, Exegesis* (Hildesheim: Gerstenberg, 1981).

Westermann, C., 'Arten der Erzählung in der Genesis', in *idem*, *Forschung am Alten Testament: Gesammelte Studien* (TBü, 24; Munich: Kaiser Verlag, 1964), pp. 9-91.

—'Promises to the Patriarchs', *IDBSup*, pp. 690-93.

—'נפש *næfæš* Seele', *THAT*, II, pp. 71-96.

Wicke, D.W., 'The Literary Structure of Exodus 1.2–2.10', *JSOT* 24 (1982), pp. 99-107.

Wiéner, C., *Le livre de l'Exode* (Cahiers Evangile, 54; Paris: Casterman, 1985).

Wijngaards, J., 'הוציא and העלה: A Twofold Approach to the Exodus', *VT* 15 (1965), pp. 91-102.

Williams, J.G., 'The Beautiful and the Barren: Conventions in Biblical Type-Scenes', *JSOT* 17 (1980), pp. 107-19.

Williams, R.J., *Hebrew Syntax: An Outline* (Toronto: University of Toronto Press, 2nd edn, 1976).

Wilson, J.A., 'Egypt', *IDB*, II, pp. 39-66.

—'Pharaoh', *IDB*, III, pp. 773-74.

Wintermute, O.S., 'Joseph, Son of Jacob', *IDB*, II, pp. 981-86.

Yalon, H., 'The Meaning of ידע, למד', *Tarbiz* 36 (1966–67), pp. 396-400 (Hebrew).

Zeligs, D.E., *Moses: A Psychodynamic Study* (New York: Human Sciences Press, 1986).

Indexes

Index of References

Old Testament

INDEX OF AUTHORS

JOURNAL FOR THE STUDY OF THE OLD TESTAMENT

Supplement Series

79 GIBEAH
THE SEARCH FOR A BIBLICAL CITY
Patrick M. Arnold, S.J.

80 THE NATHAN NARRATIVES
Gwilym H. Jones

81 ANTI-COVENANT
COUNTER-READING WOMEN'S LIVES IN THE HEBREW BIBLE
Edited by Mieke Bal

82 RHETORIC AND BIBLICAL INTERPRETATION
Dale Patrick & Allen Scult

83 THE EARTH AND THE WATERS IN GENESIS 1 AND 2
A LINGUISTIC INVESTIGATION
David Toshio Tsumura

84 INTO THE HANDS OF THE LIVING GOD
Lyle Eslinger

85 FROM CARMEL TO HOREB
ELIJAH IN CRISIS
Alan J. Hauser & Russell Gregory

86 THE SYNTAX OF THE VERB IN CLASSICAL HEBREW PROSE
Alviero Niccacci
Translated by W.G.E. Watson

87 THE BIBLE IN THREE DIMENSIONS
ESSAYS IN CELEBRATION OF FORTY YEARS OF BIBLICAL STUDIES
IN THE UNIVERSITY OF SHEFFIELD
Edited by David J.A. Clines, Stephen E. Fowl & Stanley E. Porter

88 THE PERSUASIVE APPEAL OF THE CHRONICLER
A RHETORICAL ANALYSIS
Rodney K. Duke

89 THE PROBLEM OF THE PROCESS OF TRANSMISSION
IN THE PENTATEUCH
Rolf Rendtorff
Translated by John J. Scullion

90 BIBLICAL HEBREW IN TRANSITION
THE LANGUAGE OF THE BOOK OF EZEKIEL
Mark F. Rooker

91 THE IDEOLOGY OF RITUAL
SPACE, TIME AND STATUS IN THE PRIESTLY THEOLOGY
Frank H. Gorman, Jr

92 ON HUMOUR AND THE COMIC IN THE HEBREW BIBLE
Edited by Yehuda T. Radday & Athalya Brenner

93 JOSHUA 24 AS POETIC NARRATIVE
William T. Koopmans

94 WHAT DOES EVE DO TO HELP? AND OTHER READERLY QUESTIONS TO THE OLD TESTAMENT
David J.A. Clines

95 GOD SAVES:
LESSONS FROM THE ELISHA STORIES
Rick Dale Moore

96 ANNOUNCEMENTS OF PLOT IN GENESIS
Laurence A. Turner

97 THE UNITY OF THE TWELVE
Paul R. House

98 ANCIENT CONQUEST ACCOUNTS
A STUDY IN ANCIENT NEAR EASTERN AND BIBLICAL HISTORY WRITING
K. Lawson Younger, Jr

99 WEALTH AND POVERTY IN THE BOOK OF PROVERBS
R.N. Whybray

100 A TRIBUTE TO GEZA VERMES
ESSAYS ON JEWISH AND CHRISTIAN
LITERATURE AND HISTORY
Edited by Philip R. Davies & Richard T. White

101 THE CHRONICLER IN HIS AGE
Peter R. Ackroyd

102 THE PRAYERS OF DAVID (PSALMS 51–72)
STUDIES IN THE PSALTER, II
Michael Goulder

103 THE SOCIOLOGY OF POTTERY IN ANCIENT PALESTINE
THE CERAMIC INDUSTRY AND THE DIFFUSION OF CERAMIC STYLE IN THE BRONZE AND IRON AGES
Bryant G. Wood

104 PSALM STRUCTURES
A STUDY OF PSALMS WITH REFRAINS
Paul R. Raabe

106 GRADED HOLINESS
A KEY TO THE PRIESTLY CONCEPTION OF THE WORLD
Philip Jenson

107 THE ALIEN IN THE PENTATEUCH
Christiana van Houten

108 THE FORGING OF ISRAEL
IRON TECHNOLOGY, SYMBOLISM AND TRADITION IN ANCIENT SOCIETY
Paula M. McNutt

109 SCRIBES AND SCHOOLS IN MONARCHIC JUDAH
A SOCIO-ARCHAEOLOGICAL APPROACH
David Jamieson-Drake

110 THE CANAANITES AND THEIR LAND
THE TRADITION OF THE CANAANITES
Niels Peter Lemche

111 YAHWEH AND THE SUN
THE BIBLICAL AND ARCHAEOLOGICAL EVIDENCE
J. Glen Taylor

112 WISDOM IN REVOLT
METAPHORICAL THEOLOGY IN THE BOOK OF JOB
Leo G. Perdue

113 PROPERTY AND THE FAMILY IN BIBLICAL LAW
Raymond Westbrook

114 A TRADITIONAL QUEST
ESSAYS IN HONOUR OF LOUIS JACOBS
Edited by Dan Cohn-Sherbok

115 I HAVE BUILT YOU AN EXALTED HOUSE
TEMPLE BUILDING IN THE BIBLE IN THE LIGHT OF MESOPOTAMIAN AND NORTH-WEST SEMITIC WRITINGS
Victor Hurowitz

116 NARRATIVE AND NOVELLA IN SAMUEL
STUDIES BY HUGO GRESSMANN AND OTHER SCHOLARS 1906–1923
Translated by David E. Orton
Edited by David M. Gunn

117 SECOND TEMPLE STUDIES
1. PERSIAN PERIOD
Edited by Philip R. Davies

118 SEEING AND HEARING GOD WITH THE PSALMS
THE PROPHETIC LITURGY FROM THE SECOND TEMPLE IN JERUSALEM
Raymond Jacques Tournay
Translated by J. Edward Crowley

119 TELLING QUEEN MICHAL'S STORY
AN EXPERIMENT IN COMPARATIVE INTERPRETATION
Edited by David J.A. Clines & Tamara C. Eskenazi

120 THE REFORMING KINGS
CULT AND SOCIETY IN FIRST TEMPLE JUDAH
Richard H. Lowery

121 KING SAUL IN THE HISTORIOGRAPHY OF JUDAH
Diana Vikander Edelman

122 IMAGES OF EMPIRE
Edited by Loveday Alexander

123 JUDAHITE BURIAL PRACTICES AND BELIEFS ABOUT THE DEAD
Elizabeth Bloch-Smith

124 LAW AND IDEOLOGY IN MONARCHIC ISRAEL
Edited by Baruch Halpern and Deborah W. Hobson

125 PRIESTHOOD AND CULT IN ANCIENT ISRAEL
Edited by Gary A. Anderson and Saul M. Olyan

126 W.M.L. de Wette, Founder of Modern Biblical Criticism
An Intellectual Biography
John W. Rogerson

127 The Fabric of History
Text, Artifact and Israel's Past
Edited by Diana Vikander Edelman

128 Biblical Sound and Sense
Poetic Sound Patterns in Proverbs 10–29
Thomas P. McCreesh, OP

129 The Aramaic of Daniel in the Light of Old Aramaic
Zdravko Stefanovic

130 Structure and the Book of Zechariah
Michael Butterworth

131 Forms of Deformity
A Motif-Index of Abnormalities, Deformities and Disabilities in Traditional Jewish Literature
Lynn Holden

132 Contexts for Amos
Prophetic Poetics in Latin American Perspective
Mark Daniel Carroll R.

133 The Forsaken Firstborn
A Study of a Recurrent Motif in the Patriarchal Narratives
R. Syrén

135 Israel in Egypt
A Reading of Exodus 1–2
G.F. Davies